LOVE, MYSTERY, AND MISERY
FEELING IN GOTHIC FICTION

LOVE, MYSTERY, AND MISERY

Feeling in Gothic Fiction

by

CORAL ANN HOWELLS

ATHLONE
London and Atlantic Highlands, NJ

Paperback edition first published 1995 by
THE ATHLONE PRESS
1 Park Drive, London NW11 7SG
and 165 First Avenue,
Atlantic Highlands, NJ 07716

© Coral Ann Howells 1978, 1995

British Library Cataloguing in Publication Data
*A catalogue record for this book is available
from the British Library*

ISBN 0 485 12111 5 pb

Library of Congress Cataloging in Publication Data
Cataloging in publication data applied for

Printed and bound in Great Britain by
the University Press, Cambridge

Contents

Preface
to the paperback edition

For all its obsession with ghosts and ruins and fears of death, the Gothic genre has shown remarkable powers of survival over the past two hundred years since its earliest appearance in late eighteenth-century novels and stage melodramas up to its present flourishing in popular paperback fiction, Gothic graphics and horror films like Francis Ford Coppola's *Dracula*. An important component of the contemporary Gothic revival is the revisionist fiction by feminist writers on both sides of the Atlantic like Margaret Atwood, Angela Carter and Anne Rice with *The Vampire Chronicles*. To look back at the novels of Ann Radcliffe, 'Monk' Lewis and Charles Robert Maturin as the prototypes of contemporary Gothics is to come face to face with some easily recognisable conventions of a genre which has undergone many transformations (it has been psychoanalysed, feminised and postmodernised) but which has retained its original transgressive energies.

As the first popular fiction in English, Gothic was always closer to romance than to realism for it marked a decisive shift of emphasis away from the everyday world of social conventions towards the subjective life of feeling and imagination, so opening up the wilder territories of fantasy and the dream life which had been traditionally regarded as the domain of poetry and the drama rather than of fiction. Not surprisingly, the Gothic developed as a hybridised genre devising its conventions to represent such excessive materials by pillaging from Shakespearean drama, graveyard poetry, ballads and folk-tales, as well as from landscape painting in a project which highlighted narrative artifice and produced morbidly senti-mental or melodramatically sensational fiction. The Gothic obsession with mysteries and secrets, together with its threat of disruption and its frequent eruptions of violence focussed readers' attention not only on the unreliability of appearances but on the unstable boundaries between fictional conventions of realism and fantasy. Gothic occupies borderline territory where there is always the possibility of transgression (both in the sense of crossing borders and of trespass), as dream and nightmare spill over into the waking life. It is precisely this attention to narrative representations of the uncanny and the fantastic which appeals so strongly to our late twentieth-century sensibility, with our sense of radical insecurity and our excited interest in fictive constructions and virtual realities.

Gothic novels have a different status in the mid 1990s than they had when I wrote this book nearly twenty years ago, at the beginning of the revaluation of our Gothic inheritance. (It began as a University of London Ph.D. thesis under the supervision of Professor Barbara Hardy and was first published in the late 1970s.) Then one had to argue for the legitimacy of Gothic as a proper subject of literary study; now that is no longer necessary, with major Gothic texts all easily available and with Gothic novels featuring as recognised components in courses on popular culture and on women's writing and feminist theory. These are substantial gains, but the disadvantage is that we may not pay such close attention to the slippages and oddities in these texts now that we have ready made theoretical perspectives through which to read them. This study works as a direct confrontation with a group of texts that differ in all kinds of odd ways from the conventions of realistic fiction. It was this awareness of the problematics of fictional representation which led me to such a close reading of these novels in order to illustrate the variety of narrative techniques through which the disruptions of subjectivity and fantasy are registered in Gothic fiction. Such evidence reveals certain obsessional motifs and repetitive patterns which construct a profile of distinctively 'Gothic' kinds of feeling and which relate the genre quite specifically to its historical context. With its emphasis on emotional crisis and behaviouristic display Gothic fiction develops a new relationship between sentimental romance and theatrical performance, transforming the novel into spectacular entertainment which combines melodrama and bizarre comedy with the topography of psychic disturbance and the landscape of nightmare. My study traces a map of sexual and social neurosis which extends from the ambiguities of Ann Radcliffe's shifting moonlit perspectives through the buried life of male passion in Lewis's *The Monk* to the way-out romanticism of Maturin's *Melmoth the Wanderer* where isolation and torment constitute both an aesthetics of terror and the grounds for psychological and metaphysical speculation.

It is not that we have learned to look more closely at texts over the last twenty years but that we have learned to read them through different lenses. Feminism, psychoanalysis and postmodernism have all made a difference to our methodologies of reading and to our critical perceptions. Thanks to the influence of feminist criticism with its heightened gender awareness, we find that there is now much more to be said about Gothic constructions of the feminine and about the sexual politics of these novels with their different figurings of desire in female fantasies of persecution and resistance and in male power fantasies with their threats of violence and bodily harm. Interestingly, it is only in those novels written by men that heroines are actually raped or murdered. These are very much in the minority, for Gothic was the first kind of fiction where women writers outnumbered men and where feminine perspectives had a decisive influence on shaping the distinctive characteristics and plot configurations of a literary genre. Our critical vocabulary has also changed, and the influence of the language of psychoanalysis is plain in frequent references to 'writing subjectivity' together with a variety of resources for inscribing what is 'unspeakable' and 'uncanny' through the body hieroglyphics of hysteria and the representation of the 'monstrous Other'. If there is one chapter of my book which I would now write differently it is the last one on *Jane Eyre*, for I believe it is a much stranger novel than I perceived twenty years ago when I was not paying enough attention to the mad wife and to Jane's dreams. These are features which were first brought to our attention through Sandra Gilbert and Susan Gubar's classic study *The Madwoman in the Attic: The Woman Writer and the Nineteenth-Century Literary Imagination* (1979) and developed in feminist readings of the Gothic during the 1980s and 90s.

My study focuses on particular moments of crisis in early Gothic texts, highlighting these novelists' efforts to represent material hitherto unaccommodated in fiction, spelling out narrative strategies and motifs which may be reused and theorised at this time of Gothic revival. Gothic fiction is curiously amenable to shifts in critical fashion, for its indeterminate signifiers and its slippages between the familiar and the bizarre make it endlessly available for interpretation and revisionary readings.

Coral Ann Howells
London
August, 1994.

Further Reading
Selected Gothic Criticism of the 1980s and 90s

Day, William Patrick, *In the Circles of Fear and Desire: A Study of Gothic Fantasy*. Chicago & London: University of Chicago Press, 1985.

Ellis, Kate Ferguson, *The Contested Castle: Gothic Novels and the Subversion of Domestic Ideology*. Urbana & Chicago: University of Illinois Press, 1989.

Graham, Kenneth W., ed., *Gothic Fictions: Prohibition/Transgression*. New York: AMS Press, 1989.

Jackson, Rosemary, *Fantasy, the Literature of Subversion*. London & New York: Methuen, 1981.

Masse, Michelle, *In the Name of Love: Women, Masochism and the Gothic*. Ithaca, New York & London: Cornell University Press, 1992.

Miles, Robert, *Gothic Writing 1750–1820: A Genealogy*. London & New York: Routledge, 1993.

—— *Ann Radcliffe: The Great Enchantress*. Manchester: Manchester University Press, 1995.

Napier, Elizabeth R., *The Failure of Gothic: Problems of Disjunc-

tion in an Eighteenth-Century Literary Form. Oxford: Clarendon, 1987.

Sedgwick, Eve Kosofsky, *The Coherence of Gothic Conventions*. London & New York: Methuen, 1986.

Women's Writing, 2, 1 (1994): Special Issue on Female Gothic Writing.

Introduction

When we think of English novelists at the end of the eighteenth century and the beginning of the nineteenth, the names that spring first to mind are Jane Austen, Fanny Burney and Sir Walter Scott. Only on second thoughts would we add Mrs Radcliffe, Monk Lewis and C. R. Maturin, and probably we wouldn't even remember the names of the host of minor writers whose novels Jane Austen reminds us of in *Northanger Abbey*. Yet, between 1790 and 1820, the Gothic novel, with which all these secondary names are connected, was the most popular kind of fiction in England. The obvious reason why interest in Gothic fiction declined was that the things these writers attempted to do were all done better later, by Sir Walter Scott and the Romantic poets and by Dickens, the Brontës and Poe. Encouraged by the current Gothic revival to look at these novelists again, we realise that they are important and memorable for they made the first experimental attempts to write a new kind of fiction which dealt primarily with emotional and imaginative awareness, something that had been regarded as the domain of poetry and drama, not of the novel.

The title of this book, taken from that of a Minerva Press novel written by Anthony Frederick Holstein in 1810, may be argued to be emblematic of Gothic fiction for it defines the precise combination of feelings which are distinctively Gothic, and moreover it hints at the dangers of sensationalism and emotional cliché to which novels of this kind were particularly liable. The Romantic novel as a genre has most to contribute to English fiction in the area of feeling, by which I mean the whole non-rational side of experience—emotional, imaginative and sensational—and within this genre the Gothic novel makes its own distinctive explorations. It is with these explorations into the mysterious irrational side of the human personality and with the language these novelists used to articulate their new insights

that I am concerned. My main interest is in the literary crafts-
manship of Gothic writers and in trying to evaluate their experiments in the presentation of feeling in the novel form. I have
followed a chronological arrangement in my discussion in order
to suggest the developmental nature of the changes that occurred
in Gothic fiction between 1790 and 1820. Within the recurrent
emotional crises and sensationalism so characteristically Gothic
there were attempts by some novelists to work out a more precise
emotional and imaginative vocabulary, and the ones I have
chosen show the slow but consistent line of this development.

In my first chapter I have attempted to show the importance
that Gothic novelists themselves assigned to emotion and
imagination, and with what kinds of feeling they were most
consistently concerned. I have also discussed some of the most
typical Gothic techniques for presenting feeling and have
indicated some of their obvious strengths and weaknesses, suggesting possible reasons why such insights and such myopia
occurred together.

My general conclusions are illustrated in the following chap-
ters by a detailed examination of particular novels. Most of
these are now quite readily available, though I have given short
plot summaries of each one as I discuss it and have also included
frequent quite lengthy quotations, for with the evidence immediately before us it is easier to see how these writers defined
and explored their material. Gothic novels are particularly suitable for this kind of selective treatment, for loose and discursive
as they are, they include wide variations in pace and in the
degree of attention demanded. They are essentially situational
novels, which is perhaps the necessary consequence of depending for effect on emotional crises, while I think it also indicates
on the writer's part a realistic assessment of the reader's powers
of attention. The Jamesian dictum 'Try to be a reader on whom
nothing is lost' is certainly not appropriate when reading a
Gothic novel. These are novels that are meant to be read
quickly, and there is always a clear indication when close
attention is required; elsewhere the effects are those of relaxa-
tion or of vague anxiety where the reader, like the characters
in the novel, is kept in a state of suspense. Jane Austen sum-
marised the charges against Gothic fiction when she character-

ised Mrs Radcliffe's effect as 'a raised, restless, and frightened imagination', but with her usual fairness she also showed that of course this was precisely its fascination for circulating library readers. In many of the passages I have chosen there is a marked similarity of content and treatment, which bears witness not necessarily to authorial incompetence but to the familiarity writers could expect their readers to have with Gothic conventions, while the repetitiveness argues most persuasively for the obsessional nature of their subject matter. Throughout I am emphasising the need for us as readers to discriminate and to vary the kind of attention we give to different parts of these novels; I am not proposing a radical reassessment of their value as literary artefacts but of their importance as experiments in imaginative fiction.

I begin with Mrs Radcliffe and M. G. Lewis, although Horace Walpole had made an excursion into Gothic territory thirty years before with *The Castle of Otranto*. However, it was not until the 1790s with these two writers that the implications of a fantasy literature embodying contemporary neuroses began to be thoroughly explored and exploited. Their definition of 'terror' and 'horror' fiction set the pattern of anxious ambivalence which characterised the Gothic novel for the next twenty years. Mrs Radcliffe and M. G. Lewis are the great Gothic experimentalists, and after them the public demand for morbidly sensational fiction was catered for by a host of minor writers, many of whom wrote for publishers who had set up circulating libraries like Lackington's, Bell's, and most notorious of all, Lane's Minerva Press and Library. Though we would not call these productions distinguished literature, it is interesting to consider a couple of the Minerva novels as an indication of tastes and trends in Gothic fiction in the ten-year period following the success of Mrs Radcliffe and Lewis. I have chosen Regina Maria Roche's *The Children of the Abbey* and Mary-Anne Radcliffe's *Manfroné; or the One-Handed Monk* to suggest the extremes of sentimentality and sensationalism which characterised Minerva Gothic. Jane Austen's criticism of 'Horrid Novels' in *Northanger Abbey* is the inevitable response.

As a result of the gratuitous repetitiveness of most of this minor fiction, by the second decade of the nineteenth century

'Gothic' had become a derogatory if not an abusive word, so when a writer of serious intent like C. R. Maturin took up the form he felt the need to disclaim authorship of 'mere' terror novels. In treating *Melmoth the Wanderer* I have tried to show how Gothic conventions were assimilated into the imaginative literature of Romanticism.

In my last chapter I have leapt ahead another thirty years to consider Charlotte Brontë's *Jane Eyre*. This novel is not really a development of Gothic fiction but a coda to it. In showing the full realisation of the Gothic potential, where fact and fantasy can be fused into a statement about total human awareness, *Jane Eyre* may be called the best Gothic novel. At the same time it marks the breakthrough for this kind of imaginative fiction into the everyday world which the earlier Gothic novelists had either rejected or failed to realise. By its excellence *Jane Eyre* also serves an important evaluative function, illuminating the rest while placing their experiments and achievements in perspective.

I

Gothic Themes, Values, Techniques

One must have taste to be sensible of the beauties of
Grecian architecture; one only wants passions to feel
Gothic.   (Horace Walpole, *Anecdotes of Painting*)

I want to adopt Horace Walpole's emphasis on feeling as the
distinctive attribute of Gothic—feeling as it is explored and enacted in the fictions themselves, and feeling as the primary
response elicited from the reader. As its name suggests with its
medieval associations, Gothic is allied with everything which is
the opposite of Augustan: instead of notions of order and decorum and rational judgement, it represents the darker side of
awareness, the side to which sensibility and imagination belong,
together with those less categorisable areas of guilt, fear and
madness which are such important and terrifying components
of the earlier Augustan anti-vision and of Romanticism. Gothic
fiction with its castles and abbeys, persecuted heroines, ghosts
and nightmares, projects a peculiarly fraught fantasy world of
neurosis and morbidity, and if we take a close look at the kinds
of feeling in which these novelists were especially interested we
begin to perceive how anti-Enlightenment anxieties were actually 'felt on the pulses' of a whole generation. There is nothing
confident or optimistic about Gothic fiction: its main areas of
feeling treat of melancholy, anxiety-ridden sentimental love and
horror; it is a shadowy world of ruins and twilit scenery lit up
from time to time by lurid flashes of passion and violence. All
the time we have the uncomfortable sense of being in a fantasy
world which is about to reveal secrets of the human personality
—indeed straining towards these revelations—and yet constantly kept in check by the negative forces of guilt and repression. It is this sense of an imprisonment which is both
psychological and linguistic that Robert Kiely defines as a
quality of all Romantic fiction:

The emotions on which they dwelt were too imperfectly understood or too threatening to be systematically rational-ised, except by someone as daring as the Marquis de Sade. They explored feelings and compulsions which were not merely impolite to mention but often difficult to label and describe.   (*The Romantic Novel in England*, 1973, p. 11)

His statement has particularly interesting implications for the Gothic novelists, the very bizarreness of whose fiction shows how daring their attempts were to articulate some of the more dis-concerting features of the life of the feelings. It is their vocabu-lary of emotional and imaginative experience and what it reveals about the Gothic state of mind that I intend to explore.

Gothic fiction is a literature full of curiosity, doubt and anxiety, and at this distance in time we can see working through it the same subversive forces that produced the French Revolu-tion, the Marquis de Sade and the Romantic poets. The trouble was that the Gothic novelists didn't know what to do with their feelings of frustration and rebelliousness. Many of them were middle-class women, while Lewis was the son of the Deputy Secretary of War and Maturin was an Irish clergyman; all they knew was that they were dissatisfied and anxious. Their fiction is both exploratory and fearful. They are not always totally in control of their fantasies, for having opened up new areas of awareness which complicate life enormously, they then retreat from their insights back into conventionality with the rescue of a heroine into happy marriage and the horrible death of a vil-lain. There is a profound unease and fear of anarchy which runs side by side with expressions of frustration at conventional re-straints throughout Gothic fiction. These novelists feared the personal and social consequences of any release of passion or instinctual drives, as we can see in those narratives where the action is taken to its conclusion in the self-destruction of Lewis's Monk or the damnation of Maturin's Melmoth. As the result of their deep suspicions of the affective life, what they frequently did was to betray the forces they felt so strongly for they suffered from the worst kind of fear which trivialises important issues and ends by being totally reactionary—socially, politically and morally.

These tensions may explain why the Gothic novelists chose romance as their fictional form. By adopting a mode which is recognised as being separate from everyday life, they were free to create a fictional world which embodied their fears and fantasies and offered a retreat from insoluble problems, while at the same time it rendered their fears ultimately harmless by containing and distancing them in a fantasy. Gothic fiction is a most ambiguous form, for like romance it emphasises the intuitive, the arbitrary and the supernatural—what Henry James calls 'the disconnected and uncontrolled experience' (Preface to *The American*). However, the feelings out of which such fantasies spring are recognisably late eighteenth-century: they are all areas of anxiety relating to the same dilemmas that Richardson and Jane Austen acknowledged—problems of personal moral responsibility and judgement, questionings of restrictive convention, and a troubled awareness of irrational impulses which threatened to subvert orthodox notions of social and moral propriety. These anxieties occur with obsessional frequency in Gothic fiction and though sublimated into forms which appear fabulous and unlikely, they are at the same time distorted images of real emotional tensions and moral dilemmas. Because of the ambiguities of content and treatment and the confusion between the terms 'Novel' and 'Romance', I have decided to refer to Gothic fictions as 'Novels', for that term rightly suggests the literary mode into which these experiments fit.[1]

Gothic writers were certainly expressing attitudes which were hostile to eighteenth-century Enlightened views of human potential, but so timidly that they undermined the significance of their own insights. As a result we find serious writers like Coleridge and Jane Austen criticising Gothic fiction for its artificiality and irresponsibility. In *Northanger Abbey* Jane Austen tries to laugh her readers out of extravagant imaginings into right judgement, while Coleridge, himself capable of writing *Christabel*, condemned the shrieks and murders of Gothic and in *Biographia Literaria* said he objected to being implicated in somebody else's private delirium.[2] And he was right, for much of the Gothic fiction of the 1790s insists on the reader's complicity in an obsessionally self-enclosed world. Unlike the work of the Romantic radicals it always looks away from the here and now, into past times or distant lands (or to put it more accurately, into a fantasy world which was both timeless and placeless); never does it look directly at the present or forward to the future.

Gothic fiction represents the extreme development of the eighteenth-century cult of Sensibility, as if Richardson's heroines had finally lost all sense of objective reality and had retreated into their own fantasy worlds only to find that the anxieties of real life were monstrously exaggerated within their own isolated nervous consciousness. Certainly there is nothing new in the Gothic novelists' fascination with emotional dynamics; novelists from Defoe onwards had been interested in 'the wild wonders of the heart of man'. Defoe's Roxana had her dark reflections and her death's-head hallucinations; although Richardson said that his aim was to 'inform the judgment rather than fire the imagination', Pamela and Clarissa had suffered acutely from nervous hysteria as the result of persecution, while the Lady Clementina in *Sir Charles Grandison* had even run mad under the stresses of religion and love; in Fanny Burney's *Cecilia* the heroine temporarily lost her senses when an attempt was made to seduce her, and ran wildly through the alleys of London's East End. However, all these novelists managed to suggest that such behaviour was only aberration, and they put the emphasis on society's ways of assimilating and annihilating it. With Gothic fiction there is a radical shift in emphasis; the neurotic and the obsessional become the central preoccupations, and the view of experience recorded is so exclusively subjective that individual awareness loses touch with everyday life or at least exists in a very uncertain relationship to it. By the 1790s sensibility seems to have become a nervous disease, as Michel Foucault suggests in *Madness and Civilisation*. In his detailed accounts of melancholia, madness, hysteria and hypochondria drawn from eighteenth-century treatises dealing with disorders of the nerves, he frequently provides a very apt clinical diagnosis of what are characteristically Gothic states of mind, though of course these raw materials are often sublimated in the process of giving them fictional form.[3] We cannot help noticing evidence of this sickness in the exacerbated sensibility of Gothic heroines in whom there is an extraordinarily heightened sense of the inter-relatedness between physical and emotional responses. To be 'aware' of something meant to 'feel' it through the whole organism, so that 'feeling' was truly a matter of sensation as much as of emotional or imaginative perception. Many of the Gothic descriptions of strong feelings are certainly behaviouristic and physiological: fear always reduces its victims to 'ashy paleness' accompanied by fits of trembling and stifled groans; people tend to 'totter' and 'stagger' as they gaze around with 'a wildness of aspect', and a sudden shock first of all induces 'deathy cheeks' and then the crimson blood rushes to the face with 'suffocating violence'. As a way of total response, sensibility could be cultivated as the irrational alternative to judgement, and frequently for the Gothic heroine intuition provides the only criterion for decision making. In this highly introspective state, heroines (and indeed heroes and villains as well) react with an intensity which often affects them physically so that they fall ill or faint from overpowering feeling. The relation between sensibility and insensibility is alarmingly close, and it is no accident that the cult of sensibility merges with a cult of debility in its most extreme manifestations at the end of the eighteenth century.

The Gothic heroine is the prime example of this febrile temperament, being always in a state of intense awareness yet peculiarly isolated from her circumstantial context and from personal relationships, existing as she does in a self-contained fantasy world. Constantly threatened by emotional and physical assault, she is so delicately elusive that she deprives aggression of its reality and her sufferings impinge on her no more than the events of nightmare. Her experiences in no way lead to the growth of her self-awareness or a modification of any of her attitudes; at the end she emerges with sensibility intact, even if on rare occasions, physically violated. She is the familiar figure in women's fiction of any age, embodying all the fashionable feminine fantasies and neuroses. The Gothic novelists were particularly fortunate in having a real model for their heroines in the person of the actress Mrs Sarah Siddons, 'that most picturesque of women' as her biographer James Boaden describes her; and it is instructive to compare his description of Mrs Siddons with Mrs Radcliffe's description of Emily the heroine of *The Mysteries of Udolpho*. Of Mrs Siddons, Boaden says:

2

There never, perhaps, was a better stage figure than that of Mrs. Siddons. Her height is above the middle size, though not at all inclined to the em-bon-point . . . Her attitudes are distinguished equally by energy and grace. The symmetry of her person is exact and captivating. Her face is peculiarly happy, the features big and finely formed . . . so expressive when impassioned that most people think her more beautiful than she is. So great too is the flexibility of her countenance, that the rapid transitions of passion are given with a variety and effect that never tire upon the eye. Her voice is naturally plaintive, and a tender melancholy in her level speaking denotes a being devoted to tragedy.

(*Memoirs of Mrs. Siddons*, 1827, I, 287)

And of Emily, Mrs Radcliffe says:

In person, Emily resembled her mother; having the same elegant symmetry of form, the same delicacy of features, and the same blue eyes full of tender sweetness. But lovely as was her person, it was the varied expression of her countenance, as conversation awakened the nicer emotions of her mind, that threw such a captivating grace around her.

(*The Mysteries of Udolpho*, 1794, OEN, 1, i, 5)

Quite apart from the fact that Mrs Radcliffe admired Mrs Siddons more than any other actress of her time,[4] the resemblance is, I suggest, more than coincidental, for Boaden reports that there developed during the 1780s a distinctive Siddons style:

It was not delusion which led me to notice in the loveliest faces in the world a strongly marked *sensibility*, derived from the enjoyment of this fascinating actress . . . Mrs. Siddons became the glass 'in which our noble youth did dress themselves'; and those who frequented her exhibitions, became related to her look, to her deportment and her utterance; the lowest point of imitation, that of the dress, was early and wisely too adopted; for it was at all times the praise of Mrs. Siddons to be exquisitely chaste and dignified in her exterior —simplex munditiis.

(op. cit., I, 301)

Not surprisingly we find in popular fiction the mirror image of the current taste in beauty and manners.

Just as the Gothic heroine was the idealised image of beauty, so was she the image of sublimated sexual fantasy. She innocently arouses the admiration of practically every man she meets, but usually escapes the penalties of commitment until the end, when she is happily married and promised a future of unalterable bliss. True, she is presented with the alternatives of sensibility and passion in the persons of her hero and the villain, but there is never any doubt about which she will accept; of course she chooses the first, and despite the terrible risks she runs from the villain remains blissfully ignorant of the second. Mrs Radcliffe's heroines turn with disgust from any suggestion of sexuality even when shown by the hero, and later on, Maturin's heroines who fall in love with Byronic figures never explore the implications of the magnetic attraction to which they respond. Maturin's Immalee who actually marries her demon lover Melmoth never understands him, remaining totally innocent and ignorant and dying untainted by her contact with him.

Clearly, idealisation and repression go together in the heroine; to be angelic and robed in white is only the romantic side of eighteenth-century convention, the other side of which is the condemnation of woman to a passive role in which she can be sacrificed by society for sexual and economic interests. As there was little if any initiative that she could take, she was forced to be negative and out of her inhibitions to construct a convenient fictive world of fragile sensibility and self-deception. In the Gothic novels we find an awareness as acutely realised as Richardson's or Jane Austen's of both sides of woman's image, where adulation is balanced by anxiety-ridden isolation and inviolate purity by persecution mania. As a beautiful orphan of uncertain economic and social status, the heroine frequently sees herself as a kind of Clarissa figure alone and beleaguered with only her own intuitions and feelings to guide her as she eludes male exploitation. The mainspring of her adventures is persecution by the villain, whose sinful desires are underlined by the unnaturalness of his situation. He is often a father figure, either in a priestly role like Lewis's Monk or an elderly mentor like Mrs Radcliffe's Schedoni and Maturin's Melmoth; in order to satisfy his 'impious passions' he would have to transgress his religious vows or ties of blood (in some cases both). The disconcerting transformation of protector into sexual aggressor is one that heroines experience with dreadful consistency, from Walpole's Isabella who finds herself pursued down labyrinthine ways by her bridegroom's father to Lewis's pathetically innocent heroine Antonia who is drugged and then raped by her confessor. The pattern of heroine as deceived victim caught up in an endless series of flights from her persecutor is so often repeated that we soon realise the close connection between masochistic fantasy and repressed sexuality, which is as fundamental here as in *Clarissa* (though Lovelace is a more subtle threat than any Gothic villain). The obsessive fear of sex is dramatised again and again, though usually given overtones of Christian suffering. Just as Clarissa's adversity was her 'shining time' so the Gothic heroines glory in their sufferings as proof of their angelic natures and their 'patient resignation to the will of Heaven'. Only rarely is any attempt made to suggest sexual responsiveness in the heroine herself. Invariably these attempts, timid and slightly bizarre as they tend to be, are discounted.

However, even Mrs Radcliffe, that most discreet of writers, once makes the suggestion in *Udolpho* that the heroine is secretly in love with the villain, though as the accusation comes from a jealous lover it is easily deniable (which is probably just as well for the heroine's pride, as the villain himself rejects the idea). In Lewis's *The Monk*, where male guilts and fears connected with sexuality are the basic stuff of the novel, the innocent heroine is strangely attracted to the monk, as she confesses: 'I am myself astonished at the acuteness of my feelings'. After a most turbulent narrative culminating in the rape of this heroine by the monk, the attraction is explained by the fact that he is her brother, at once underlining and condemning the ambiguity of the initial feelings. Tough passionate women with overt sexual appetites are vigorously condemned, like Signora Laurentini in *Udolpho* who suffers agonies of repentance in a nunnery, or Victoria in Charlotte Dacre's *Zofloya* who is hurled headlong down a dreadful abyss by Satan himself. It was to be expected that as sexual passion was associated with danger and bestiality its only full expression in Gothic fiction would be rape, murder, incest, death or damnation. However, tentative as they are, the few early examples of the ambiguities of sexual attraction are interesting forerunners to the appearance of the Byronic figure in Maturin's *Melmoth* where the attraction of opposites comes to play a significant part in the development of the love story—though even there, sex is still linked with violation, and death not life is its proper consummation.

Charlotte Brontë revolted against these restrictive conventions for treating sexual love, but even Mr Rochester still has some of the devilish fascination of the traditional Byronic hero-villain about him. Neither Charlotte nor Emily was entirely free of convention in this respect, and the earlier Gothic novelists writing novels of fantasy and emotional indulgence were more timid than the Brontës. There are implications of sexuality in a superficial and stylised way: the heroine is always beautiful and passive, the hero is good-looking and energetic, and the villain's flashing eyes and powerful physique suggest his passionate nature. The implications are seldom developed or if they are, the outcome is inevitably tragic. By this method conventional morality was vindicated while still exploiting the emotional appeal of what was regarded as immoral.

I believe that the dread of sex runs right through Gothic fiction and is basic to many of its conventions of anxiety and terror. Gothic heroines suffer incessantly from persecution mania, and there is a high incidence of hysteria and madness among them which goes with much threatened brutality on the part of the villains. However, the causes of such violent feeling are never adequately explained, for Gothic novelists flirt with sexuality treating it with a mixture of fascination and coy withdrawal from its implications. With the treatment of sex which we find in Charlotte Brontë, for example, dread and desire are identified as being two sides of the same coin; but Gothic novels for all their daring, lack this frankness. They are full of unresolved conflicts and repressions, packed with crises which are the outward signs of inward tensions, but consistently avoiding any clear analysis of the relation between startling effects and their possible causes. This failure can be only partially explained by the difficulty of finding a language to talk about passion and instinct; more importantly it is a failure to

come to terms with such feelings on the part of novelists themselves. They wanted to explore and exploit violent emotions,
but at the same time they were not certain enough of their own
values to revolt against eighteenth-century moral and literary
conventions. The world of emotions was the real centre of their
interest, but they treated it with such a mixture of coyness and
hysteria that the impact of genuine insights into the springs of
feeling is too often buried.

Perhaps the real embarrassment to Gothic writers was their
sense of their duty as moralists, for as writers of quasi-romance
they were caught in the difficult position of trying to satisfy two
entirely different demands: on the one hand the claims of orthodox Christian morality and its extension into social propriety,
and on the other hand their own imaginative imperatives leading them in the opposite direction into the dynamics of impulse
and irrationality, aided and abetted, of course, by their reading public's appetite for excitement. The effect of these two
conflicting pressures is frequently quite disastrous, robbing their
work both of moral conviction and of imaginative truth. They
still adhered to the Johnsonian doctrine of the didactic purpose
of fiction:

> In narratives where historical veracity has no place, I can-
> not discover why there should not be exhibited the most per-
> fect idea of virtue . . . Vice, for vice is necessary to be shown,
> should always disgust; nor should the graces of gaiety, or the
> dignity of courage, be so united with it as to reconcile it to
> the mind.   (*Rambler* Essay no. 4, 31 March 1750)

All the Gothic novelists are inheritors of this moralistic doctrine,
claiming as Richardson had done that their novels were written
for the sake of 'Example and Warning' (Richardson's letter to
Lady Bradshaigh, 15 December 1748).[5] The only trouble was
that in fiction whose appeal was so obviously to the imagination
rather than to the judgement and where the criteria of judgement were themselves called into question, the interpretation of
events at the end in Christian moral terms frequently looks
inappropriate as a comment on the moral and emotional issues
raised within the novels. They do not enact a moral argument
as Richardson or Fielding had done in their very different ways;

instead of the sense of a problem being worked through, what we have is a series of partial insights into dilemmas, the implications of which are finally abandoned as the writers give up and give in to conventions endorsed by society and by the traditions of novel writing.

The ambivalent attitude of Gothic writers inevitably affected the way they presented emotion. Though they always insist on the powers of feeling and imagination they tend to concentrate on external details of emotional display while leaving readers to deduce for themselves complex inner psychological movements, from such evidence as a 'certain wildness of aspect' or a 'settled paleness of the countenance'. Their splendid displays of strong feeling often seize our attention but only add to the mystery of the feelings which could have provoked them. Take the two following passages, written twelve years apart:

> The desperate courage which the Marchese had assumed now vanished; he threw himself back upon the pillow, his breath shortened, the cold dews paced each other down his forehead, he veiled his face, which exhibited a cadaverous paleness, with the coverture; and stifled groans, and irregular respiration, were all the symptoms of remaining existence.
>
> (Eleanor Sleath, *The Orphan of the Rhine*, 1798.
> Folio Press edition, 1968, iii, 269)

> Terrified by the sudden violence of her manner, the soul-harrowing expression of her yet supremely-lovely features, our heroine remained motionless—one hand of her mother she yet retained within her own tremulous grasp; but it was the next moment withdrawn, and the convulsed form of Madame de Saussure staggered toward the sofa.
>
> (A. F. Holstein, *Love, Mystery, and Misery!* 1810, i, 85–6)

Both these descriptions are typical of the way Gothic novelists record emotion: there is a precise recognition of its violent physical effects and at the same time perceptible on the author's part a shocked withholding of sympathy or a perplexed incomprehension like that of 'our heroine' in the second passage. As readers we are consistently placed in the position of literary voyeurs, always gazing at emotional excess without understanding the why of it: what we are given are the gestures of feeling rather than any insight into the complexity of the feelings themselves. The springs of these emotions elude us, so that we can only look on with appalled fascination as floods of feeling rush through the characters distorting their physical features with alarming rapidity:

> Pride, grief, horror, amazement, indignation, dismay, alternately agitated, alternately glowed in every feature.
> (Louisa Sidney Stanhope, *The Confessional of Valombre*, 1812, i, 167)

As the result of this preoccupation with externals Gothic novels have frequently been criticised for being sensational, theatrical and melodramatic. It seems to me that these three words ought not to be taken only as adverse criticism, for they exactly describe the peculiar quality and the contemporary appeal of Gothic fiction. Gothic techniques are essentially visual in their emphasis on dramatic gesture and action and in their pictorial effects, giving the reader an experience comparable to that of a spectator at the theatre. Indeed, at no other period has the English novel been so close to the drama as it was between 1790 and 1820. We may think that the wholesale transplanting of dramatic techniques into prose fiction is uncomfortable or inappropriate, but as an experiment in widening the emotional rhetoric of the novel what the Gothic writers did is undeniably interesting.[6] When we consider that these novelists from Walpole to Maturin without exception acknowledged Shakespeare as the major influence on their work, and that some of them, for example Lewis and Maturin, wrote more plays and melodramas than novels, not to mention the ease with which Gothic novels were adapted for the stage (e.g. Boaden's melodramas *Fontainville Forest* and *The Italian Monk* from Mrs Radcliffe's novels, and *Aurelio and Miranda* from Lewis's *Monk*), we begin to realise how accurately the word 'theatrical' can be used to describe the techniques and the effects of Gothic fiction.

It is easy to understand the appeal that Shakespeare would have had for these novelists when we relate Walpole's remarks in his *Otranto* prefaces to the way in which Dr Johnson interprets the qualities of Shakespearean drama in his *Preface to Shakespeare* (1765). Both of them saw his genius as essentially English and outside the classical orders of art, belonging to the English nation and its literature in its infancy when people were mainly interested in tales of 'adventures, giants, dragons, and enchantments'. All that 'Gothick mythology of fairies', as Johnson calls it, was outside the ordered social and moral ethos of the modern age, back in the 'barbarous times':

> He had no regard to distinction of time or place, but gives to one age or nation, without scruple, the customs, institutions and opinions of another, at the expense not only of likelihood but of possibility.

Johnson's scrupulous weighing of Shakespeare's looseness against his 'endless variety' and his concern with 'the general passions and principles by which all minds are agitated' was assimilated by novelists later in the century in so far as they saw Shakespeare as the image of freedom in literature. His plays pointed to the direction they wanted to follow, in subject matter and in methods of presentation. Speaking of Shakespeare's use of the marvellous, Johnson said:

> His plots, historical or fabulous, are always crowded with incidents, by which the attention of a rude people was more easily caught than by sentiment or argumentation and such is the power of the marvellous, even over those who despise it, that every man finds his mind more strongly seized by the tragedies of Shakespeare, than of any other writer; others please us by particular speeches, but he always makes us anxious for the event, and has perhaps excelled all but Homer in securing the first purpose of a writer, by exciting restless and unquenchable curiosity and compelling him that reads his work to read it through.

What Johnson did was to free Shakespeare from the charges of irregularity brought against him by neo-classical formalism, while Walpole showed how his plays could be used as models for fiction. In so doing, they made Shakespeare available to a new generation of writers who interpreted him and used him according to their own liking. Using his plays as models they borrowed his plots, his dramatic situations and his character types. The most cursory glance through Gothic novels will reveal the extent of Shakespearean borrowings: three of the 'Horrid Novels' mentioned in *Northanger Abbey* are prefaced by Shakespearean quotations, even though they may be as inapposite as Francis Lathom's description of his Gothic thriller *The Midnight Bell* (1798) as a 'round unvarnish'd tale'; and Lewis actually reveals the secret of *The Monk* in his quotation from *Measure for Measure* at the head of Chapter I. Shakespearean scenery with its wild Scottish heaths, storms and shipwrecks, funereal vaults and castle ramparts, influenced the landscape of terror fiction, combining as it did with other current enthusiasms for Ossian, the sublime and medieval architecture.

Macbeth and *Hamlet* appear to have been the most popular plays with novelists, providing as they do models for almost every kind of dramatic crisis by which men's passions are revealed, from supernatural fear to murder, revenge, madness, distracted love, melancholia, and agonised penitence. There are an abundance of Gothic murder scenes which bear a close resemblance to Hamlet's midnight visit to Claudius or to the murder of Duncan, while Lady Macbeth's tormented vision of the blood on her hands is the model for all those scenes where women who have committed crimes of passion are tortured by their guilt. Signora Laurentini in *Udolpho* and Lady St Clair in Mrs Kelly's *Ruins of Avondale Priory* (1796) are women of the Lady Macbeth type, while in *The Midnight Bell* the image is used quite literally: the hero is awakened by his mother, her hands covered in blood, her eyes wildly fixed and her hair dishevelled, who tells him to fly the castle instantly, 'as you value life, as you value heaven'. Then of course there are any number of agonised villains like Macbeth, distracted lovers in the dishevelled Hamlet style, and heroines of a distinct Ophelia cast in their sweetly pathetic expressions of wandering wit. Ghosts wander on battlements in the moonlight world of *Udolpho* and of Mrs Sleath's *Nocturnal Minstrel* (1810), while Scottish heaths peopled by mysterious figures veiled in mist are regular scenic features from Mrs Radcliffe's *Castles of Athlin and Dunbayne* (1789) right through the 1790s and into the nineteenth century with novels like Mrs Kelly's *Baron's Daughter* (1802) and Horsley-Curteis's

Scottish Legend (1802), Francis Lathom's *Romance of the Hebrides* (1809) and Jane Porter's *Scottish Chiefs* (1810). Sir Walter Scott's poems and the Waverley Novels when they began to appear in 1814 were enthusiastically received by a reading public who had become accustomed by a long literary tradition to associate Scotland with mystery and adventure.

These random examples suggest how pervasive the Shakespearean influence was, for Shakespeare's plays provided a picturesque vocabulary of feeling which satisfied the current taste for highly-wrought emotions and inflated language. The Gothic novelists imitated Shakespeare's methods for showing passions in action, though they ignored his subtle investigations of those passions which made violence convincing. They were also hampered by the moral restriction of dealing with passions only in order to condemn them, so the result was often a reduction of Shakespeare to eighteenth-century moral cliché. Perhaps the most complete example of Shakespeare *moralisé* was Mrs Eliza Parsons' *The Mysterious Warning* (1796) based on *Hamlet*. She took the play and transformed it into a moral fable about the destructive effects of the passions on man's happiness and hopes of salvation. Despite the nature of her original, she was able to declare her honourable intention and her own negative merits in her Dedication to the Princess of Wales: 'I have never written a line tending to corrupt the heart, sully the imagination, or mislead the judgment of my young readers.' Taking as her motto 'Thus conscience can [sic] make cowards of us all', Mrs Parsons shapes her narrative into a triumphant conclusion of virtue over vice which she then celebrates in the lines

> Foul deeds will rise
> Though all the earth o'erwhelms them, to men's eyes.

The balance of *Hamlet* is drastically altered to fit in with Mrs Parsons' moral thesis about the infallible workings of Providential justice, so that though the themes of revenge, incest and fraternal treachery are preserved, moral and emotional qualities are re-allotted. The revenge motif is transferred from the hero to his wicked brother, and Hamlet's gloom and cynicism become the dominant traits of the penitent villains. Ferdinand, Mrs Parsons' Hamlet figure, emerges as the noble sentimental hero, the champion of virtue who performs the sacred trust of bringing unnatural behaviour to light and seeing that it is punished. Unlike Hamlet he is a man of decisive action who accomplishes his purpose and is rewarded by marriage to the girl he loves. The ghost figure gives the mysterious warnings about his brother's treachery which the hero receives, though finally the phenomenon is revealed to have been extraordinary rather than supernatural. (All the time it was the voice of a faithful old retainer who, like the ghost of Hamlet's father, knew the truth about secret evil deeds done by members of the family.) Mrs Parsons' belief in the unsearchable ways of Providence has something in common with Hamlet's fatalism, recommending as it does endurance, patience and acceptance, though only, I feel, because she believed that Providence was synonymous with poetic justice:

> In vain may the wicked hope to deceive the virtuous and unsuspecting mind, unobserved and undiscovered; there is a watchful and unerring eye, to whom all their black and artful schemes are laid open, and who, in its own good time, defeats the machinations of the wicked, and brings the offenders to the punishment they deserve.
>
> (*The Mysterious Warning*, Folio Press, 1968, iv, 375)

In comparison with its prototype, *The Mysterious Warning* is inferior in every respect except its sensationalism.

Shakespearean borrowings were not only literary, however; the presentation of feeling in Gothic fiction is so closely related to theatrical performances of Shakespeare in the eighteenth century that as we read we have the impression of watching a group of actors who are imitating the styles of Mrs Siddons or J. P. Kemble, and later Eliza O'Neill and Edmund Kean.[7] The instinct of Gothic novelists in turning for their models to the theatre and its most popular contemporary exponents was a fine one, for in choosing the language of gesture they found a vocabulary which appealed directly to their readers' imagination (many of whom incidentally would have formed the theatre audiences and so were already familiar with its conventions). The language of gesture is passion animated, as so much eighteenth-century drama criticism suggests, with its insistence on refined mimetic techniques which demanded total physical, emotional and imaginative responsiveness from an actor. Garrick, for example, was praised by Dr Fordyce for the noble scope of his genius in his portrayal of King Lear in 1763, where the correspondence between emotions and their behaviouristic manifestations is the feature singled out for special praise:

> They [diverse and vehement feelings] possessed by turns all your frame, and appeared successively in every word, and yet more in every gesture, but most of all in every look and feature; presenting, I verily think, such a picture as the world never saw anywhere else.[8]

We can place beside this comments made on dramatic performances throughout the eighteenth century and into the early nineteenth, in order to see the continuous line of theoretical assumptions and indeed of vocabulary which the Gothic novelists assimilated:

> Every passion or emotion of the mind has from its nature its proper and peculiar countenance, sound, and gesture; and the whole body of man, all his looks, and every sound of his voice, like strings on an instrument, receive their sounds from the various impulses of the passions.
> (C. Gildon, *The Life of Thomas Betterton*, 1710, p. 43)

> To act a passion well, the actor never must attempt its imitation, 'til his fancy has conceived so strong an image, or idea, of it, as to move the same impressive springs within his mind, which forms that passion, when 'tis undesigned, and natural.
> This is an absolutely necessary, and the only general rule ... And the truth of its foundation, that it is wholly built on nature, is evident beyond dispute, upon examining its effects, in this deduction, from their causes.
> First, the imagination must conceive a *strong idea* of the passion. Secondly, but that idea cannot *strongly* be conceived, without impressing its own form upon the muscles of the *face*. Thirdly, nor *can* the look be muscularly stamp'd, without communicating instantly the same impression, to the muscles of the body. Fourthly, the muscles of the body (brac'd, or

slack, as the idea was an active or a passive one) must, in their natural and not to be avoided consequence, by impelling or retarding the flow of the animal spirits, transmit their own conceiv'd sensation, to the sound of the *voice*, and to the disposition of the *gesture*.

And this is a short abstract of the Art, in its most com-prehensive and reduced idea.

(A. Hill, *Essay on the Art of Acting*, 1754, pp. 355–6)

There are also Mossop's annotations for his soliloquy as Cardinal Wolsey in *Henry VIII* (published in the *Monthly Mirror* in 1799):

O negligence
(quick and high ... wild, sudden, speaks spitefully and
peevishly)
Fit for a fool to fall by. What cross Devil
(hurried spirit and all in a breath)
Made me put this MAINSECRET in the Pacquet
(pause)
I sent the King. Is there no way to cure this?
(side look ... cunning face full to the audience ... fret-
ful, to himself and musing)[9]

The line of criticism continues substantially unchanged in Hazlitt and in Boaden's Memoirs.

Inevitably in the novels as in the theatre certain patterns of facial expression and gesture came to be associated with certain feelings just as appearance indicated certain character types, and it is needless to detail the many 'fearful despairing groans' of the villains, the 'chilly agues of terror', the 'distracted looks' and 'deathy cheeks', or 'streaming tears of rapture' that pro-ceeded from true lovers reunited. There is no doubt some vali-dity for depicting extreme states of emotion according to a fixed pattern; the very choice of extremes limits the possibility of varied reactions. As Virginia Woolf points out, there are not many possible ways of registering shock and terror:

It is unlikely that a lady confronted by a male body stark naked, wreathed in worms, where she had looked, maybe, for a pleasant landscape in oils, *should* do more than give a loud cry and drop senseless. And women who give loud cries and drop senseless do it in much the same way. That is one of the reasons why it is extremely difficult to write a tale of terror which continues to shock and does not first become insipid and later ridiculous.

(*Granite and Rainbow*, ed. L. Woolf, 1958, p. 59)

The Gothic novelists always tended to exaggerate emotional responses, so we find them more often depicting unusual heights and depths than showing the vast intermediate area of variable feeling which constitutes much of everyday life experience. Their repertoire was in fact limited by their preference for hysteria and emotional violence, a feature which became exaggerated in the minor fiction written between 1800 and 1810 into a wallowing in emotional display. (Incidentally, similar criticisms of overacting in the theatre were more frequently made at the same time, against the successors of Mrs Siddons and J. P. Kemble.) Hysterical insistence on emotional reaction finds its most superb rationale in the statement made in 1810 by A. F. Holstein in *Love, Mystery, and Misery*: 'If a frame is convulsed by deepest emotion, and the countenance with anguished suffering, the depiction is too strong to be misinterpreted.'

The absurdity to which physical display could lead is illustrated in the amusing account of how Thomas Babington Macaulay once kept a list of the number of fainting fits which occurred in a five-volume Minerva novel of 1806 (Kitty Cuthbertson's *Santo Sebastiano*). His list of faintings reads as follows:

Julia de Clifford	11
Lady Delamore	4
Lady Theodosia	4
Lord Glenbrook	2
Lord Delamore	2
Lady Enderfield	1
Lord Ashgrove	1
Lord St. Orville	1
Henry Mildmay	1

Macaulay's sister ends the account by selecting a typical passage from the novel 'to serve as a specimen of these catastrophes':

'One of the sweetest smiles that ever animated the face of mortal now diffused itself over the face of Lord St. Orville, as he fell at the feet of Julia in a death-like swoon.'[10]

Language is also affected by extensive borrowing from the drama so that like physical appearance and gesture it is a kind of attitudinising and cannot function as an individuated statement of feeling. The flexibility which we recognise in the dialogues of Richardson, Fielding or Sterne has vanished, for now heroes and heroines speak in elegant formulae while villains rant and rave in extravagant hyperbole. Walpole, conscientiously imitating Shakespeare, had made an attempt to give the servants dialectal speech and we find instances of liveliness in the speech of 'low' characters throughout the period, but apart from Maturin's convincing Irish peasant dialogues in *Melmoth*, it is humorous caricature rather than genuine speech. When we compare the effect of Gothic novelists' use of dialect with that of Scott or Dickens, we see very little of that delight in verbal inventiveness which characterised the greater writers. Instead of conversation giving us an insight into a character's mind and feelings, in the Gothic novel the effect is just the opposite: particulars of individual feeling are blurred by orthodox rhetoric, and conversation is restricted by decorum to being a statement of the outward appearance of emotion.

Another method much favoured by these novelists for suggesting emotional states and atmosphere was the presentation of landscape. The novels are full of sublime and picturesque scenic descriptions, sometimes evoking a purely aesthetic response in the reader, but more frequently used as a kind of visual correspondence suggestive of an inner psychological state. Like Jane Austen, we cannot imagine a Gothic novel which doesn't have a castle or an abbey—or at least a monastic cell—for there is a distinctive Gothic environment which is both fairytale and menacing. It is an aesthetically created world, a farrago of popular eighteenth-century pictorial images deriving from the paintings of Claude Lorrain and Salvator Rosa, the architectural fantasies of Piranesi, and a general enthusiasm for the medieval revival. Not only is it a world lacking in substance, but when we compare Gothic descriptions of houses and scenery with those in the novels of Fielding, Richardson or Jane Austen,

we find a disturbing shift in the authors' imaginative response
to the world outside themselves. Instead of a sense of stability
and harmony what we find in Gothic fiction is a dreadful insecurity in the face of a contingent world which is entirely
unpredictable and menacing.

It is interesting to speculate why Fielding gave Squire Allworthy a Gothic house to live in in *Tom Jones*. He called it
Paradise Hall:

> The Gothic style of building could produce nothing nobler
> than Mr. Allworthy's house. There was an air of grandeur in
> it that struck you with awe, and rivalled the beauties of the
> best Grecian architecture; and it was commodious within as
> venerable without.   (Book I, Ch. iv)

The contrast between what Gothic represents in this Augustan
novel and the disturbing connotations which such architecture
assumed in later novels is very revealing of the different authorial attitudes to the world in which they lived. Fielding transformed his Palladian models in order to emphasise certain
anti-Augustan qualities about Squire Allworthy which he
admired. Paradise Hall as its name suggests is like Eden, 'awe-
inspiring, grand, noble, venerable', and by making it Gothic
rather than Palladian Fielding is defining its difference from the
Augustan world. Gothic here is as much associated with feeling
as it would be for Horace Walpole thirty years later, but Fielding sees feeling as a good value belonging to the expansive era
of pre-Augustan innocence. Everything in the description of
Allworthy's house and his park points to harmony and stability;
Gothic actually enhances this by carrying within it the religious
connotations of cathedrals and notions of pre-Lapsarian innocence. With Richardson something of the hole-and-corner
nature of Gothic creeps in as we see Pamela imprisoned by
Squire B. in an old rambling house with owls hooting; and certainly Clarissa shares the sense of nightmarish imprisonment
with later Gothic heroines. However, for Richardson a house
still has a solid existence of its own with its whole domestic
organisation going on uninterruptedly, whatever its imaginative transformations within the heroine's mind. Jane Austen's
Palladian houses withstand any disintegration in the order of

3

things, Donwell Abbey, Pemberley and Mansfield Park remaining as the very emblems of stability and harmony. By the time we get to Jane Austen we notice that a radical change has taken place in attitudes to Gothic architecture, so that after the 1790s it would be impossible for a writer to contemplate a Gothic edifice as anything other than radically unsound.

With Gothic novels the stability of the external world breaks down in the way it had threatened to do in Richardson; it has become interiorised, translated into the private world of imagination and neurotic sensibility. Nothing is constant any more: an ordinary room can suddenly be transformed into nightmare by the unlooked-for appearance of a ghost in a chair or a waxen figure covered in worms hiding quietly behind a velvet curtain; objects look different in the moonlight from what they do in the daytime, and things are not necessarily what they seem. Stone walls are not solid any more but are full of sliding panels and secret doorways opening onto winding staircases, while the foundations of Gothic castles are honeycombed by endless labyrinthine passageways which end in cells or funeral vaults or perhaps open into the light of day. Scenery shifts arbitrarily from one episode to the next; this is not merely related to the conventions of romance landscape but more fundamentally to the general instability and impermanence of things, when even castles like Udolpho or the prisons of the Inquisition can fall down or suddenly lose their solidity and power, melting back into the landscape of nightmare. When I suggested earlier that the Gothic world was the external image of the characters' (or the novelists') own obsessions, I was trying to make clear how the configurations of Gothic have a psychological rather than a physical existence.[11] When reading Gothic fiction we have no sense of the real world even in the passages of static picturesque description, partly because they derive from the imaginary landscapes of painting and partly because they have only the most illusory stability. Even life in the countryside so nostalgically conjured up by writers like Mrs Radcliffe and Mrs Roche no longer has the peace and predictability which Fielding gave to it, for heroines can be snatched away from this security at a moment's notice by the arbitrary will of some powerful figure of authority. Everything in the Gothic world is exaggerated: the tranquil beauty of the country, the seemingly infinite corridors of castles, the dimness of moonlit landscapes, the ferocity of storms, the ruggedness of mountains—so that what began as an aesthetic response to environment becomes an imaginative recreation of the world. When we talk about dream landscape in Gothic novels we are talking about a fictive world whose topography is shaped by and is the shape given to emotional responses to uncertainty and threat—the world of nervous breakdown from which Pamela and Clarissa were saved.

Over thirty years (1790–1820) there was a vast variety in the kind and quality of Gothic novels; the preoccupations with fear and terror and all types of overwhelming emotion remained constant, but different novelists responded differently to these common impulses. If we look carefully under what at first glance appears an undifferentiated mass of sensationalism we shall see a number of remarkable attempts to explore the private hinter-land of the human personality. These explorations are expressed through intense and exaggerated imagery in which contem-porary readers found excitement, suspense and beneath it all an interplay of the passions they covertly recognised themselves as sharing.

Ann Radcliffe, *The Mysteries of Udolpho*

> Mrs. Radcliffe as an author, has the most decided
> claim to take her place among the favoured few, who
> have been distinguished as the founders of a class or
> school. She led the way in a peculiar style of composition,
> affecting powerfully the mind of the reader, which has
> since been attempted by many, but in which no-one has
> attained or approached the excellencies of the original
> inventor.[1]

Sir Walter Scott's testimony immediately invites us to ask what
are the excellencies of Mrs Radcliffe's 'peculiar style of com-
position' which enabled her to 'lead the way' in Gothic fiction.
Both Scott and Coleridge felt that she worked by a kind of
magic, Scott calling her a 'mighty magician' and Coleridge
talking about her 'spells'. Her magic is obviously a verbal one,
for her spells are made out of words dexterously woven into
narrative webs which entangle her readers' feelings and imagination in a maze of dreadful uncertainty. To start untangling
the web we would be wise to look closely at the way Mrs Radcliffe uses language to register and interpret experience; what
we shall find is a curious interweaving of Love, Mystery, and
Misery with strands of eighteenth-century rationalism and
moral judgement which produces a new pattern in fiction, a
pattern which challenges us by its ambiguity.

Mrs Radcliffe's world is a frightening one full of shifting perspectives where ways of seeing and judging are continually dis-
solving into uncertainty; it has all the contours of picturesque
fantasy or dream in its timelessness, its placelessness, and its
arbitrariness. Yet we are always aware that this world has an
outer shell around it, that of the author's controlling judgement
which places romance in a definite relationship to the everyday
world. Unlike much fantasy literature, Mrs Radcliffe's fiction
is always responsive to the hazards and problems of life, a

quality which gives it a toughness lacking in many other Gothic novels, for though she may neglect the trivia of living, she never offends her reader's common sense by denying that it exists. Frustration, disappointment and inconvenience are all there, but they are made manageable by a deliberate change in emphasis from practical realities to emotional and imaginative experience, while the formal elegance of her prose lifts the narrative out of the real world into a distanced literary mode of existence. Her novels reflect the romantic tendency to escape from immediate pressures into a private world where difficulties instead of being limitations become stimuli for imaginative flight. At the same time a hard core of rationality insisted on by the author makes it impossible for her heroines or her readers to forget that life cannot be lived for very long as escapist fantasy. The Radcliffian atmosphere of 'dreadful uncertainty' makes for a suspenseful kind of entertainment, and more importantly it creates the conditions for a somewhat anxious investigation into the relative importance of emotion, intuition and reason in human understanding. I say 'somewhat anxious', partly because of the kinds of feeling which Mrs Radcliffe treats and partly because her world of Gothic romance is so evidently one of sublimation and repression.

To get closer to the Radcliffian mystery I shall examine some of the scenes of emotional crisis in *The Mysteries of Udolpho* in order to show how her fictional techniques allow her to present the complex interplay between different kinds of awareness which constitute the peculiar excitements and dangers of her fiction. The passages I have chosen are all closely connected with the castle of Udolpho; this is Mrs Radcliffe's Heart of Darkness, the centre of anarchy and tyrannical power where all those feelings subversive of rational judgement have free range: perplexity and anxious fear on the heroine's part and aggressive hostility on the villain's. Udolpho provides an imagined landscape whose mysteries relate more to the human personality than to the environment. It is a world apart from eighteenth-century social orthodoxy with its ideals of 'order, peace, honour, and beauty' (as Lionel Trilling formulated them to describe Jane Austen's ideals) though Mrs Radcliffe does remind us of their continuous existence by containing Udolpho and its mysteries within a framework of eighteenth-century manners and domestic harmony. As a novel *Udolpho* is decorous and leisurely, 'rising from the gentlest beauty by just gradations to the terrific and sublime' then returning at the end to a picture of peace and order in the next generation very like the one with which it opened.

The mysteries of Udolpho are far away in the future when the novel opens, for we first meet the heroine Emily St Aubert living with her parents in aristocratic rural retirement in their ancestral home of La Vallée 'on the pleasant banks of the Garonne' in the south-west of France. Oddly enough, for all their late eighteenth-century sensibility and picturesque taste these characters are supposed to be living in the sixteenth century, a convention which is so obviously artificial that we do not for a moment take it as a serious historical perspective but purely as a literary device to enclose the author's imagined world within the realms of pseudo-medieval romance. Once we accept that this is a work in the romance tradition, we should not be surprised to find domestic tranquillity shattered by pressures from outside. In Gothic romance it is always the heroine who is snatched away from security to be subjected to trials which threaten the distintegration of her very identity but which she manages quite remarkably to survive. This is precisely what happens in *Udolpho*, though it is characteristic of Mrs Radcliffe's carefully controlled approach that Emily's way of life changes fairly gently and that she has an introduction to the world (albeit an inadequate one) before she is thrown upon Udolpho and its mysteries. Her first view of the outside world is in company with her father when they take a tour down through the Pyrenees to Languedoc, meeting on the way the dashing young hero Valancourt with whom she begins to fall in love. The really drastic changes in Emily's life begin with the death of her father, for as an orphan in her minority she is placed under the care of her aunt who shortly afterwards marries an Italian adventurer called Montoni. It is he who snatches Emily away from La Vallée and from Valancourt, forcing her to go with him and his household to Italy, where she and her aunt find themselves virtually imprisoned in his lonely castle of Udolpho high up in the Apennines. This castle is the centre of the novel, for it is here that Emily suffers all those terrors, real and imaginary, that distinguish her experiences from those of earlier sentimental heroines. Of course she is finally helped to escape but her return home is protracted by a complicated series of delays, including a weird encounter with a dying nun who is harassed by sexual guilt and a harrowing crisis in her relationship with Valancourt which threatens her happiness as surely as Udolpho had threatened her sanity. In the end, however, all is happily resolved: Montoni dies 'in a doubtful and mysterious manner', and even the castle of Udolpho is deprived of its power to terrify; Emily and Valancourt are restored to each other and return to La Vallée where they embark on a happily married life of 'goodness, wisdom, and domestic blessedness'.

Such a summary inevitably shows how closely the novel keeps to sentimental romance narrative. What it does not show is the strangeness of Mrs Radcliffe's world or the peculiarly enigmatic quality of her story-telling methods. Her world is always at one remove from the actual, for she is deliberately creating an imaginary landscape with a France and an Italy decorated with palaces of the imagination or of nightmare, and peopled by characters who are themselves abstractions and who feel with curiously aestheticised emotions—what Archibald Alison in 1790 called 'emotions of Taste'.[2] Everything is filtered through Mrs Radcliffe's imagination which operates like moonlight on a landscape transforming the distinct outlines of reality into obscure romantic shapes. The comparison is in fact Mrs Radcliffe's own:

> Human reason cannot establish her laws on subjects, lost in the obscurity of imagination, any more than the eye can ascertain the form of objects, that only glimmer through the dimness of night. (*Udolpho*, II, xi, 330)[3]

A later Gothic novelist, Rev. C. R. Maturin, loved 'the twilight shade' of Mrs Radcliffe's world and found her romances 'irresistibly and dangerously delightful; fitted to inspire a mind devoted to them with a species of melancholy madness'.[4] Certainly the heroine has a penchant for sentimental melancholy though perhaps Maturin's own morbid temperament led him to exaggerate the mournful aspect of Mrs Radcliffe, for her comments on moonlight suggest not madness but nostalgia:

> A clear moonlight, that succeeded, gave to the landscape what time gives to the scenes of past life, when it softens all their harsher features, and throws over the whole the mellowing shade of distant contemplation.
>
> (*Udolpho*, III, vii, 416–17)

What Mrs Radcliffe aimed to provide was a stimulus to her reader's imagination freed from the restrictiveness of rational definition—a 'negative' as she called it in her essay on the Supernatural in Poetry: 'Obscurity, or indistinctness, is only a negative; which leaves the imagination free to act upon the few hints that truth reveals to it.'[5] Her fictional technique is very close to the 'judicious obscurity' in literature which Edmund Burke praised so highly in his treatise on the Sublime.[6] It has been remarked that Mrs Radcliffe is similar to Burke in her treatment of sublimity and doubtless she was working within a framework of contemporary aesthetic assumptions.[7] I think their affinity rests on something more radical, however, and that is their shared recognition of the fundamental importance of imagination, those powers which as Burke says, 'captivate the soul before the understanding is really able either to join with them or oppose them'.[8] Burke analysed sublimity in his treatise and Mrs Radcliffe dramatised his analysis in her fiction, adding narrative interest to aesthetic speculation. Her novels are pervaded by sublime images closely associated with feelings of fear and a kind of elation won through acute tension and anxiety. The affective power of mountain landscapes and dim twilit perspectives would have struck an answering chord in her eighteenth-century readers, and while their impact on us has lost some of its force through long usage there is still enough stimulus generated by vast dim images for us to feel disconcerted as Mrs Radcliffe harasses her characters and her readers alike.

Mrs Radcliffe's method of presenting her material is a complex mixture of external and internal techniques. Sometimes she works entirely by externals, describing characters, situations and scenery to the reader so that we may react to a concrete series of images in the way we might react to paintings in a gallery. At the other extreme she may use her own modified version of indirect interior monologue, showing how a character's mind and emotions are interacting in the very process of registering experience and compelling the reader's imaginative participation by the intensity of focus on one point of view. More frequently she combines internal and external methods so that scenery or incidents arouse the reader's emotions while at the same time they reflect the feelings of characters involved and allow the author yet another voice, discreet yet distinctly evaluative. Mrs Radcliffe moves deftly from one point of view to another, stimulating and guiding her reader's expectations and responses, while managing to preserve the illusion of imaginative freedom.

The variety and subtlety of Mrs Radcliffe's technique can be seen most clearly in her scenic descriptions and especially in her treatment of architecture. The description of the castle of Udolpho is a typical example of Radcliffian Gothic. It is a long description, but as Sir Walter Scott said when quoting it in his Memoir, 'so beautiful a specimen of Mrs. Radcliffe's talents that we do not hesitate to insert it'.

Towards the close of day, the road wound into a deep valley. Mountains, whose shaggy steeps appeared to be inaccessible, almost surrounded it. To the east, a vista opened, that exhibited the Apennines in their darkest horrors; and the long perspective of retiring summits, rising over each other, their ridges clothed with pines, exhibited a stronger image of grandeur, than any that Emily had yet seen. The sun had just sunk below the top of the mountains she was descending, whose long shadow stretched athwart the valley, but his sloping rays, shooting through an opening of the cliffs, touched with a yellow gleam the summits of the forest, that hung upon the opposite steeps, and streamed in full splendour upon the towers and battlements of a castle, that spread its extensive ramparts along the brow of a precipice above. The splendour of these illumined objects was heightened by the contrasted shade, which involved the valley below.

'There,' said Montoni, speaking for the first time in several hours, 'is Udolpho.'

Emily gazed with melancholy awe upon the castle, which she understood to be Montoni's; for, though it was now lighted up by the setting sun, the gothic greatness of its features, and its mouldering walls of dark grey stone, rendered it a gloomy and sublime object. As she gazed, the light died away on its walls, leaving a melancholy purple tint, which spread deeper and deeper, as the thin vapour crept up the mountain, while the battlements above were still tipped with splendour. From those too, the rays soon faded, and the whole edifice was invested with the solemn duskiness of evening. Silent, lonely and sublime, it seemed to stand the sovereign of the scene, and to frown defiance on all, who dared to invade its solitary reign. As the twilight deepened, its features became more awful in obscurity, and Emily continued to gaze, till its clustering towers were alone seen rising over the tops of the woods, beneath whose thick shade the carriages soon after began to ascend.

The extent and darkness of these tall woods awakened terrific images in her mind, and she almost expected to see banditti start up from under the trees. At length the carriages emerged upon a heathy rock, and, soon after, reached the castle gates, where the deep tone of the portal bell, which was struck upon to give notice of their arrival, increased the fearful emotions, that had assailed Emily.   (*Udolpho*, ii, v, 226–7)

The first paragraph is one of the purple passages of Gothic scenic description, an imaginative recreation in prose of a typical Salvator Rosa painting, with the physical features of sublimity carefully arranged in a deliberately aesthetic description: in the foreground the rugged mountains surrounding and dominating a deep valley, then the 'vista' of the landscape opening out into a 'perspective' of the Apennines whose 'darkest horrors' carried specific emotional and aesthetic connotations for those familiar with the ethos of the Grand Tour. Mrs Radcliffe stresses the emotional power of the visual impression by a brief shift to Emily's point of view, 'it all exhibited a stronger image of grandeur than any Emily had yet seen'. Emphasis on light and dark, the play of sunlight and shadow, follows Burke's strict caution 'against anything light and *riant*'. The sun is setting and as the valley is plunged in shadow, the last rays of sunshine stream through an opening in the cliffs to highlight a castle built above on a precipice. This now becomes the focus of attention; in its splendour, it both satisfies us aesthetically and stimulates our emotions, like an exclamation mark on the landscape. The castle is high up, lit by the sun, while the valley below is in shadow.

'Below' is an important word, not only in the aesthetic patterning of the passage but in its emotional patterning as well, for a great deal of the force of the castle as an image derives from its position 'above' the travellers. We have the sense of winding down into a dark enclosed space: a Gothic road is never straight, and the valley into which it leads is 'surrounded' by 'steeps' which are 'inaccessible'; the labyrinthine quality of the place is hinted at in the description of the valley as 'involved' in shade (surely a word with Miltonic overtones for Mrs Radcliffe). If we look carefully at the syntax we notice a very odd thing: the subject of every sentence and clause is non-human. It is a road, mountains, vistas, the sun, or indeed the castle—there are no human agents here at all. The environment is supreme and things have an active life of their own, imposing their own conditions upon the human beings who come there. This is more than the effect of impressionistic description; it is basic to the Gothic heroine's experience of the world.

Once, it is true, we have a reference to Emily 'seeing' and that is her only response, a passive private registration. 'Seeing' and 'gazing' can be purely aesthetic activities too, closely related to late eighteenth-century experience of the sublime and the picturesque—what Dr Johnson called 'a voluntary agitation of the mind'—though sublime emotions can be rapidly transformed by a change in perspective into something much more disturbing for the beholder. This is precisely Emily's experience when Montoni announces that the splendid castle belongs to him. His speech astonishes the reader too, for his is the first human voice to break the silence of contemplation as with his terse comment he dissipates the aesthetic illusion. Now that the castle has a name and an owner it ceases to be merely a sublime object and its attributes of power and magnificence are brought uncomfortably close. His statement is the shock technique which destroys the 'delightful horror' of aesthetic distance and awakens a very real sense of menace.

In the next paragraph there is a shift to Emily's point of view, but the quality of her gazing has been altered by her knowledge that Udolpho belongs to Montoni. Now gazing with 'melancholy awe' she sees its sublimity as 'gloomy', while the onset of darkness is described in words evocative of her own feelings: the 'melancholy' purple tint spreads 'deeper and deeper', describing not only colour and density but also harking back to the 'depths' of the first paragraph. In the 'solemn' duskiness, the castle takes on an 'awful' power as it rises 'silent, lonely, and sublime', a presence which 'frowns defiance'. The adjectives and the personification of the castle show the curious fusion that has taken place in Emily's mind between the attributes of the edifice and its owner, so that by the time the light fades there is no separation between the outer world and Emily's inner world; the 'terrific images' of sublimity have multiplied and transformed themselves in her imagination so that she 'almost expected' to see banditti rise up as fearful presences in a nightmare landscape. Her fears may have had some rational basis in sixteenth-century Italy, but Emily's reaction is primarily an imaginative one, more likely based on an authorial memory of Salvator Rosa's paintings than on anything in actuality. Udolpho has become for her the symbol of dread and everything associated with it shares the attributes of danger, so that even the 'deep' tone of the portal bell increases her 'fearful emotions'. These fears are exaggerated to such a pitch that she sees her arrival at Udolpho as her entry into a prison.

At this point Mrs Radcliffe quietly comments: '. . . her imagination, ever awake to circumstance, suggested even more terrors than her reason could justify.' It is the first remark the author has permitted herself since the point of view became Emily's. As frequently happens in *Udolpho*, the heroine's feelings have been presented in such detail and the reader's identification with those feelings so encouraged that we find we are accepting something as fact which is, or could be, merely a projection of the character's imagination. The author's balanced comment at the end of the paragraph is likely to be missed, quietly stated as it is within the context of Emily's fears. I think this is

intentional: Mrs Radcliffe wanted to exploit the emotional possibilities of the scene, but her rational comment is there too,
posing the antithesis between the suggestions of imagination and
the justifications of reason, implying that there may be other
ways of judging than the one chosen by the heroine and un-
obtrusively keeping the way open for a return via commonsense
to the familiar world. (For the wittiest appreciation of Mrs
Radcliffe's virtuoso performance we must turn to Jane Austen's
Northanger Abbey where in the frustration of Catherine's hopes in
her approach to Northanger there is a recognition both of the
emotional power of the description and of its dimension of
conscious artificiality.)

The description of Udolpho is very much a late eighteenth-
century set piece appealing to the reader's love of the sublime
and the picturesque. The idiom, with its emphasis on emotional
and imaginative response to scenery and architecture, would be
familiar to contemporary readers from landscape painting,
poetry and Burke's aesthetic theory. The castle itself was also a
familiar feature. It had appeared in fiction from Walpole's
Otranto onwards and had been celebrated by Reynolds in his
Academy lectures, by William Gilpin in his picturesque *Tours*,
and by Archibald Alison in his discussions on the sublime:

> The Sublimest of all the Mechanical Arts is Architecture,
> principally from the durableness of its productions: and these
> productions are in themselves Sublime, in proportion to their
> Antiquity, or the extent of their Duration. The Gothic Castle
> is still more sublime than all, because, besides the desolation
> of Time, it seems also to have withstood the assaults of War. [9]

Mrs Radcliffe did not really have to coerce her readers into
sympathising with Emily's reactions; all she had to do was to
direct their predictable responses. What is remarkable about
the passage is the interplay between visual and emotional perspectives: visual continuity is combined with a shift in point of
view from authorial scenic description to the heroine's subjective
and emotionalised view of the castle. The latter is in fact a projection of her own fears. What begins as an appeal to the reader's
aesthetic sense becomes through Mrs Radcliffe's subtle per-
suasions a way of emotionally involving us with the heroine's

predicament, by what Burke called 'the contagion of the passions'. By the time Montoni's party enters the castle of Udolpho we are prepared to accept, and indeed to expect, 'long suffering and murder within its walls'. From a suspension of the action in the aesthetic contemplation of the novel's focal image, Mrs Radcliffe has prepared the way for setting her narrative in motion again, exciting our expectations and darkening the imaginative associations around the castle.

Given the complex interaction between visual surfaces and emotional response in this description, it is worth considering the implications of Scott's shrewd comment on the image of Udolpho:

> It affords a noble subject for the pencil; but were six artists to attempt to embody it upon canvas, they would probably produce six drawings entirely dissimilar to each other, all of them equally authorised by the printed description.
>
> (Memoir, xxx)

And indeed, three different paintings of the castle of Udolpho were exhibited at the Royal Academy in 1797, 1798 and 1799.[10] Mrs Radcliffe's description is one of subjective response to the castle rather than a close observation of it. We are inevitably reminded of Burke's distinction between painting and poetry as imitative and emotive arts, for as he claims, 'words may affect without raising images':

> In reality, poetry and rhetoric do not succeed in exact description as well as painting does; their business is to affect rather by sympathy than by imitation; to display rather the effect of things on the mind of the speaker, or of others, than to present a clear idea of the things themselves.
>
> (Sublime, v, vi, 215)

Certainly Mrs Radcliffe's technique is poetical and rhetorical; when Scott called her 'the first poetess of romantic fiction' he was drawing attention to the strong imaginative appeal of her writing, for her methods are in many ways close to lyric poetry. What she does is establish a direct link between the reader and the feeling generated by a scene, frequently by encouraging our sympathetic identification with an intensely focussed though totally one-sided point of view. With increased emotional involvement, a 'clear idea of things themselves' recedes as much for us as for the hypersensitive heroine. Curiously, the more we become involved in her self-enclosed world, the less clearly we see the heroine herself. She too dissolves as a personality and remains with us only as a sensibility, a sensitive refracting medium for our own feelings. Mrs Radcliffe's power over her readers' imaginative sympathies was remarked on very early in her career; in 1792 the *Monthly Review* critic described *The Romance of the Forest* as a tale 'very skilfully constructed, to hold the reader's curiosity in suspense, and at the same time to keep his feelings in perpetual agitation',[11] and in an appreciation of her work written shortly after her death in 1826 the critic of the *New Monthly Magazine* made a similar observation on her affective powers:

> There was a fine knowledge of the pulses of curiosity and fear in the human heart; and a nice discrimination in apportioning the degree and kind of excitement which would call forth their fondest throbbings, which has never elsewhere been employed by the novelist. It may be true that her persons are cold and formal; but her readers are the virtual heroes and heroines of her story as they read; and when they rise from the perusal, instead of having become intimate with a rich troop of characters, they seem to have added a long series of adventures to their individual history. It is idle however, to dispute about the means, when the end is so apparent; to contend that that which has endured so long had no principle of vitality; that books which have been devoured by thousands, have no legitimate hold on the sympathies; or that an effect is easily produced, which a hundred well-trained imitators have attempted to produce in vain.[12]

Mrs Radcliffe went to great lengths to draw her readers into her fictions, even on occasions experimenting with static situations whose appeal was rather like that of a painting. Instead of being presented with the anxious imaginary world of the heroine, the reader is faced with a picture painted by the author, in which the characters are little more than formal elements and where the point of view we are invited to share is the author's entirely.

There is a very good example of this 'picturesque' presentation of feeling in the description of the funeral of Emily's aunt Madame Montoni at Udolpho. The scene is full of feeling, yet it is neither moral nor religious. It is no meditation on death like Gray's *Elegy* or Young's *Night Thoughts*, nor does it embody the Christian feeling of Clarissa's death, though doubtless Mrs Radcliffe believed in an afterlife and in the notion that death is part of the Providential pattern: 'In death there is nothing new, or surprising, since we all know, that we are born to die; and nothing terrible to those, who can confide in an all-powerful God' (*Udolpho*, 1, vii, 76). Certainly a good conscience and a serene faith could reconcile man to death, but it could not alleviate the effects of the mysterious confrontation with non-being which made death the primary cause of imaginative fear. Burke had called it 'the king of terrors' and the Graveyard poets had given death and the fear of death a vocabulary which united all men's fears of the mysterious, the dark and the unknown. It is the frisson of our immediate response to the phenomenon of death that Mrs Radcliffe is trying to evoke in the funeral scene. She was no less keenly aware of the physical horrors of death than M. G. Lewis, as is clear in the glimpses at Udolpho of bloodstained corpses and waxen images crawling with worms, though unlike Lewis she saw horror as productive of nothing but revulsion and preferred suggestive images which would enliven rather than freeze the reader's imagination:

They must be men of very cold imaginations with whom certainty is more terrible than surmise. Terror and horror are so far opposite, that the first expands the soul, and awakens the faculties to a high degree of life; the other contracts, freezes, and nearly annihilates them. Neither Shakespeare nor Milton ... nor Mr. Burke anywhere looked to positive horrors as a source of the sublime, although they all agree that terror is a very high one; and where lies the great difference between *Terror* and *Horror* but in the uncertainty and obscurity that accompanies the first respecting the dreaded evil?   (*On the Supernatural in Poetry*, 149)

In the funeral scene Mrs Radcliffe begins with the ritual accompaniments of death and then so structures her presentation that the reader is led away from the actual narrative situation towards his own morbid speculations:

At the moment, in which they let down the body into the earth, the scene was such as only the dark pencil of a Domenichino, perhaps, could have done justice to. The fierce features and wild dress of the *condottieri*, bending with their torches over the grave, into which the corpse was descending, were contrasted by the venerable figure of the monk, wrapt in long black garments, his cowl thrown back from his pale face, on which the light gleaming strongly shewed the lines of affliction softened by piety, and the few grey locks, which time had spared on his temples: while, beside him, stood the softer form of Emily, who leaned for support upon Annette; her face half averted, and shaded by a thin veil, that fell over her figure; and her mild and beautiful countenance fixed in grief so solemn as admitted not of tears, while she thus saw committed untimely to the earth her last relative and friend. The gleams, thrown between the arches of the vaults, where, here and there, the broken ground marked the spots in which other bodies had been recently interred, and the general obscurity beyond were circumstances, that alone would have led on the imagination of a spectator to scenes more horrible, than even that, which was pictured at the grave of the misguided and unfortunate Madame Montoni.   (III, v, 377–8)

Mrs Radcliffe catches our attention by showing us the very moment of burial, that time of extraordinary transformation from humanity to earth which spells 'deadness' in all its brutal realism. The passage is full of the characteristic Gothic movement downwards that we noticed in the journey through the valley to Udolpho, here enacted in the 'bending' of the *condottieri* and the 'letting down' of the body into the earth, later to be emphasised by the vaults and the other newly-made graves. If the description were only this it would be pure graveyard horror, but Mrs Radcliffe encourages her readers to use a wider variety of imaginative responses by introducing a deliberately aesthetic dimension. With the word 'scene' and the reference to

4

the seventeenth-century Italian painter Domenichino in the first sentence, she freezes the action in a tableau designed to appeal to a public who knew and liked the Bolognese school, among whom were Domenichino and Guido Reni. (Reynolds commented rather tartly on the popularity of this school in his XVIth Discourse in 1786: 'If excellence of this kind is to be valued according to the *number*, rather than the *weight and quality* of admirers, it would assume an even higher rank in Art.') Just as she had borrowed from the compositional techniques of landscape painting in her description of Udolpho, now Mrs Radcliffe adopts Domenichino's technique of arranging figures in strongly contrastive groups. She gives us a detailed study of forms, with the fierce *condottieri* bending over the open grave 'contrasted by' the monk in his black robe and the veiled Emily beside him, the perfect emblem of grief. It is a totally static embodiment of feeling contained within the architectural cadre of the 'arches of the vaults', very similar in its picturesque effect to those views framed by Gothic windows or by long Venetian mirrors which are found elsewhere in the novel. The strong *chiaroscuro* effects of the last sentence complete the visual appeal of this scene 'pictured' at the grave of the 'unfortunate and misguided Madame Montoni'. Surely the most perfunctory epitaph in Gothic fiction, this suggests that Mrs Radcliffe was not really interested in the feelings of grief and loss attached to death but mainly in the morbid stimulus to the imagination it can provide. Being keenly aware of the multi-dimensional appeal of her verbal medium, she does not stop at the funeral tableau but initiates a movement away from this particular scene through the 'general obscurity beyond' into her readers' own minds where they will conjure up scenes even more 'horrible' than this one. (The word 'horrible' is an interesting and unusual one for Mrs Radcliffe to use and surely derives from Burke's usage in a similar context: 'The ideas of pain, sickness, and death fill the mind with strong emotions of horror', *Sublime*, p. 91.) As always it is the mechanics of 'terror' which interest Mrs Radcliffe, to induce in her readers that feeling which 'awakens the faculties to a high degree of life' by images of 'uncertainty and obscurity'.

In such a presentation the technique is closer to visual art than to the novel, where we are accustomed to find feeling linked directly to the experience of particular characters; here Mrs Radcliffe is working entirely outside her characters, using them like the objects in a picture to reflect emotion outwards in order to stimulate our own patterns of emotional association. The peculiar combination of graveyard gloom, religiosity and aesthetic treatment makes this passage absolutely seminal for Gothic fiction. Mrs Radcliffe quite consciously provides a model which urges readers to create their own morbid fantasies for themselves, and indeed this is exactly what other Gothic novelists did (for they were all, like Monk Lewis, readers of Gothic fiction too). We can see the pattern of Madame Montoni's funeral repeated with variations in much of the fiction and poetry about burials throughout the nineteenth century, extending through the graveyard horrors of Lewis and Shelley to the poetry of Rossetti.

If Mrs Radcliffe's skill as a writer shows itself undeniably in the way her descriptions play with surfaces and appearances, it is also apparent when she portrays the registering consciousness of one of her characters. Those characters whose minds she gets closest to are her heroines, especially when they are in solitude. We learn very little about these girls in public situations for their manners are so delicate that their response to other people is very stylised and formal; it is only when the heroines are alone that we get a freer play of mind and a kind of anxiety-ridden emotional reverie is revealed, made all the more intense by their own self-enclosure. Mrs Radcliffe registers the obsessive quality of such mental activity with a precision which comes very close to the technique of interior monologue, though the presentation is always indirect, allowing a subtle interplay between the points of view of character and author. An excellent example of the combination of inner action with authorial intervention occurs in the incident where Emily, a prisoner in Udolpho, hears mysterious music under her window at midnight and jumps to the conclusion that the unknown singer is her lover Valancourt whom she had left behind in France:

Her sighs were deep and convulsed; she could no longer listen to the strain, that had so often charmed her to tranquillity, and she withdrew from the casement to a remote part of the chamber. But she was not yet beyond the reach of the music; she heard the measure change, and the succeeding air called her again to the window, for she immediately recollected it to be the same she had formerly heard in the fishing-house in Gascony. Assisted, perhaps, by the mystery, which had then accompanied this strain, it had made so deep an impression on her memory, that she had never since entirely forgotten it; and the manner, in which it was now sung, convinced her, however unaccountable the circumstance appeared, that this was the same voice she had then heard. Surprise soon yielded to other emotions; a thought darted, like lightning, upon her mind, which discovered a train of hopes, that revived all her spirits. Yet these hopes were so new, so unexpected, so astonishing, that she did not dare to trust, though she could not resolve to discourage them. She sat down by the casement, breathless, and overcome with the alternate emotions of hope and fear; then rose again, leaned from the window, that she might catch a nearer sound, listened, now doubting and then believing, softly exclaimed the name of Valancourt, and then sunk again into the chair. Yes, it was possible, that Valancourt was near her, and she recollected circumstances, which induced her to believe it was his voice she had just heard. She remembered he had more than once said that the fishing-house, where she had formerly listened to this voice and air, and where she had seen pencilled sonnets, addressed to herself, had been his favourite haunt, before he had been made known to her; there, too, she had herself unexpectedly met him. It appeared, from these circumstances, more than probable, that he was the musician, who had formerly charmed her attention, and the author of the lines, which had expressed such tender admiration;—who else, indeed, could it be? She was unable, at that time, to form a conjecture, as to the writer, but, since her acquaintance with Valancourt, whenever he had mentioned the fishing-house to have been known to him, she had not scrupled to believe that he was the author of the sonnets.

As these considerations passed over her mind, joy, fear and

tenderness contended at her heart; she leaned again from the casement to catch the sounds, which might confirm or destroy her hope, though she did not recollect to have ever heard him sing; but the voice, and the instrument, now ceased.

(III, v, 387–8)

Here we see the interior monologue becoming a refined technique for arousing suspense, for not only does it enact Emily's doubts and uncertainties but it has all the trappings of sentimental mystery which encourages the reader to engage with her in her dilemma. The process of emotionalised logic is registered so intensely and so exclusively from Emily's point of view that we lose all sense of how feeling may be distorting judgement. From the beginning we are caught up in Emily's restlessness of mind and body as the lonely girl reacts to a familiar song in a very unfamiliar place. Nostalgia combined with her sense of isolation encourages her to try to identify the unknown singer, and Mrs Radcliffe minutely traces the stages by which Emily succeeds in creating an emotionally satisfying solution to an incomprehensible mystery. Her memory of the past and her sensations on hearing the song provide such a powerful stimulus to her feelings that Emily's judgement is very quickly dominated by emotion. Indeed by the fourth sentence feeling seems to have taken over completely: Emily is no longer the subject of the sentence; instead we have 'surprise', 'a thought' which 'darts like lightning', and a 'train of hopes'. There is still some feeble attempt on Emily's part to withhold judgement as the 'yet' at the beginning of the next sentence suggests, but the balance soon tips toward feeling for 'she could not resolve to discourage' hope. Torn between the opposing impulses of hope and fear, 'now doubting, then believing', Emily actually does something: she calls out to the singer. It is her one dynamic action, and it carries her towards conviction while convincing us too. From now on the step from 'it was possible' to 'it was more than probable' that the unknown singer is Valancourt is very easy to make, and her rhetorical question convinces her of what she had wanted to believe, 'Who else, indeed, could it be?'. By this time the reader like Emily is so caught up in her fictive structure that, forgetting its uncertain basis in fact and her real

ignorance of events in the fishing-house, we adopt the satisfying conclusion that the mysterious singer must be Emily's
lover.

There is no doubt any longer in Emily's mind as 'joy, fear
and tenderness contended at her heart', and she leans out of the
window again. However, the structure of this long sentence is
very curious; clauses are juxtaposed in such a way as to generate
uncertainty in any mind not already emotionally committed.
Her leaning out of the window is revealed to be a totally pur-
poseless inquiry on two counts: first, she 'did not recollect' to
have ever heard Valancourt sing; second, she is met by total
silence, 'for the voice, and the instrument, now ceased'. Emily
is really up against blankness; where there had been little
external information before, there is now none at all. The two
final clauses cast into doubt her whole solution to the mystery
and contain an implied authorial comment on her reasoning
process. Silence may be interpreted as grounds for hope from
Emily's point of view—or alternatively as grounds for doubt
from the author's.

It is Mrs Radcliffe's intention to appeal to our curiosity and
sentimental interest in the lovers' fate so as to secure our sympathetic involvement. As so often happens, the authorial doubt
so slyly expressed at the end is passed over unnoticed, the reader
being so close to Emily's thoughts. We shall probably be as disappointed as Emily when she later discovers that the singer was
not Valancourt after all. We have been persuaded to accept as
argument a structure of restless longings and memories, for all
that has been dramatised is Emily's self-enclosed consciousness,
intensely active but not really relating to the outside world at
all. She cannot influence her environment in any way and
indeed the outside world is unresponsive to her at very crucial
times. It is from this sense of Emily's powerlessness that we
derive our image of her as the victim of circumstances and perhaps it is her own awareness of it that generates her deep
melancholy and frustration. This passage reveals the double
point of view which is operating so much of the time in Mrs
Radcliffe's fiction: Emily's emotionalised view and a more
objective view which is the author's, for though quiet and self-
effacing Mrs Radcliffe is a distinctively separate presence

always in control of the movement of her narrative and always manipulating her readers' responses.

Emily so often gets things wrong that we are forced to ask what Mrs Radcliffe meant by giving her an over-active imagination—by making her an 'imaginist' in fact, like Jane Austen's Emma. I have borrowed Jane Austen's vocabulary here because I want to point to the similar assumptions behind Mrs Radcliffe's and Jane Austen's treatment of their heroines. Mrs Radcliffe clearly has a double purpose: on the one hand she is sympathetic enough with the life of the feelings to trace Emily's in detail and to encourage her readers to indulge in sentimental fantasy; but on the other, like Jane Austen, she is attempting to show the unreliability of conclusions based on feeling and first impressions rather than on rational judgement. One of the things Emily must battle against throughout the novel is her strong natural propensity towards emotionalism, and one of the most interesting attempts at continuity of theme is the educational process by which Emily must learn to balance reason and feeling in order to gain 'rational happiness'. Her father, who 'had too much good sense to prefer a charm to a virtue', had tried 'to strengthen her mind, to inure her to habits of self-command; to teach her to reject the first impulse of her feelings and to look with cool examination on the disappointments he sometimes threw in her way' (i, v, 5). This learning programme in its precise outline places Mrs Radcliffe squarely in the line of eighteenth-century moralists such as Richardson and Dr Johnson and leads straight on to Jane Austen. Indeed, it is close in word and spirit to 'that subjection of the fancy to the understanding' that Mr Knightley thought would be so advantageous to Emma. Mrs Radcliffe was not by any means the first novelist to condemn emotional indulgence,[13] but she was one of the few novelists before Jane Austen whose authorial condemnation had any effect on her fiction—though Jane Austen evidently did not think it had enough, and we might be inclined to agree with her. Emily tends to oscillate between polar opposites, sometimes succumbing to excessive feeling and at others keenly self-aware and stringently self-critical:

She blamed herself for suffering her romantic imagination

to carry her so far beyond the bounds of probability, and
determined to endeavour to check its rapid flights, lest they
should sometimes extend into madness.   (III, i, 342)

The author's own judgement is hardly more severe:

It was lamentable, that her excellent understanding should
have yielded even for a moment, to the reveries of superstition,
or rather to those starts of imagination, which deceive the
senses into what can be called nothing less than momentary
madness. Instances of this temporary failure of mind had
more than once occurred since her return home; particularly
when wandering through this lonely mansion in the evening
twilight, she had been alarmed by appearances, which would
have been unseen in her more cheerful days.   (I, x, 102)

Mrs Radcliffe is on the way to creating an Emma in Emily,
for she is interested in examining how a girl's mental and emotional isolation may breed fantasies. However, her romance
form with its extravagant crises of action and feeling works
against her. Too often what is shown is a correspondence rather
than a contrast between imagined fears and the reality of the
romance world. There is no opportunity for a coherent drama-
tisation of Emily's development; so what we have is the exploration of certain aspects of personality within a very limited
emotional framework. Unlike Emma, Emily does not grow any
wiser; in the end she is merely rescued from the world of
Udolpho and brought back to ordered society. There is no
more relatedness between her experiences at Udolpho and at
La Vallée than there is between a nightmare and an awakening
in the light of day. Mrs Radcliffe does not even stress what must
surely be Emily's remarkable powers of recovery; after all,
Jane Eyre remembered her terrible childhood experiences in
the Red Room for the rest of her life. We are forced to conclude
that Emily St Aubert is not a character of flesh and blood like
Emma Woodhouse or Jane Eyre but only a linear series of responses to outlandish situations. Although balanced judgement
triumphs at the end, it is not enacted by the heroine but belongs
solely to the author's argument and to her manipulative skill in
shaping her narrative.

Although it is true that we have no coherent sense of Emily as a personality, her sensibility does provide the focus for that emotional area where Mrs Radcliffe's own sensitivity and skill are most acute: in the detailed exploration of certain anxiety states which are identifiably feminine and closely associated with isolation, dependence and sexual fears. The pretence at setting the story in the late sixteenth century gives Mrs Radcliffe the freedom to choose forms which both embody and disguise contemporary neuroses, and as Emily pursues her elusive way through the terrors of a world of romance her adventures are very evidently an analogue for the predicament of the late eighteenth-century woman. Like the heroines of Richardson, Fanny Burney and Jane Austen, Emily is forced to meet a series of challenges which are social and moral in origin and in which the only guidance on how to act comes from her own feelings. Under the pressures of isolation and loneliness she is harassed into acute states of anxiety where her good sense sometimes gives way to crises of hysteria and panic, as is made explicit in her behaviour at Udolpho where she momentarily loses the ability to distinguish between real and imaginary dangers:

> Long-suffering had made her spirits peculiarly sensible to terror, and liable to be affected by the illusions of superstition ... Yet reason told her that this was a wild conjecture, and she was inclined to dismiss it; but, with the inconsistency so natural, when imagination guides the thoughts, she then wavered towards a belief as wild.   (II, xi, 330–1)

Certainly conditions at Udolpho are extreme, for Emily is literally imprisoned there under a tyrant's control. The real-life predicament, however, is not difficult to see under the romance disguise: Emily is an unmarried girl, an orphan in her minority, left to the care of an irresponsible aunt and her aunt's tyrannical husband, who first tries to strip his wife of her property and marry off his niece to his own advantage; he then takes the two women away to his secluded castle, where he is the sole arbiter of justice, and after worrying his wife to death tries to extort the inheritance from his niece. Put in these terms, Montoni looks rather like Le Fanu's Uncle Silas in a plot concerned with male exploitation of economically defenceless women, a common enough theme in sentimental fiction. What is unusual about *Udolpho* however is the extravagant fantasy forms in which the situation is dramatised: Montoni is not only mercenary but an Italian brigand who suffers from a power fantasy, while his secluded castle is a fortified defence post high in the Apennines filled with armed desperadoes where the dangers of assault and possibly of murder are far from imaginary. In the arranged marriage Emily's suitor is neither an 'odious Solmes' nor a dashing Henry Crawford but the hot-blooded Italian Count Morano who cannot be restrained in his pursuit until he has tried to abduct Emily and in consequence been severely wounded by Montoni. Everything is dramatised in terms so violent that anxiety often verges on hysteria and hallucination:

> She beheld herself in the remote wilds of the Apennine, surrounded by men, whom she considered to be little less than ruffians, and their worst associates, amid scenes of vice, from which her soul recoiled in horror. It was at this moment, when the scenes of the present and the future opened to her imagination that the image of Valancourt failed in its influence, and her resolution shook with dread. She thought she understood all the horrors, which Montoni was preparing for her, and shrunk from an encounter with such remorseless vengeance, as he could inflict. (III, v, 384)

Emily's own cast of sensibility is peculiarly melancholy. Robert Kiely refers to her 'fine sense of danger', and it is true that she not only expects the worst at all times but that her most acute feelings are those of misery and fear. Everything in Emily's make-up is an exaggeration of those negative responses which were often the only ones available to the late eighteenth-century woman who wished to preserve her own individuality. The danger for such a woman was that any ability she might have to act positively and spontaneously was liable to be corrupted by constant opposition and resistance from those around her. In Emily's case the corruption takes the form of her own prudential fears exaggerated to the point of neuroticism, and so often getting the better of her. It is characteristic of Emily that she is much more susceptible to Montoni's image than to that of her own true love Valancourt. Indeed what she feels most

acutely in her relationship with Valancourt are the miseries
rather than the joys of love—the pains of forced separation and
the dreadful desolation when later she rejects him. Indeed, at
the end when Valancourt comes running into her lonely tower
to claim her as his wife, Emily has no intuition whatever either
of his approach or his intention. On the other hand she is
obsessed by Montoni from the very first time she sees him:

> This Signor Montoni had an air of conscious superiority,
> animated by spirit, and strengthened by talents, to which
> every person seemed involuntarily to yield; the quickness of
> his perceptions was strikingly expressed on his countenance,
> yet that countenance could submit implicitly to occasion;
> and, more than once in this day, the triumph of art over
> nature might have been discerned in it. His visage was long,
> and rather narrow, yet he was called handsome; and it was,
> perhaps, the spirit and vigour of his soul, sparkling through
> his features, that triumphed for him. Emily felt admiration,
> but not the admiration that leads to esteem; for it was mixed
> with a degree of fear she knew not exactly wherefore.
>
> (I, xii, 122)

The longer Emily is in his house the more she allows her imagination to magnify his power over her. In a curious way Emily
and Montoni are counterparts to each other in the same fantasy: he with his will to power and his display of 'conscious
superiority' has the ideal foil in Emily, filled as she is with
admiration for his exceptional qualities and at the same time
terrified by the mysteriousness of a temperament diametrically
opposite to her own:

> Her sufferings, though deep, partook of the gentle char-
> acter of her mind; hers was a silent anguish, weeping, yet
> enduring; not the wild energy of passion, inflaming imagina-
> tion, bearing down the barriers of reason and living in a
> world of its own. (II, x, 329)

Mrs Radcliffe's language suggests that their antagonism finds
its parallel in the aesthetic antithesis between the sublime and
the beautiful, an idea supported by Lionel Trilling's comment

on the sexual polarities contained in Burke's notion of Sublimity:

> He [Burke] explicitly connects the sublime with masculinity, with manly ambition; the defining characteristic of the sublime, he tells us, is its capacity for arousing the emotion of 'terror' which calls forth in us the power to meet and master it; the experience of terror stimulates an energy of aggression and dominance. Beauty, on the contrary, is to be associated with femininity; it seduces men to inglorious indolence and ignoble hedonism.[14]

Certainly the antagonism between Montoni and Emily has a sexual resonance as well, all the more neurotic for being treated so evasively and indirectly. All the time Emily is under Montoni's protection she is obsessed by ideas of vice, rape and murder, though Montoni himself hardly seems to be aware of her except as an object to be exploited economically. Sexuality comes to the surface only on one extraordinary occasion, with Count Morano's jealous accusation that Emily has refused him because she is in love with Montoni. However, there is no attempt either by Emily or by the author to explore the mixed feelings of instinctual attraction and exaggerated irrational fear that Emily has for Montoni. Indeed, there is no overt acknowledgement of sexual feeling in the novel at all; there is merely the recognition of a nameless power which is a frightening, potentially destructive force capable of assaulting both the body and the will. This fearful awareness is surely at the basis of the threats of rape and murder which pervade Gothic fiction but which for Mrs Radcliffe hover only as nightmarish forms to torment the innocent minds of her heroines as they 'recoil in horror' and 'shake with dread' at the prospect of the villain's 'remorseless vengeance'.

In what is probably Emily's worst crisis of fear we see the enacting of these neuroses as she is helplessly caught in a situation of dramatic isolation and possibly of real danger. On the occasion when Udolpho is about to be attacked, Montoni sends Emily away to a cottage in Tuscany, though whether for her safety or with the intent to have her murdered Emily does not know. What is most dreadful is the situation of uncertainty in which Emily finds herself, where it is impossible to balance the claims of fearful imaginings against rational awareness:

Emily now breathed with difficulty, and could scarcely support herself. When first she saw these men, their appearance and their connection with Montoni had been sufficient to impress her with distrust; but now, when one of them had betrayed himself to be a murderer, and she saw herself, at the approach of night, under his guidance, among wild and solitary mountains, and going she scarcely knew whither, the most agonizing terror seized her, which was the less supportable from the necessity she found herself under of concealing all symptoms of it from her companions. Reflecting on the character and the menaces of Montoni, it appeared not improbable, that he had delivered her to them, for the purpose of having her murdered, and of thus securing to himself, without further opposition, or delay, the estates, for which he had so long and so desperately contended. Yet, if this was his design, there appeared no necessity for sending her to such a distance from the castle; for, if any dread of discovery had made him unwilling to perpetrate the deed there, a much nearer place might have sufficed for the purpose of concealment. These considerations, however, did not immediately occur to Emily, with whom so many circumstances conspired to rouse terror, that she had no power to oppose it, or to enquire coolly into its grounds; and, if she had done so, still there were many appearances which would too well have justified her most terrible apprehensions . . .

The dread of what she might be going to encounter was now so excessive, that it sometimes threatened her senses . . . So romantic and improbable, indeed, did her present situation appear to Emily herself, particularly when she compared it with the repose and beauty of her early days, that there were moments, when she could have almost believed herself the victim of frightful visions, glaring upon a disordered fancy. (III, vi, 406–7)

We are plunged into Emily's self-enclosed world of dreadful surmise where she is scarcely able to perform the most elementary vital functions, obsessed as she is by her present danger. Mrs Radcliffe carefully builds up dread to a crescendo, tracing its origin in Emily's fear of Montoni and then piling up unnerving details phrase by phrase as Emily's growing sense of her own vulnerability is heightened into 'the most agonising terror'. The situation is certainly very alarming; it is close to the abduction scenes in many Gothic novels and is a situation whose potential Mrs Radcliffe exploits in her next novel *The Italian* (1796) where the aim of such a journey *is* to take the heroine to an out-of-the-way place to have her murdered. Emily is again trapped by her enforced passivity so that the only possible activity available to her is a mental one, 'reflecting on the character and menaces of Montoni'. He is the strongest argument for her terrors and all she can do is augment her fear of him by surmise. The authorial voice does intrude with one rational suggestion where Mrs Radcliffe makes some attempt to distance herself and the reader from Emily's anxious imaginings: 'These considerations did not immediately occur to Emily' who is as usual so overcome by 'circumstances' that she cannot inquire 'coolly'. But the commentary never contradicts Emily and appearances are so strong that they undercut any attempt at rational appraisal, even the author's. Emily's fears are so pervasive that the sense of dread infects even the last sentence quoted, where she seems for one fleeting moment to share the author's own rational doubts: 'she could almost have believed herself the victim of frightful visions glaring upon a disordered fancy'. But these moments of sanity that cut like shafts across Emily's mind suggesting that her present situation is both 'romantic' and 'improbable' only take on an ironic force at a time when anxious fear seems to be the most reasonable response to present circumstances. There is no reliable way of judging and by the end the author's and Emily's points of view seem to merge so that the reader, like Emily, is plunged into total uncertainty. There is no decisive movement here from one point of view to another as there was in the passage about the singer quoted earlier; instead, both the possibility of safety and the possibility of death are given equal weight and objective reality remains elusive. While the passage is cast in the form of reasoned argument with one sentence depending on and balancing the other, it has really only the

appearance of judiciousness; what we have in effect is the drama-
tisation of a process very close to obsession, going round and
round the same point and finding no escape or release from the
central anxiety.

A passage like this which sticks so closely to the minutiae of
subjective experience demonstrates conclusively that we ought
not to underrate Mrs Radcliffe's understanding of the com-
plexities of emotion nor her recognition of the powers of the
imagination. Indeed this is precisely what she is exploiting in
her heroine and in her readers: 'That love, so natural to the
human mind, of whatever is able to distend its faculties with
wonder and astonishment' (IV, vi, 549). She deliberately creates
situations of uncertainty out of which readers and characters
alike will try to construct meaningful patterns, usually like
Emily frightening themselves more than Mrs Radcliffe could
have done. Like Burke, Mrs Radcliffe believed that 'it is our
nature when we do not know what may happen to us, to fear
the worst that can happen' (*The Sublime*, II, xix, p. 134). Scott
remarked that her romances gain their powerful effect 'by an
appeal in one word to the passion of *fear*, whether excited by
natural dangers or by the suggestions of superstition' (*Memoir*,
p. xviii). She exploited the imaginative appeal of the apparently
inexplicable, but her scepticism always compelled her to destroy her fantasy world and return her readers to a world they
recognised, where rationality reigned supreme. Scott did not
like her method of explaining everything away and talked of the
reader's 'disappointment and displeasure'; he was 'angry with
his senses for having cheated him, and with his reason for having
acquiesced in the deception':

> A principal characteristic of Mrs. Radcliffe's Romances, is
> the rule which the author imposed upon herself, that all the
> circumstances of her narrative, however mysterious, and
> apparently superhuman, were to be accounted for on natural
> principles, at the winding up of the story.   (*Memoir*, p. xxiv)

Coleridge confessed to a similar sense of frustration:

> Curiosity is raised oftener than it is gratified; or rather, it
> is raised so high that no adequate gratification can be given

it; the interest is completely dissolved when once the adventure is finished, and the reader, when he is got to the end of
the work, looks about in vain for the spell which had bound
him so strongly to it.[15]

Mrs Radcliffe's explanations are perhaps due to her being
very alive to the *dangers* of abandonment to intense feeling. She
attempts to suggest that these intensities are fairytale, daydream
or even madness, and that real life is something different and
much more ordinary—all of which perhaps accounts for our dis-
satisfaction at the end when we are asked to accept 'real life'
again, a life which possesses the solid virtues of rational happiness but none of the excitements of the world of Udolpho. We
feel that with the passing of Montoni and Udolpho into the
world of darkness all the excitement has gone from Emily's
life:

> Montoni, too, often rose to her fancy, such as she had seen
> him in his days of triumph, bold, spirited and commanding;
> such also as she had since beheld him in his days of vengeance;
> and now, only a few short months had passed—and he had no
> longer the power, or the will to afflict;—he had become a
> clod of earth, and his life was vanished like a shadow!
>
> (IV, x, 580)

All that is left for Emily is to make her peace with Valancourt
and to live happily ever after like the heroine of any sentimental
novel. However, with Emily's rather morbid sensibility there is
not much chance for Mrs Radcliffe to celebrate happiness in
love. Emily has always behaved towards Valancourt with ut-
most circumspection, a policy continued on her return to
France when she believes he is no longer morally estimable.
There is something rather chilly about her decorum when on
their first meeting after long separation she carefully explains
that she will not be able to marry him if his character is not as
blameless as it used to be:

> 'I sincerely forgive you', replied Emily. 'You best know
> whether I shall continue to love you, for you know whether
> you deserve my esteem. At present, I will believe that you do.

It is unncessary to say', added she, observing his dejection, 'how much pain it would give me to believe otherwise.'

(III, xiii, 504)

Her statement illustrates the proper way a young lady ought to behave in such an event, though of course it also gives Emily the opportunity for another crisis of refined masochism and Mrs Radcliffe the chance to exploit tensions between appearances and the reality under the surface of behaviour. Her prudent rejection is totally at variance with her feeling for Valancourt so that on the one hand she refuses to see him and on the other suffers in her own watertight world as intensely as she did at Udolpho: 'When she attempted to think, her mind refused controul, and she could only feel that she was miserable' (III, xiii, 509). Again the dilemma is basically a moral one, this time complicated by the possibility that feeling may for once be the only adequate criterion of judgement. Emily is so miserable that she comes to doubt the very principles on which she has acted:

> In these moments, she could not congratulate herself on the prudence, that had saved her; she could only lament, with bitterest anguish, the circumstances, which had conspired to betray Valancourt into a course of life so different from that, which the virtues, the tastes, and the pursuits of his early years had promised; but she still loved him too well to believe that his heart was even now depraved, though his conduct had been criminal. (IV, x, 584)

Interestingly, the heroine in Mrs Radcliffe's later novel *The Italian* has a similar perception of the dubious value of reason and prudence when faced with the recognition of purely emotional claims:

> Her very virtues, now that they were carried to excess, seemed to her to border upon vices; her sense of dignity appeared to be narrow pride; her delicacy, weakness; her moderated affection, cold ingratitude; and her circumspection, little less than prudence degenerated into meanness.[16]

Mrs Radcliffe could never openly reject reason and prudence though the structure of antithesis holds a suggestion here, as we

5

find later in Jane Austen's *Persuasion*, that reason may be inadequate to determine the proper value of an emotional relationship. After giving up Valancourt, Emily is faced with a dreadful
emotional blankness in which all her nervousness is exacerbated
by isolation and frustration, while Valancourt hovers on the
edge of her vision in a variety of romantic roles: a robber in the
night, a figure dashing out into the storm, and finally returning
as the successful lover to invade her lonely tower in the dusk of
evening. If Mrs Radcliffe had been writing a different kind of
novel the conclusion of Emily's virtuous decision could well
have been righteous misery, but as she is writing a sentimental
romance whose criteria are those of wish-fulfilment and moral
optimism, all comes right in the end—an ending which is a
vindication of Emily's moral integrity, a disarming of Valancourt's romantic posturing as a rebel, and also an ending where
social order and domestic harmony are the norms:

> Round the supper-table appeared a group of faces, smiling
> with felicity, but with a felicity, which had in each a different
> character. The smile of Blanche was frank and gay, that of
> Emily tender and pensive; Valancourt's was rapturous, ten-
> der and gay alternately; Mons. St. Foix's was joyous, and
> that of the Count, as he looked on the surrounding party,
> expressed the tempered complacency of benevolence; while
> the features of the Countess, Henri, and Mons. Bonnac, dis-
> covered fainter traces of animation.   (IV, xviii, 670)

This picture of smiling faces around the supper table is worth
our careful attention, for it is the image of Mrs Radcliffe's
picturesque resolution of her narrative. Her attempt to individu-
ate and characterise by facial gesture is a most interesting one,
as much for its failures as for its successes. Qualities of character
are suggested entirely through the anecdotal evidence of a
smile, the only one possessing any real animation being Valancourt's, which manages to combine Emily's 'tenderness' with
Blanche's 'gaiety' together with his own energetically romantic
quality of 'rapture'. I think Mrs Radcliffe's attempt at the
family portrait fails; we have the same sense here, as in a faded
old photograph, of the inherent limitations of this method for
capturing identity and feeling. The moment is so fixed that we

cannot read below its surface or beyond it into the future: it spells the closure of narrative action.

In the final chapter all we hear is the author's voice as she takes farewell of her characters and of her readers. The tale modulates back into normality by several stages: first the marriage feasts with their conventional Gothic pageantry but still held at a distance from present reality through the device of a servant-girl's imaginings and an old woman's memories of the past; then the sentimental return home of Emily and Valancourt to La Vallée, and after that the decisive shift into the real world with the economic tidying up of inheritances and property. Montoni has disappeared and even the dreadful castle of Udolpho is domesticated: it serves a useful function when Emily gives it to a worthy friend of her husband's: 'Thus affluence restored his long oppressed spirits to peace, and his family to comfort' (IV, xix, 672). Emily quite forgets Udolpho, her experiences there of the primitive forces of sexuality and aggression, and her fears of violent death. Mrs Radcliffe pushes aside the uncomfortable psychological insights and moral problems raised so that at the end the emotional resonance is rather disappointingly reduced and decorum is reasserted in the bland authorial voice justifying her tale for its entertainment value and its moral worth. The joy she celebrates is her joy at the restoration of a civilised humane order and the moral message she states so judiciously (indeed judicially) is the orthodox one that the antithesis between good and bad shall be shown to be resolved in the triumph of innocence and patience. With a last wave of her hand, Mrs Radcliffe bids farewell to her readers:

> And, if the weak hand, that has recorded this tale, has, by its scenes, beguiled the mourner of one hour of sorrow, or, by its moral, taught him to sustain it—the effort, however humble, has not been in vain, nor is the writer unrewarded.

The ending of *Udolpho* is very close to conventional eighteenth-century assumptions but this should not blind us to the very real ambivalence in Mrs Radcliffe's attitude and technique. She exploits almost continuously a double point of view: her heroine's and her own, that of the participant and of the objective

observer, or that of the feelings and that of the rational judgement, points of view which lead to totally different conclusions.
At best, this produces the controlled ambivalence and 'dreadful
uncertainty' which is the distinctive Radcliffian manner; at
worst, it produces contradictions and the feeling of disappointment which Scott and Coleridge registered and which we feel at
the end of *Udolpho*. The underlying design of her fiction rests on
the contest between her imagination and her sense of reality
and in the course of the narrative we sense the pull in opposite
directions as her imagination rises and then sinks back again
under more rational control. In the last chapter we see a very
striking enactment of this to-and-fro movement where the
double point of view is stated in the author's own voice, for the
celebration of 'rational happiness' is prefaced by a most subversive quotation from *Comus* glorifying the imagination:

> Now my task is smoothly done,
> I can fly, or I can run
> Quickly to the green earth's end,
> Where the bow'd welkin low doth bend,
> And, from thence, can soar as soon
> To the corners of the moon.

It carries the suggestion that now her literary 'task' is finished
the author can 'soar' having earned her imaginative freedom,
surely a disquieting admission from a novelist whose stated intention is to argue for the claims of decorum and rational
self-control.

Ultimately Mrs Radcliffe abandons us to radical uncertainty;
Robert Kiely is right when he suggests that she really does cast
doubts on the conventional notions of order and harmony with
her insights into the irrational arbitrary nature of our subjective
life (*The Romantic Novel*, p. 80). If Mrs Radcliffe is like Jane
Austen in so many of her assumptions about the relationship
between private feeling and public living, she is also like her contemporary Joanna Baillie who in her *Plays of the Passions* (First
Series, 1798) attempted to delineate 'those great disturbers of
the human mind' in order to evaluate their proper place in
total experience.[17] Both Miss Baillie and Mrs Radcliffe find
themselves forced to acknowledge that the forces of love, sex,

fear and death actually lie under the surface of civilised life but both of them fear the consequences of excessive feeling and finally insist on a mannered world of social relationships which allows no room for other more dangerous insights. Mrs Radcliffe's unease with this compromise is evident throughout her narratives in her ambiguous recording of experience and reinforced by the anxiety-ridden self-enclosure of her heroines. She cannot stop herself making positive claims for imagination and feeling, even if she has to hide behind a mask to do it, as in *Comus*, or indeed in an extraordinary outburst in her next novel *The Italian*. Here the disguise is so complete that she can speak out directly on the necessity and dangers of the imagination in a statement which is all the more illuminating when we remember that it is the villain who says it and that it is the young sentimental hero who blushes at the 'reproof' it contains:

> What ardent imagination ever was contented to trust to plain reasoning, or to the evidence of the senses? It may not willingly confine itself to the dull truths of this earth, but, eager to expand its faculties, to fill its capacity, and to experience its own peculiar delights, soars after new wonders into a world of its own! (*The Italian*, pp. 397–8)

M. G. Lewis, *The Monk*

Dreams, magic terrors, spells of mighty power,
Witches, and ghosts who rove at midnight hour.
(Epigraph to *The Monk*, trans. from Horace)[1]

The Monk is the most daring, the most shocking and the most Gothic of eighteenth-century English Gothic romances. It is daring in its treatment of sexual fantasy and violence; it is shocking in the luridly sensational sense as well as in its radical insights into criminal psychology; and it is Gothic in its presentation of a dark subterranean world filled with supernatural terrors and the odours of death. The areas of feeling with which *The Monk* is concerned go far deeper than the confines of Radcliffian sensibility; they plunge into the murkier regions of Gothic neurosis, especially the dangerous and violent excesses of the erotic imagination which Mrs Radcliffe had scrupulously repressed. It is a fantasy of the buried life of passion and instinct, where the wanderings of unreason are contained and concealed within the Gothic cadre of ecclesiastical architecture. Monastic cells, burial vaults and underground passages provide a frighteningly extensive area for the tortuous exploration into forbidden feelings, making the daylight world look pallid and mediocre. The looming figures in the narrative all belong to the subterranean world, against which the forces of reason and humanity are totally ineffectual. *The Monk* comes close to being a Gothic nightmare but curiously it is not one; instead, it is a Gothic entertainment. What saves *The Monk* from giving us an attack of the horrors is its presentation as pure fantasy for it is a tale of exaggeratedly Gothic dimensions told with immense narrative energy and a gusto which both embellishes the conventions of horror and at the same time subverts them by ridicule. The authorial voice ranges restlessly and wittily over Gothic conventions, engendering in the reader a kind of radical insecurity

about the limits of nightmare and reality, but finally denying
any connection between the fictive world of the novel and the
real world outside it. *The Monk* has the double appeal of allowing us to indulge in extravagances of feeling while protecting us
from their consequences by locating such extravagances quite
specifically in the remote reaches of fantasy.

Matthew Gregory Lewis was only nineteen when he wrote
The Monk and although inspired by *The Mysteries of Udolpho* it
is much more sensational and horrible than Mrs Radcliffe's
novels ever were. Indeed it was roundly condemned at the time
for its violence and obscenity. Coleridge in a hostile review condemned it for its 'figures that shock the imagination and narratives that mangle the feelings', and thought its 'images of naked
horror' more appropriate for a military hospital than for a
novel.[2] Lewis was forced to recall and expurgate the third
edition and *The Monk* became a by-word for wicked fiction.[3]
Lewis had studied in Germany in 1792 and he was a great
reader of German romances and ballads before he wrote his
own Gothic romance.[4] With *The Monk* we have for the first
time a novel by an English writer which has the German
emphasis on fantasies of sexual brutality and on the horrors of
physical corruption. This corrupt fleshliness is really very un-
English: the main influence on Gothic fiction before Lewis was
arguably Shakespearean and Jacobean drama and indeed the
influence of Shakespeare is pervasive in *The Monk* as well; there
were plenty of murders and ghosts in the English dramatic
tradition but not the emphasis on sensual horror or the combination of sexuality and diabolism which Lewis introduced.
The Monk is much more overtly concerned with suffering and
horror than anything produced in the English novel before and
the critical question that it raises for us is how the author manages to mediate and control these painful feelings through his
literary art.

Lewis is a highly self-conscious storyteller working within a
recognisable literary tradition to which he constantly alludes.
The resonance of English and German Gothic romance is
strongly felt throughout the novel, as he plays with certain predictable responses in his readers, sometimes exploiting Gothic
conventions when he wants sensationalism and horrific effects

and sometimes drawing attention to their artificiality through comic burlesque. His literary range extends beyond contemporary Gothic to include the folkloric world of ballads and older romances whose titles and characters are woven into the texture of his narrative, with reminders to the reader of Tristan and Iseult, Dr Faustus and Blondel. These all serve as models through which the raw materials of emotion are refracted to us. Some critics have discerned the shade of the Marquis de Sade in *The Monk*; Sade certainly liked the novel,[5] though I agree with Maurice Lévy that Sade's influence is no more than a plausible hypothesis. The obvious model for the main narrative of sexual obsession is Richardson's *Clarissa*; there is ample evidence for this not only in the central enormity of the rape but in details of the action, through the heroine's terrible resurrection among the tombs (which recalls an early nightmare of Clarissa's) to the dying torments of the villain (where the physical horrors of Mrs Sinclair's death are combined with the frenzies of Lovelace); we might even see the Monk as a cruder Lovelace pursuing his male fantasies without the hindrance of a woman of Clarissa's calibre! Such constant allusions to a literary hinterland help to control the emotional experiences recorded by distancing them into art just as effectively as do the highly artificial theatrical techniques of presentation. Lewis was addicted to sensational stagey effects and following the publication of *The Monk* revealed his considerable talents as a playwright in the large number of successful melodramas he wrote for Covent Garden and Drury Lane between 1797 and 1811. His narrative is presented with all the animation of a theatrical performance, the action progressing by a series of highly charged scenes interspersed with ballads and songs in a mode which is consciously theatrical and artificial. Even Ambrosio the Monk is very likely modelled in his appearance and gestures on the contemporary actor J. P. Kemble, Mrs Siddons's brother.[6] Lewis had ample opportunity to play with a wide range of responses in his readers but the responses he evokes are always those appropriate to fantasy rather than to a direct confrontation with the pressures of real life.

The narrative itself hardly encourages us to see it as the imitation of real life; it is highly sensational and unlikely from

beginning to end, as this plot summary taken from the title page
of a pirated abridgement of *The Monk* in 1818 indicates:

> The Monk, a Romance; in which is depicted the Wonderful
> Adventures of Ambrosio Friar of the Order of Capuchins,
> who was diverted from the track of Virtue by the Artifices of
> a Female Demon, That entered his Monastery disguised as a
> Novice, and after seducing him from his Vow of Celibacy,
> Presented him with A Branch of Enchanted Myrtle, to
> obtain the person of the beautiful Antonia of Madrid; How
> he was Discovered in Her Chamber by Her Mother, whom
> he Murdered, To keep his Crime a Secret; And the Particulars
> of the Means by which he caused the Body of Antonia to be
> conveyed in a Sleep to the Dreary Vaults of his own Convent,
> where he Accomplished his Wicked Machinations on the
> Innocent Virgin, whom he then Assassinates with a Dagger,
> presented to him by his Attendant Fiend, Who afterwards
> Betrays him to the Judges of the Inquisition, In the Dungeons
> of which he is Confined, and Suffers Torture; and how, to
> Escape from thence, he Assigns over his Soul and Body to
> the Devil, Who Deceives him and Inflicts a Most Ignominious
> Death.[7]

This skeletal account captures the emphasis on sex and violence that we find in the original, especially the urgency of
sexual feeling and its recklessness; it also focusses on the anti-
clericalism and diabolism that are so important in Lewis's creation of a Gothic underworld of morbid fantasy which pushes
inexorably towards death. But by its sheer crudity of language it
transforms *The Monk* into a piece of lurid Gothic pornography,
totally neglecting the narrative artifice of the novel together
with its wit and range of tone. Certainly male sexual fantasy
seems to be the informing principle of *The Monk* and the pornographic stimulus is clearly there in the thrill of illicit sex; but
the sustaining interest is a narrative one, for the novel deftly
weaves several subplots in and out of the main one concerning
the Monk to contrive a whole range of variations on the theme
of sexual disaster. By weaving in the literary strands of ghost
stories, German robber stories, ballad narratives of demon lovers
and tales of monastic tyranny, Lewis gives his narrative a

resonance beyond that of sexual nightmare. Indeed the narrative interest extends beyond the tale to the teller, into the contemplation of authorship as an activity, a subject which is handled humorously and compassionately in the case of the poetry-writing young page Theodore who is caught up in the 'mania of authorship'. As his master explains:

> In short to enter the lists of literature is wilfully to expose yourself to the arrows of neglect, ridicule, envy, and disappointment. Whether you write well or ill, be assured that you will not escape from blame ... Authorship is a mania to conquer which no reasons are sufficiently strong; and you might as easily persuade me not to love, as I persuade you not to write. (II, ii, 199)

The language and sentiments are reminiscent of Lewis's verse Preface to *The Monk* and we cannot help identifying the voice of Theodore's amiable critic with the author's own voice in a private and prophetic dialogue with himself.

The authorial presence in *The Monk* is both pervasive and disturbing. As Robert Kiely remarks:

> *The Monk* derives much of its interest from the curious division between a narrative voice which seems wittier, subtler and more human than the narrative framework to which it has committed itself. One often has the feeling in reading *The Monk* that it is about to become a much funnier or sadder book than it is. (*The Romantic Novel*, p. 106)

Lacking Mrs Radcliffe's discretion as a manipulator of the reader's feelings, Lewis insists on peeping out from behind his Gothic scenarios to make witty or moral comments on the action, or simply to draw attention to his own cleverness. We are continually reminded of the artificiality of the conventions he uses but at the same time his acknowledgement of their limitations points the way to real insights into the neuroses which underlay Gothic sensationalism.

I have said that *The Monk* was daring in its treatment of sexual fantasy, for it dares to be explicit about desire as it speculates on the dangerous connections between the erotic imagination and the darker instinctual urges towards violence, destruction and death. Like *The Mysteries of Udolpho*, *The Monk* was a response to an oppressive social milieu, but it is much more aggressive than *Udolpho* with striking extensions into criminal pathology as Lewis explores male sexual guilts rather than female sexual fears. Lewis did not write sentimental fiction illustrating the triumph of female virtue but a savage story about the forces of destruction. While treating that conflict between reason, conscience and feeling which is so characteristically Gothic, he turns the conventional moral structure on its head, presenting us with the disturbing possibility that the forces of passion and instinct are stronger than the forces of reason and conscience. All his emphasis is on the power of passion over judgement so that the novel registers a keen sense of moral shock—not only on the part of his characters but on the author's part too—at the revelations of the destructive potential contained within the self. What makes the fantasy so sombre and terrifying is the claustrophobic sense of imprisonment; in a world which Lewis sees as 'base, perfidious and depraved' passion can find no safe place where tenderness and sexuality could flourish and produce life; instead, the sexual instincts have to be kept secret, hidden underground in monastic cells or furtively concealed beneath flowing ecclesiastical robes where they flourish into a bizarrely destructive existence, asserting their power in ways attended by the torments of remorse, guilt and misery. *The Monk* is about sexual obsession but it is not erotic: in no other novel is sex presented more forlornly, as Lewis catches the syndrome of desire, consummation and its aftermath in all its incessant repetitiveness and frustration.

It is in the figure of the Capuchin abbot Ambrosio that sexual desire is imaged most frighteningly. Certainly it was no frivolous choice on the author's part to make his main character a monk, for monkishness with its rigid polarisation of sex and religion and its contempt for the desires of the flesh strikes exactly the right note for dark erotic fantasy. Clearly *The Monk* is anti-Catholic (as most English Gothic fiction was) but hostility to the tyranny and repressiveness of monastic institutions is here directed specifically against their denial of the emotional imperatives of the individual, and it is the vow of chastity that comes in for special attack. Lewis, like Milton, cannot praise a fugitive and cloistered virtue; he criticises as false the virtue of sexual purity when it is only the result of ignorance and lack of contact with the world. Indeed, the simplest part of the narrative shows the destruction of this kind of innocence—as Ambrosio is seduced by a novice in the monastery who turns out to be a woman! The author is certainly keen to persuade his readers of the erotic appeal of illicit sex in a monastic cell by moonlight as the cowls are flung back but Ambrosio's indulgence carries more serious overtones as well. Not only does it falsify his public image of sanctity but it also destroys his fragile self-image, torturing him with guilt and fear till he actually becomes the hypocritical monster that the monks of anti-clerical fiction so often are.[8] From being a worshipper of the Virgin Mary's ideal image, Ambrosio is initiated into the mysteries of sex by the disguised novice who is really a female demon with the Virgin's face, then by tormented stages he gradually becomes a criminal psychopath who rapes and murders an innocent girl after strangling her mother. What is so terrifying to the reader of this lurid history is that we watch Ambrosio degenerating, totally blinded to the inevitability of his crises of feeling, consistently shocked by his own criminal propensities yet powerless to escape from his guilt-ridden obsession. To claim that it is finally not 'obsession' but demonic 'possession' as the author does is, I think, to dodge the issue about the monk's compulsive behaviour which is expressive of repressed desires and fears; but then Lewis was no analyst of feeling like Maturin—he rejects emotional complexity for the shock value of dramatic scenarios.

Ambrosio looms over the novel as a dark tormented figure. Kiely sees him as the type of the Romantic rebel fighting against the forces of repression to seek fulfilment of the infinite possibilities within himself, a being for whom reform and salvation are unthinkable as he pursues his reckless course. But in Ambrosio we also have the spectacle of a crippled hero, whose energies have been so constricted by his monastic upbringing that they have turned inwards, creating the self-imprisonment of obsession. The architectural structures that Ambrosio inhabits become in the course of the novel images of his own tortuous psychology; instead of being places of retreat they turn into places of death and imprisonment as his course leads him out of the cathedral and the monastic cell into the funeral vaults and finally to the prisons of the Inquisition. Through it all, Lewis traces the course of frustrated sexual desire, perverted by monkish repression from its romantic yearnings and imaginative idealisation into a dark destructive lust for power. For Ambrosio, the sexual impulse has been so contaminated by deception and guilt from the beginning that it is productive of nothing but an inveterate hostility towards women as the betrayers and humiliators of men. This in turn encourages the dreadful complicity between him and his first mistress, who is a *femme fatale* in the literal sense. Their partnership is much more evil than its mechanics of diabolism suggest for it consistently denies and betrays natural human feeling. The real shock to the reader is not the thrill of monkish sexuality but the revelation of Ambrosio's potential for cruelty and violence. In him desire can only find its consummation in rape and murder in the funeral vaults of a convent, a terrible image of sexuality dehumanised but not deprived of its instinctual energy.

Behind his sanctified public image Ambrosio is remarkably unstable, for human character as Lewis reveals it is not something fixed, as most Gothic novelists pretended to believe. The initial warning about the Monk in the *Measure for Measure* quote[9] should alert us to the fact that the self, made up as it is of contradictory impulses, is unpredictable and capable of unrealised possibilities. For Lewis inconsistency and instability are part of the nature of things, not only of human beings and feelings but of the whole contingent world. *The Monk* is organised on this principle, not on the static notion that appearances and reality are different but that reality itself is a very shifty concept and at any time we are likely to be confronted by something entirely outside our expectations and which undermines all our assumptions about the way things ought to be. The narrative forces on us these shocks of confrontation in its incidents, its revelations about feeling and motive and in its changes of tone, striking through our accustomed responses into new apprehensions of insecurity.

A startling instance of the subversive nature of Lewis's fiction occurs in a ghost story, one of the sub-plots in *The Monk*, about two lovers Raymond and Agnes who plan to elope from a German castle together with Agnes disguised as the ghost of a nun. The narrative context deliberately parodies Gothic romance, mocking the legend of the ghostly nun with Agnes's own 'burlesqued gravity' and joking about romances like *Tristan and Iseult*, 'those unmerciful volumes' as Raymond calls them. The lovers' adventure promises to be played out as high farce, with Agnes calmly walking past the superstitious inhabitants of the castle in her disguise; everything looks like a comic exploitation of Gothic and the lovers drive away in their carriage. Only then does the tone change: the carriage begins to fly away at breakneck speed (in a way that foreshadows the terrible ride in Bram Stoker's *Dracula*) and when it is smashed to pieces in a storm Raymond is struck senseless by a piece of flying flint. It is not till he recovers that the bizarre truth of his adventure begins to dawn on him: it is not his beloved Agnes with whom he has eloped but the Bleeding Nun herself! His terrible realisation is recorded as a Gothic nightmare.

I continued to toss about from side to side, till the Clock in a neighbouring Steeple struck 'one'. As I listened to the mournful hollow sound, and heard it die away in the wind, I felt a sudden chillness spread itself over my body. I shuddered without knowing wherefore; Cold dews poured down my forehead, and my hair stood bristling with alarm. Suddenly I heard slow and heavy steps ascending the stair-case. By an involuntary movement I started up in my bed, and drew back the curtain. A single rush-light, which glimmered upon the hearth shed a faint gleam through the apartment, which was hung with tapestry. The door was thrown open with violence. A figure entered, and drew near my Bed with solemn measured steps. With trembling apprehension I examined this midnight Visitor. God Almighty! It was the Bleeding Nun! It was my lost Companion! her face was still veiled, but She no longer held her Lamp and dagger. She lifted up her veil slowly. What a sight presented itself to my startled eyes! I beheld before me an animated Corse. Her countenance was long and haggard; Her cheeks and lips were bloodless; The paleness of death was spread over her features, and her eye-balls fixed stedfastly upon me were lustreless and hollow.

I gazed upon the Spectre with horror too great to be described. My blood was frozen in my veins. I would have
called for aid, but the sound expired, ere it could pass my
lips. My nerves were bound up in impotence, and I remained
in the same attitude inanimate as a Statue.

The visionary Nun looked upon me for some minutes in
silence: There was something petrifying in her regard. At
length in a low sepulchral voice She pronounced the following words.

'Raymond! Raymond! Thou art mine!
Raymond! Raymond! I am thine!
In thy veins while blood shall roll,
I am thine!
Thou art mine!
Mine thy body! Mine thy soul!—'   (II, i, 159–60)

This is a conventional Gothic scenario with appropriate
sound and lighting effects so that we are provided with all the
cues for a thrill of horror as we follow Raymond's sensations.
Lewis traces them in the behaviouristic detail of a theatrical
performance, with the 'sudden chillness' of premonitory dread,
the 'shuddering' and the hair 'bristling with alarm'. Then the
ghost herself appears, impassive and slow-moving as befits the
animated corpse that she is, and we have the nightmare description of the demon lover who is commonly portrayed as a
ghost or a corpse or a vampire. The figure whom Raymond and
the reader had assumed to be part of legend suddenly leaps out
into a different kind of existence. Lewis insists on keeping close
to physical notation as we watch Raymond transformed by
sheer terror into the mirror image of the ghost herself: his 'stillness', 'the blood frozen in his veins' and his 'nerves bound up
in impotence' convert him into a death image too. Their
encounter is the ghastly parody of a lovers' meeting, where
Raymond's rivetted stare and the nun's 'petrifying' regard are
the hideous opposite of the lovers' gaze. When the silence is
broken, the parody is continued in a way both horrible and
ludicrous as the nun repeats Raymond's ditty to Agnes when
he had sworn his oath of fidelity to her. Instead, he finds himself bound to the Bleeding Nun herself and is only rescued later

by the Wandering Jew who happens to be passing through Germany at the time!

It is typical of Lewis to create a grotesque Gothic entertainment like this, filled with the clichés of dread and horror and amusingly amplified by the ghost's own words singing a silly rhyme in a 'sepulchral voice'.[10] As he boasted a few years later (in his Postscript to *Adelmorn the Outlaw*, 1801), he could if he liked 'deluge the town with such an inundation of ghosts and magicians, as would satisfy the thirst of the most insatiable swallower of wonders'. He seems here to be making fun of Gothic nightmares—and then we find he has turned around and undermined all our comfortable assumptions: the supernatural really is there all the time! It engenders a kind of radical insecurity when we discover that at crucial points nightmare and reality merge. For Lewis there are no limits to fantasy but fantasy becomes a way of plumbing the psyche to the area of those forces which lie below rational comprehension and whose images are available only through nightmare. What is so shocking about the supernatural nun, for Raymond and for us, is the way she corresponds to a vision of sexuality as being something dangerous to life. The shadow of disaster that Raymond believes he has escaped when the nun is eventually exorcised continues to hang over his love affair with Agnes. She is forced to become a nun and then violates her vow of chastity when she and Raymond meet clandestinely; as a result, she undergoes dreadful monastic persecution, being incarcerated in a funeral vault where she has nothing to do but adore the decaying corpse of her baby. When Agnes's release finally does come and the lovers are reunited in marriage, their happiness, though achieved, is still muted in a world full of risks and pain.

The history of the Bleeding Nun provides a kind of warning to the reader about Ambrosio's career with its furtive monastic sexuality. Once the Monk has been awakened to the possibilities of sex through his seduction in the monastery, he is caught up in a web of guilt-ridden erotic fantasy from which he cannot escape, and when the young girl Antonia comes to him begging for a confessor for her dying mother he sees her, whose 'affliction seemed to add new lustre to her charms' (241), as the perfect victim. Though his feeling for her begins as the most conventional

romantic fantasy, the impossibility of a love relationship
with her rapidly transforms tenderness into desperate lust;
to fulfil his ambitions in such repressive conditions he has to
resort to diabolical arts. He goes into an infernal partnership
with his first mistress Matilda and together they plan the rape
of Antonia. From this point on, the sexual fantasy becomes
truly Gothic, with forbidden feeling driven underground into
the regions inhabited by death to pursue in secret its violent
consummation.

The rape of Antonia reads like a demonic distortion of the
final scene of *Romeo and Juliet,* with Antonia drugged and buried
in the funeral vaults of the convent and 'resurrected' by Ambrosio. Lewis knew that he could rely on his readers' literary
expectations to respond to the gloomy horror of echoing vaults,
funeral trappings and dimly receding architectural perspectives,
just as he could exploit the common Gothic situation of a beautiful heroine persecuted by a lustful villain. What shocked his
readers out of their comfortable literary horrors was that he
went far beyond conventional Gothic fears to the ultimate assault of rape, showing both its physical brutality and its dimensions of nightmare fantasy. There is the authentic Gothic
love-among-the-tombs frisson generated by the image of
Antonia's return to life surrounded by rotting bodies and all the
odours of physical corruption:

> By the side of three putrid half-corrupted Bodies lay the
> sleeping Beauty. A lively red, the fore-runner of returning ani-
> mation, had already spread itself over her cheek; and as
> wrapped in her shroud She reclined upon her funeral Bier,
> She seemed to smile at the Images of Death around her.
>
> (III, iv, 379)[11]

The strong suggestion of necrophilia is extended in Ambrosio's
tormented fantasies of guilt and desire as, lifting Antonia from
her coffin, he addresses the unconscious girl in language which
clearly belongs not to eroticism but to sexual pathology:

> 'For your sake, Fatal Beauty!' murmured the Monk, while
> gazing on his devoted prey; 'For your sake, have I committed
> this murder [of Antonia's mother], and sold myself to eternal

6

tortures. Now you are in my power: The produce of my guilt
will at least be mine. Hope not that your prayers breathed in
tones of unequalled melody, your bright eyes filled with tears,
and your hands lifted in supplication, as when seeking in
penitence the Virgin's pardon; Hope not, that your moving
innocence, your beauteous grief, or all your suppliant arts
shall ransom you from my embraces.'   (III, iv, 379)

The subterranean vaults define the contours of Ambrosio's
obsession, imprisoning him and Antonia in a world far removed
from the light of day and rational feeling, within which Antonia's terror merely acts as a stimulus to his mad lust for sexual
power over his victim.

The rape itself is presented as a totally destructive act:

'Can I relinquish these limbs so white, so soft, so delicate;
These swelling breasts, round, full, and elastic! These lips
fraught with such inexhaustible sweetness? Can I relinquish
these treasures, and leave them to another's enjoyment? No,
Antonia; never, never! I swear it by this kiss, and this! and
this!'

With every moment the Friar's passion became more
ardent, and Antonia's terror more intense. She struggled to
disengage herself from his arms: Her exertions were unsuccessful; and finding that Ambrosio's conduct became still
freer, She shrieked for assistance with all her strength. The
aspect of the Vault, the pale glimmering of the Lamp, the
surrounding obscurity, the sight of the Tomb, and the objects
of mortality which met her eyes on either side, were ill-
calculated to inspire her with those emotions, by which the
Friar was agitated. Even his caresses terrified her from their
fury, and created no other sentiment than fear. On the contrary, her alarm, her evident disgust, and incessant opposition,
seemed only to inflame the Monk's desires, and supply his
brutality with additional strength. Antonia's shrieks were
unheard: Yet She continued them, nor abandoned her en-
deavours to escape, till exhausted and out of breath She sank
from his arms upon her knees, and once more had recourse
to prayers and supplications. This attempt had no better
success than the former. On the contrary, taking advantage

of her situation, the Ravisher threw himself by her side: He clasped her to his bosom almost lifeless with terror, and faint with struggling. He stifled her cries with kisses, treated her with the rudeness of an unprincipled Barbarian, proceeded from freedom to freedom, and in the violence of his lustful delirium, wounded and bruised her tender limbs. Heedless of her tears, cries and entreaties, He gradually made himself Master of her person, and desisted not from his prey, till He had accomplished his crime and the dishonour of Antonia.

Scarcely had He succeeded in his design, than He shuddered at himself and the means by which it was effected.

(III, iv, 383–4)

As an account of sexual outrage this comes very close to pornography, with its excited insistence on the illicit thrills of monkish sensuality and its attempts to shock us by the display of physical cruelty. Ambrosio and Antonia are reduced to the level of rapist and victim, stripped of any other feelings but those directly related to this act of violation: Ambrosio's tormented rhapsody of the flesh only acts as a stimulus to his brutal assault, while Antonia like a true victim can do nothing but aggravate his lust by her 'evident disgust' and 'incessant opposition'. There is no question of gratification or delight on anybody's part—the characters' or the readers'—but there is for us the voyeuristic fascination of watching how far conventional limits can be transgressed, as the Monk dares to proceed along ways that are forbidden until the rape is accomplished. The authorial language of moral opprobrium at the end merely underlines the shockingness of the rape.

Even after the rape there is no release from the dark fantasy world for Ambrosio's frenzies of self-recrimination flower into his nightmarish project to keep Antonia as a prisoner in the vaults so that he can secretly come to do penance to her in yet another convolution of his deranged and perverted idealism. There is deadlock between them, until suddenly voices from the outside world break in and Antonia attempts to escape. However, Ambrosio catches her by her streaming hair and stabs her twice as she clings to a pillar crying out for help. This stabbing is the only possible ending to such a nightmare, where sexual desire has been perverted from a life-giving to a death-dealing force: orgasmic destruction is the appropriate consummation. The rape and murder can surely be described as 'obscene' within the term of Susan Sontag's definition of the word in her essay on 'The Pornographic Imagination': 'It's towards the gratifications of death, succeeding and surpassing those of eros, that every truly obscene quest tends.'[12] If obscenity is, as she suggests, a question of the moral tone with which sexual experience is treated, and if the extremes of obscene erotic experience expose a close connection between sex and death, then 'obscene' is the right word in this context. Obsessed as it was with sexual feeling as a forbidden but fascinating area of speculation, Gothic fiction always leans towards pornography; Lewisian Gothic takes the further step of making the connection between sex, guilt and death quite explicit.

The final movement of the novel is also towards death as it pushes through a labyrinth of Gothic terrors to Ambrosio's destruction. After his unmasking he is thrown into the prison of the Inquisition, that place of mysterious persecution which fascinated not only Lewis but Gothic novelists from Mrs Radcliffe to Maturin. Totally cut off from the outside world, Ambrosio moves through his nightmare of damnation, tormented in body by the Inquisition and tempted by Matilda on the plea of their 'mutual guilt and danger' to sell his soul to the Devil for release. He signs the Faustian pact at the very moment that the guards enter to take him away to be ceremonially burned as a heretic and the conventional Gothic machinery of sensationalism and diabolism once more stifle any exploration of the psychological drama. Ambrosio's adventure can be relegated to the status of a nine days' wonder:

> The story, how a Sorcerer had been carried away by the Devil, was soon noised about Madrid; and for some days the whole City was employed in discussing the subject. Gradually it ceased to be the topic of conversation: Other adventures arose whose novelty engaged universal attention; and Ambrosio was soon forgotten as totally, as if He never had existed.
>
> (III, v, 438)

By totally alienating Ambrosio from society, the author seems concerned to deny any connection between his tormented career and real-life problems. In his last-minute revelation that Ambrosio had been the victim of diabolical stratagems from the beginning, he implies that nothing in the Monk's history relates to sexual or religious oppression but that it is all demonic. He actually identifies the irrational with the supernatural, a shocking instance of authorial bad faith when we consider that the stuff of the novel has been the exploration of the buried life of passion and instinct.

At last Ambrosio is carried away by the devil out of the dark underground world into a place of glaring light, to a 'precipice's brink, the steepest in Sierra Morena', a landscape whose barren desolation images his state of utter despair. There follows Ambrosio's terrible dying, as the devil perpetrates his final outrage:

'Villain, resign your hopes of pardon. Thus I secure my prey!'

As He said this, darting his talons into the Monk's shaven crown, he sprang with him from the rock. The Caves and mountains rang with Ambrosio's shrieks. The Daemon continued to soar aloft, till reaching a dreadful height, He released the sufferer. Headlong fell the Monk through the airy waste; The sharp point of a rock received him; and He rolled from precipice to precipice, till bruised and mangled He rested on the river's banks. Life still existed in his miserable frame: He attempted in vain to raise himself; His broken and dislocated limbs refused to perform their office, nor was He able to quit the spot where He had first fallen. The Sun now rose above the horizon; Its scorching beams darted full upon the head of the expiring Sinner. Myriads of insects were called forth by the warmth; They drank the blood which trickled from Ambrosio's wounds; He had no power to drive them from him, and they fastened upon his sores, darted their stings into his body, covered him with their multitudes, and inflicted on him tortures the most exquisite and insupportable. The Eagles of the rock tore his flesh piecemeal, and dug out his eye-balls with their crooked beaks. A burning thirst tormented him; He heard the river's murmur as it

rolled beside him; but strove in vain to drag himself towards
the sound. Blind, maimed, helpless, and despairing, venting
his rage in blasphemy and curses, execrating his existence,
yet dreading the arrival of death destined to yield him up to
greater torments, six miserable days did the Villain languish.
On the Seventh a violent storm arose: The winds in fury rent
up rocks and forests: The sky was now black with clouds, now
sheeted with fire: The rain fell in torrents; It swelled the
stream, The waves overflowed their banks; They reached the
spot where Ambrosio lay, and when they abated carried with
them into the river the Corse of the despairing Monk.

(III, v, 441-2)

The spectacle of suffering is meant to shock us for this is
Gothic fantasy that has leapt beyond the bounds of suggestive
terror into an extravaganza of horror. The German influence is
again plain here though there are Richardsonian moral echoes
as well in the recall of the villainous Mrs Sinclair's death
(*Clarissa*, iv, 379–80). The account of Ambrosio's death agonies
is very close to the ending of Veit Weber's *The Sorcerer*, translated into English 1795, which was probably known to Lewis
in the original German, as Peck, Lévy and Ritter suggest. The
focus on physical, not metaphysical, anguish is quite unambiguous in *The Sorcerer*, where the villain's dying torments are the
result of an unsuccessful suicide attempt:

> Towards the evening of the second day, the rising winds
> howled a note of comfort to the wretched sufferer; the sea
> curled into higher waves, and the distant thunder growled
> in hoarse murmurs. The miserable object of such accumu-
> lated tortures implored Heaven to bury him beneath the
> ocean; or to hurl its flaming bolts at his head. The tempest
> grew more obstreperous; the winds raised the waters moun-
> tains high, and hoisted them far over the rock, where lay the
> suffering sinner. One of the waves on its return bore his
> mangled body into the sea, and completed and terminated
> his punishment.[13]

Lewis's rhetoric of sensationalism with its 'tortures most exquisite and insupportable' almost obscures Ambrosio's genuine

moral anguish, for he does achieve some knowledge in his commerce with the devil, an insight into human fallibility which confirms his despair. The horrors are so extreme that they mask any understanding of his suffering; the language is not the notation of real life but entirely literary in its resonance. It links Ambrosio's suffering with that of other great sinners of Christian and pagan myth, from the echoes of Satan in the debased Miltonic of 'Headlong fell the Monk through the airy waste' to the torments of Prometheus and Tantalus. The exaggerated claims made for the Titanic proportions of Ambrosio's sin and its punishment culminate in his death on the seventh day presented as a savage inversion of the Creation. After such a grandiose display we are left in a state of shock as the 'despairing Monk' and all his concerns are swept off the face of the earth. A kind of catharsis has been achieved in the liberation of violent feelings within Gothic horror fantasy.

Lewis is shocking and subversive in a way that Mrs Radcliffe never was in his exploration of the dark irrational hinterland of the human mind whose glooms and terrors find an appropriate image in the labyrinthine Gothic underworld. Far from restricting his imagination, the rhetoric of Gothic fantasy gives him the freedom to explore an extensive range of hidden feelings within the escapist world of romance. It may even be argued that Lewis's storytelling in· *The Monk* consciously exploits the secret appeal of Gothic fiction, whose deliberate mode is to separate passion and instinct from everyday life, so allowing their indulgence but effectively controlling the threat of the irrational by forcing it back into the realms of fantasy.

Minerva Press Fiction, 1796-1819: Regina Maria Roche, *The Children of the Abbey* and Mary-Anne Radcliffe, *Manfroné; or, The One-Handed Monk*

'But are they all horrid? are you sure they are all horrid?'
'Yes, quite sure.'   (Jane Austen, *Northanger Abbey*)

The taste for Gothic fiction, first established in the 1790s by Mrs Radcliffe and Monk Lewis, made it for over twenty years the most popular form of light reading in England. Even as late as the second decade of the nineteenth century the public still wanted tales of the marvellous, as was clear from the popularity of Gothic melodrama. However, the appeal of the Gothic novel was flagging and when Scott's *Marmion* (1808) and *The Lady of the Lake* (1810) appeared, followed by the first two cantos of Byron's *Childe Harold's Pilgrimage* in 1812 and the first Waverley novel in 1814, readers were enthusiastic in welcoming the new writers. The number of parodies of Gothic fiction increased after 1813 and though tales about black monks, oaths of vengeance and Italian mysteries were still appearing in 1820 the Gothic novel had become something of a laughing-stock.

The heyday of Gothic was the great age of the circulating libraries—Bell's, Lackington's, and most notorious and successful of all, Lane's Minerva Library.[1] Beginning in 1791 with one library in Leadenhall Street, London, at the offices of the Minerva Press, Lane rapidly established lending libraries at all the fashionable resorts in the provinces, Scotland and Ireland; there were even Minerva libraries in New York, Jamaica and India by 1810. When we consider that Lane dealt mainly in 'Novels, Tales, Adventures, and Romances', and that between

1795 and 1810 more than a third of his yearly output had Gothic titles, we can appreciate the sort of demand he cultivated and supplied. It is Jane Austen's world where the Isabella Thorpes, Catherine Morlands and Harriet Smiths read avidly and uncritically.

Although Lane's authors were on the whole very minor figures (he did not publish Mrs Radcliffe or Lewis and even by 1800 the authors of half his books remained anonymous), the homogeneous nature of the Minerva Press novels makes them the most coherent field for surveying the qualities of Gothic fiction *en masse*. Minerva Press fiction was a barometer of public taste so it is not surprising that rather than new departures we should see the patterns already established by Mrs Radcliffe and Lewis repeated with infinite variations to satisfy a consistent public demand. Inevitably such a process degenerates; by 1810 there was a notable increase in sensationalism to supplement flagging inventiveness. Authors became very concerned with the superficial attractiveness of titles which promised more excitement than their novels could fulfil. Sentimental novels were presented to the public under provocative names like Mrs Martin's *The Enchantress; or Where Shall I Find Her?* (1801), while Mrs Meeke (who had no less than five novels published by Minerva in 1803) chose titles which encouraged her readers —quite misleadingly—to expect thrills rather than sentiment: *Amazement, Something Odd!* and *The Nine Days' Wonder* appeared in 1804, followed in 1806 by *Something Strange!* and in 1808 by *There Is a Secret, Find It Out!* The challenge of this list is capped only perhaps by Mrs Llewellyn in 1813 with *Read, and Give It a Name*. Titles tend to stress the bizarre, the thrilling and the horrible, like Eleanor Sleath's *Who's the Murderer? or The Mystery of the Forest* (1802), *The Idiot Heiress* (1805), A. J. Crandolph's *The Mysterious Hand; or Subterranean Horrors* (1811), and Francis Lathom's *Italian Mysteries; or, More Secrets than One* (1820). Some authors were even attentive to chapter headings as a way of whetting their readers' appetites, as we find A. F. Holstein doing in *Love, Mystery, and Misery!* with the come-hitherish: 'Misery continues, Mystery not lessened, and Love still apparent'. These are all fairly cheap devices to stimulate interest but Lane knew that his readers would leaf rapidly through, one of his library rules being that a new book could be borrowed for only four days.

Lane liked his readers to be titillated but he did not encourage violence and it is noticeable that most Minerva Press writers imitated Mrs Radcliffe's sentimental fantasies rather than Lewis's brutal sensationalism. Apart from *Horrid Mysteries* (a translation from the German which he published in 1796), the few 'fleshly' Gothic novels produced in the period were not published by Lane. The most notorious were Lewis's *Monk*, published by Bell of Oxford Street, and Charlotte Dacre's *Zofloya; or, The Moor* (1806), published by Longman, which Shelley later enjoyed. Lane always paid ample lip-service to the morally improving value of novels, and of this his Prospectus printed in the *Morning Advertiser* (8 February 1794) gives an eloquent example: he stated that the Minerva printing office was to be 'open to such subjects as tend to public good—the pages shall never be stained with what will injure the mind or corrupt the heart—they shall neither be the instrument of private damnation or Public Inquiry'.[2] This did not prevent his library becoming known as the most notorious purveyor of melodramatic fiction, but if it did not restrict the fantasies of his writers at least it ensured very moral prefaces and conclusions in all Minerva novels.

I have chosen two Minerva novels from opposite ends of the emotional spectrum: *The Children of the Abbey* emphasises sentimentality and nostalgia in the Radcliffian manner, while *Manfroné; or, The One-Handed Monk*, owing much to Lewis, points in the direction of melodrama which the Gothic novel took in the early nineteenth century. Though there are radical differences between the brands of Gothic they represent, they indicate the range of popular fiction over which Minerva extended its protective name to cater for the demands of circulating library readers.

The Children of the Abbey

The Children of the Abbey was one of the most enduringly popular Minerva novels; published in 1796, it had reached its tenth edition by 1825 and was still in print in 1882. We can easily see why the novel had such a wide appeal: it is Radcliffian Gothic domesticated, entertaining readers with the charms of sentimental indulgence and escapist fantasy plus the occasional frisson of terror, all set reassuringly in the familiar context of late eighteenth-century polite society. Though alive to the delights of sublime and picturesque scenery which Mrs Radcliffe's admirers loved, Mrs Roche never goes further afield than the British Isles, while her situations and character types are derived from the contemporary social scene, and even the conventional Gothic apparatus—*de rigueur* in a tale about an Abbey—seems much closer to an enthusiasm for medieval architecture than to any fascination with the supernatural. Indeed, appeals to superstitious fear are used very sparingly, Mrs Roche revealing herself as a moralist and social critic to whom human relationships are more important than any fear of ghosts. But *The Children of the Abbey* is still unmistakably Gothic in feeling, with the characteristic strains of morbid anxiety and repressed hysteria giving it its distinctive tone—though, interestingly, this is not so much a property of narrative action as of language. Like Mrs Radcliffe and Lewis, Mrs Roche is well aware that feelings are more powerful forces than decorum or rational discourse will admit, so she turns to the available Gothic vocabulary of terror or the language of sentimental novels to find a way of communicating intensities of feeling beneath the world of social convention. With its detailed accounts of social surfaces and its hints at the underlying passional realities, *The Children of the Abbey* is a very interesting attempt to solve the old dilemma of the Gothic novelist formulated by Walpole in *Otranto* when he talked about his desire to blend two kinds of Romance: 'the Ancient, all imagination and improbability, and the Modern, where Nature is intended to be copied'. What Mrs Roche has produced is a curiously hybrid form where the anxious fears of Radcliffian Gothic are re-enacted in the world of Fanny Burney as the shade of Richardson hovers in the background pointing forward to the world of Jane Austen.

The Children of the Abbey is a very civilised novel, lacking all the violence and arbitrariness that we find in so much Gothic fiction. Though it is a celebration of feeling, the feelings with which it deals are those belonging to the gentler region of

Sensibility: nostalgia, love of nature, friendship and most importantly, honourable sexual love. It is this last which gives the novel its separate identity for *The Children of the Abbey* is about marriage, especially about the ideal of the good marriage and how it can be achieved. This theme makes it a very feminine novel, with its main focus on women's feelings about sexual love and marriage in a world where to be married was the highest point of a woman's aspirations. Inevitably Mrs Roche's use of the conventional language of sensibility leads to a very traditional presentation with much play on sentimental excess and romantic feeling, but her firm belief in the value of marriage as a social institution means a shift in emphasis away from the neurotic isolation of a Radcliffian heroine (whose feelings were much less directly related to the marriage theme) and a total absence of the hysterical guilt-ridden sexuality of *The Monk* (where marriage is not mentioned at all!). And because this is a novel about marriage and its importance, it is much more directly related to social issues in the real world than Mrs Radcliffe's fiction or indeed any other novel I shall consider till *Jane Eyre*.

In true sentimental fashion the narrative tends to highlight romantic love, but Mrs Roche tries to toughen sentimentality by insisting that love must be tested by bitter worldly experience before it is allowed to form the basis of a married relationship, at which point it is assimilated into the recognised fabric of social institutions. Whatever flights of fantasy Mrs Roche may indulge in, she is an author who never disregards worldliness and the importance of wealth, social status, class and reputation, so that in her narrative sentimental love stories are interwoven with a legal intrigue about a lost inheritance, together with a great deal of commentary on contemporary social conventions and problems of conduct. The solutions she comes to are all very much in accord with received opinion, though on the way she offers some acutely critical insights into a society which allows insincerity, hypocrisy and social ambition to flourish.

The Children of the Abbey, Oscar and Amanda Fitzalan, are the dispossessed heirs of the title and estate of a wealthy Scottish family whose seat is Dunreath Abbey. Much of the novel is concerned with the struggles of these two to maintain their honour against the combined pressures of family jealousy, social hostility, poverty and sexual aggression, in a plot where the love affairs of Amanda and Lord Mortimer and of Oscar and Adela Honeywood, a general's daughter, are worked out in a curious counterpoint of romance and realism. The greater part of our attention is engaged by the trials of Amanda in the traditional heroine role as she suffers from the persecutions of the sexually rapacious Colonel Belgrave, her jealous relations the Roslines, and the financially desperate father of Lord Mortimer. Not only does she manage to outwit all her more socially advantaged competitors in a way that is emotionally satisfying to the reader but at the same time her sufferings and triumphs make a moral point by demonstrating the invulnerability of female innocence when supported by an unwavering faith in God. Christian moralising is not lacking in this novel, for like most Minerva authors Mrs Roche uses the ups and downs of her narrative action to reinforce notions of the instability of earthly happiness which may be granted or withdrawn as we are worthy of the care of Divine Providence. In the end the wheel comes full circle: those who have wrongfully persecuted Amanda and Oscar are brought low, while the two Children of the Abbey regain their inheritance through a missing will produced by their penitent maternal grandmother who has been secretly imprisoned in the Abbey for many years. She declares, with true confessional rhetoric: 'I have lived . . . to justify the ways of Providence to men; and prove, that however calamity may oppress the virtuous, they or their descendants shall at last flourish' (IV, x, 218).[3] Reinstated to title and fortune, Amanda and Oscar achieve their happy marriages and the novel ends as it began with a eulogy on domestic bliss and rural felicity brought about by the mysterious machinery of a Providence which is both merciful and just.

By working out her narrative in contemporary society Mrs Roche manages to be a great deal more persuasive about the threats to innocence than those novelists who translated their problems into medieval Gothic fantasy. Instead of creating an enclosed fictive world where both escapism and neurosis could flourish, Mrs Roche offers pastoral nostalgia and sentimentalism

toughened by a disturbing awareness of civilised city life and
the threat that it poses to such romantic longings; after all,
modern civilisation has produced not only a Belgrave but a
Lord Mortimer as well, and we are always conscious in the novel
of a seesaw movement between contemporary social awareness
and a retreat from reality into wish fulfilment. Though explicitly
endorsing the *status quo*, the novel gives us a curious impression
of instability, incorporating as it does patterns of opposition in
its subject matter and in its language. Just as there are incom-
patibilities in the kinds of literary convention the author uses, so
there are sharp juxtapositions throughout between innocence
and worldliness, romantic love and sexual passion, appearance
and reality, sincerity and deceit, the pastoral retreat and life in
the city. Such confrontations are arguably the stuff of most
plots but here they are so consistent and sometimes so arbitrarily
introduced that we cannot help but see them as signs of an
authorial dilemma about the relative values of different kinds
of experience.

The novel begins with a celebration of country life and childhood innocence, counterpointed by an awareness of the vulnerability of such an ideal world:

> Yellow sheafs from rich Ceres the cottage had crown'd,
>   Green rushes were strew'd on the floor,
> The casements sweet woodbine crept wantonly round,
>   And deck'd the sod seats at the door.   (Cunningham)

'Hail sweet asylum of my infancy! Content and innocence
reside beneath your humble roof, and charity, unboastful of
the good it renders. Hail, ye venerable trees! my happiest
hours of childish gaiety were passed beneath your shelter;
then, careless as the birds that sung upon your boughs, I
laughed the hours away, nor knew of evil. Here surely I shall
be guarded from duplicity; and, if not happy, at least in
some degree tranquil: here unmolested may I wait, till the
rude storm of sorrow is overblown, and my father's arms are
again expanded to receive me.'   (i, i, i)

The opening quotation, from John Cunningham's *Content*

(1781) celebrating the peaceful life of a shepherd and shep-
herdess, serves as an emblem of the idyllic country retreat, full
of sentimental appeal in its summery prettiness, which is both
extended by the heroine's lyrical outburst on her homecoming
and tempered by her adult realisation that this is indeed a
retreat from the cares of the world. The idea of coming home
always generates a powerful emotional charge, suggesting our
return to a safe familiar place where we may find again the
feelings associated with our childhood; it is such an encounter
that the heroine's reverie enacts for us here. So strong is her
sense of the past that things in the present, like her old nurse's
cottage or the trees in the lane, lose their immediate reality and
become signs pointing back to a lost world filled with laughter
and gaiety. When she does return to the present, it is over-
shadowed by the recognition that such careless happiness is no
longer possible, for experience inevitably destroys the strong
simple elations of innocence. What is so obviously appealing
here is the common romantic yearning to recapture the childish
illusion of perfect security, to be 'guarded', to be 'unmolested',
to escape if only temporarily from the pressures of the world.
Where Mrs Roche comes close to the sentimental novelists is
in her reluctance to show her heroine coming to terms with adult
experience; Amanda sees the world purely as a threat and what
is emphasised is her need for protection; she will 'wait' at her
nurse's cottage till her 'father's arms are again expanded to receive' her. 'Asylum' is the key word in this opening paragraph,
introducing an image which recurs throughout the novel. The
many refuges described usually turn out to be illusory till finally
the heroine finds her true asylum in marriage where, under the
protection of her husband, she is removed from the assaults of
the world to flourish in domestic tranquillity on a country
estate. Amanda's reverie is really as emblematic as the Cunningham quotation, setting up familiar patterns of feeling which
are to run throughout the novel, in the language of sentimental
rhapsody. For Mrs Roche's contemporary readers this opening
would have had a literary resonance too, for it is a close imitation in form and substance of the beginning of Fanny Burney's
Cecilia (1786), with the significant difference that Cecilia is
saying goodbye to the 'abode of her youth' to go out into

the world whereas Amanda is retreating to the scene of her childhood.

As we might expect, the perfect embodiment of all the virtues is the heroine Amanda Fitzalan. She is the most completely traditional character in the novel, having the inevitable sentimental attributes of 'ineffable sweetness and sensibility' and idealised by the author as a paragon of innocence and integrity. A full-length portrait of Amanda presented in the first chapter in very balanced prose and conventional imagery tells us about the temperament of the sentimental stereotype of Woman and also delineates our appropriate emotional response to such a figure:

> Though the rose upon her cheek was pale, and the lustre of her eyes was fled, she was, from those circumstances (if less dazzling to the eye), more affecting to the heart: cold and unfeeling indeed must that one have been, which could see her unmoved; for her's was that interesting face and figure, which had power to fix the wandering eye, and change the gaze of admiration into the throb of sensibility; nor was her mind inferior to the form that enshrined it.   (i, i, 7)

Such a presentation encapsulates Amanda in the ideal woman mould as surely as do the social conventions of the world in which she moves. As a woman she is schooled in the virtues of sweetness and modesty and to accept suffering and self-sacrifice as her birthright. 'Patient submission to the will of heaven' and the need to 'support her misfortunes with placid resignation' all conspire to exalt the value of suffering till it becomes a refined form of masochism:

> She spoke of the rapture attending the triumph of reason and humanity over self and passion, and mentioned the silent plaudits of the heart, as superior to all gratification or external advantages: she spoke from the real feelings of her soul.
>   (iv, iv, 76)

With such a moral code—fully endorsed by her father and by her lover, indeed inherited from her dead mother—Amanda has little chance to show herself as anything other than a victim, someone who seeks refuge and male protection; as others see her, so she always sees herself, in the dependent roles of daughter or wife, making but modest claims for herself as an individual.

It is not so much that Amanda lacks the potential for developing an individual personality; she has a strong sense of her own moral worth and indeed a 'mind' (as suggested in her portrait) which is capable of doubting the wisdom of always doing her 'duty' uncritically, but her sense of her rôle and its restrictions is so strong that it often allows her only a negative display of feeling, whose outward evidence is 'the languor of her face', a 'universal trembling' of her frame, or silence, the most eloquent and at the same time the most inarticulate of all. To sustain a sense of identity through such negative exertions is no doubt so exhausting that we begin to understand how it is that so often Amanda, like any other sentimental heroine, has to escape from the discomforts of the present into memory or imagination as the only emotionally satisfying alternative open to her.

The author, though evidently alive to such frustrations, never questions this code of feminine submission. Amanda's reward for all her sufferings is to be married to Lord Mortimer, 'when he should be at liberty to watch over her with guardian care, soothe every weakness and soften every pain' (II, x, 158). Amanda feels herself

> ill-qualified . . . to struggle with a world where she would be continually liable to such shocks; she had yet a hope of escaping them—a hope of being guarded by the tutelary care of Lord Mortimer and of being one of the happiest of her sex.
> (III, v, 94)

The language and the sentiments are so totally conventional that they reduce the individuality of both Amanda and Mortimer, in spite of the fact that the latter 'entertained high notions of the independence that a rational mind has a right to maintain . . . he would neither be controlled by others nor merely allured by the advantages of fortune' (II, vii, 92). However, when Mortimer spells out his ideal of marriage to Amanda there is nothing independent or original about it; he endorses all the received assumptions about marriage and ends by praising Amanda as a force for social good:

7

I naturally wish to secure to myself domestic happiness; but never could it be experienced, except united to a woman whom my reason thoroughly approved; who should at once possess my unbounded confidence and tenderest affection; who should be not only the promoter of my joys, but the assuager of my cares ... To you I am bound by a sentiment even stronger than love—by honour; and with real gratitude acknowledge my obligations ... Were those, my dear Amanda, of your sex, who, like you, had the resistless power of pleasing, to use the faculties assigned them by a bounteous Providence in the cause of virtue, they would soon check the dissipation of the times.   (II, x, 141–2)

Lord Mortimer may be making an oblique reference here to his own earlier mistake in asking Amanda to be his mistress rather than his wife for worldly young man that he is, 'though with a tincture of romance in his disposition' (I, v, 71), he has been touched by the pernicious influences that Amanda has been sheltered from. His presentation as the modern sentimental hero is interesting, combining an odd mixture of realistic delineation and sentimentalism, acknowledging him as a wealthy eighteenth-century gentleman with all that this implies while at the same time registering the passionate feelings of the private man underneath.

Lord Mortimer was unutterably affected by her tears; a faint sickness seized him, he sunk upon the seat, and covered his face with his handkerchief, to hide his emotion; but, by the time service was over, it was pretty well dissipated.

Amanda returned home, and his Lordship waited for Howell's coming out of church. 'What the devil, Howell,' said he, 'did you mean by giving us such an exhortation? Have you discovered any little affair going on between some of your rustic neighbours?'   (I, vii, 92)

Like Amanda, Mortimer has been educated to play a certain rôle and is quite capable of meditating on his feelings and then choosing the appropriate code in which to express—or to conceal—them, as when he believes she has been unfaithful to him:

Oh, my Amanda, my distress is surely severe! Though

> anguish rives my hearts for your loss, I must conceal it; the
> sad luxury of grief will be denied me; for the world would
> smile if I could say I now lamented you.   (II, xii, 219)

The author acknowledges that the public persona keeps in
check a seething mass of private feelings but she often insists on
allowing extremes of passion to burst out rather than confining
herself to hints and suggestions. Inhibition exhausts Mortimer
just as much as it does Amanda, and in the privacy of an inter-
view with his aunt over the question of Amanda's supposed
unfaithfulness the anguish he has kept hidden in company
bursts out:

> The agony he suffered from that deception, joined to the
> excessive agitation and fatigue he had felt the preceding
> night and the present day, so powerfully assailed him at this
> moment, that his senses suddenly gave way, and he actually
> fainted on the floor.   (II, xii, 230)

Codes of decorum break down, not only for the hero but for the
author as well, as she turns from the language of social restraint
to sentimental excess, indulging in overwrought display as
extreme as anything that we would find in Gothic fantasy.

The shift in conventions that characterises Mortimer's presentation is even more marked in that of the villain Colonel
Belgrave. Here we find a real discrepancy between the realistic
assessment of him as an eighteenth-century libertine using his
superior social position to exploit women sexually and economically and the other romantic view of him in his rôle as villain,
the predatory male whose deceitfulness and lust are so exaggerated by the heroine's fear that he becomes the embodiment of
evil in her eyes. True, Amanda is sexually threatened by Belgrave, who really is as bad as Manfroné or any other Gothic
villain and as assiduous in his persecutions. The very sight of
him always brings on a crisis of horror for her; he is likened to
an evil genius dogging her footsteps and when she sees him she
turns as pale as if she had seen a ghost:

> The terror his presence inspired, was too powerful for
> reason to conquer, and raised the most gloomy presages in
> her mind: she believed him capable of any villainy—his

looks had declared a continuance of illicit love. She trembled
at the idea of his stratagems being renewed . . . To Heaven
she looked up for protection.   (II, x, 159)

Traditional Gothic language is perhaps the most appropriate
register of Amanda's neurotically heightened fears here, with a
certain piquancy deriving from the fact that her crisis is set in
the very civilised context of a society ball where the sight of
Belgrave's 'invidious eyes fastened on her' is a very disorienting
experience. Though there is no castle in the Apennines, the dis-
solute laughs of unprincipled ruffians are still to be heard in
eighteenth-century London. Belgrave does attempt to seduce
Amanda, not in a remote castle but in the private dressing-
room of a London house. His words echo those of Ambrosio,
Manfroné, or any other villain about to triumph in his wicked
designs:

> 'Neither cries nor struggles, Amanda,' said he, 'will be
> availing: without the assistance of a friend, you may be con-
> vinced I could not have entered this house; and the same
> friend will, you may depend upon it, take care that our tête-
> à-tête is not interrupted.'   (II, xii, 199)

The language becomes entirely Gothic, and though used only
figuratively, it is very effective in its suggestion of violence and
intensity of feeling:

> Had Death, in his most frightful form, stared her in the
> face, she could not have betrayed more horror: she looked
> towards it with a countenance as expressive of wild affright
> as Macbeth's, when viewing the chair on which the spectre
> of the murdered Banquo sat.   (II, xii, 206)

Amanda herself is forced by the stereotype into the traditional
rôle of Gothic helplessness:

> 'To Heaven I leave the vindication of my innocence: its
> justice is sure, though sometimes slow, and the hour of retribu-
> tion often arrives when least expected.'   (II, xii, 211)

Clearly, events in actual life deny the comfortable assertions of
a Henry Tilney that atrocities do not occur in Christian England and his 'neighbourhood of voluntary spies' do not protect

innocence but collaborate with wickedness for the sheer delight of being spiteful. Amanda is made to look guilty, which is a measure of success for Belgrave in a society where to have a compromised reputation is almost as bad as having no reputation at all; the real measure of such villainy is spelt out by another gentleman later in the novel: 'You are not only the violater, but the defamer, of female innocence!' (IV, vi, 123).

Belgrave's individuality is gradually eroded, mainly through the language in which he is presented to us, so that by the end he has assumed the resonance of Richardson's Lovelace as his agonies of guilt suggest:

> 'Dying!' he repeated; 'Amanda Fitzalan dying! But she will be happy; her's will be a pure and ministering spirit in Heaven, when mine lies howling—the angels are not purer in mind and person than she is.'—'Then you are an execrable villain!' cried Sir Charles, laying his hand on his sword.
>
> (IV, vi, 124)

And of course Belgrave, like any repentant Gothic villain, falls victim to the greatest agony of mind and body: 'His senses were restored a short time before he died; but what excruciating anguish, as well as horror, did he suffer from their restoration!' (IV, xi, 241). (Incidentally, England is rid of him, for he crosses to Calais where he dies of a fever brought on by agitation of mind and 'inebriety'.)

While preserving a breath of actuality in the situation, Mrs Roche uses conventional language to convey extremes of feeling which lead away from and beyond the confines of ordinary experience. This technique is strikingly clear in the one truly Gothic episode in the novel, which occurs in the ruined chapel of Dunreath Abbey, the ancestral home to which Amanda returns 'afflicted and unknown' as a lady's companion.

> If at all inclined to superstition, you are now going to a place which will call it forth. Dunreath Abbey is gothic and gloomy in the extreme, and recalls to one's mind all the stories they ever heard of haunted houses and apparitions.
>
> (III, xi, 215)

Starting from this ironic almost anti-Gothic perspective, the

author treats the Abbey first as an architectural phenomenon
and then as a moral emblem of the instability of things; only
gradually does she move into the murkier regions of Radcliffian
terror. All the Gothic apparatus of fear is there in the picturesque ruined chapel overgrown with ivy which Amanda
visits alone one moonlit night looking for her dead mother's
portrait. On penetrating into the nearby deserted apartments
of the abbey where she supposes her mother to have lived,
Amanda's experience assumes a dreamlike quality where the
normal relations between appearance and reality are obscured
by 'almost total darkness' relieved only by fitful moonbeams.
As Amanda enters a 'little arched door' she is surprised to find
herself suddenly in a 'lofty hall, in the centre of which was a
grand staircase, the whole enlightened by a large gothic window'; the place is filled with the 'hollow echo' of her own footsteps, and having made her way through a long gallery 'in
almost total darkness' into a spacious room, she is shocked to
find not her mother's portrait as she had expected but a human
figure. Not unnaturally she believes that she is confronting the
legendary ghost of the abbey:

> Her horror may be better conceived than described, when
> she found herself, not by a picture, but by the real form of a
> woman, with a deathlike countenance! She screamed wildly
> at the terrifying spectre, for such she believed it to be, and
> quick as lightning flew from the room. Again was the moon
> obscured by a cloud, and she involved in utter darkness.
>
> (III, xiii, 236)

When Amanda is pursued by the figure there is a real frisson of
horror as she feels 'an icy hand upon her's'.

> She made a spring to escape through the entrance: but the
> apparition, with a rapidity equal to her own, glided before
> her; and with a hollow voice, as she waved an emaciated
> hand, exclaimed, 'Forbear to go!'.—A deadly faintness again
> came over Amanda; she sunk upon a broken seat, and put
> her hands over her eyes, to shut out the frightful vision.
>
> (III, xiii, 237)

Having wrought Amanda to this pitch, the author immediately dispels any possibility of a supernatural cause:

'Lose,' continued the figure, in a hollow voice, 'lose your superstitious fears; and in me behold not an airy inhabitant of the other world, but a sinful, sorrowing, and repentant woman!'   (III, xiii, 237)

The 'spectre' is no other than the wicked old Lady Dunreath who had deprived Amanda's mother of her inheritance and who now wishes to make reparation to her descendants by giving Amanda her grandfather's will which had been kept hidden for many years. It is the turning-point in Amanda's fortune as by this means she and her brother, the Children of the Abbey, are enabled to establish themselves as its rightful heirs. Thanks to her conditioning, Amanda is able to cope admirably with this traumatic shock, feeling not only wonder but also 'pity' and the 'tenderest compassion' for the 'unhappy woman'. And interestingly, she immediately makes the connection between righteousness and its due reward: 'A will which will entitle my brother to affluence? Oh, Providence, how mysterious are thy ways' (III, xiii, 241). It is typical of Mrs Roche's attitude and technique that in the most startling crisis in the novel she should evoke supernatural fear and then make a point which is not psychological but moral. Though she can deploy the full Gothic paraphernalia of terror, she refuses to give it any validity beyond emphasising crises in human relationships.

Her healthy scepticism about Gothic terrors does not in any way hide Mrs Roche's delight in overwrought displays of feeling and it is in love relationships full of human interest both personal and social that she most freely indulges her penchant for emotional excess. Her *pièce de résistance* is surely the reconciliation scene between Amanda and Lord Mortimer at the end of the novel where these lovers, having survived a very tempestuous affair full of misunderstandings and separations, meet again by accident and finally resolve all the difficulties in the way of their marriage.

As a love scene it is sentimental in the extreme, yet it bears such a provocative resemblance to the meeting between Elizabeth

Bennet and Darcy at Pemberley in *Pride and Prejudice* that one wonders if Jane Austen had not been inspired by this scene as her own model. She may perhaps have read *The Children of the Abbey*; after all, Harriet Smith had in *Emma*, and the hero's friend in both *Pride and Prejudice* and *Children of the Abbey* is called Charles Bingley. *Children of the Abbey* was published in 1796 and its Dedication is dated June 1 of that year so it must have appeared just before she began her first *Pride and Prejudice* draft (*First Impressions*) in October. From what we know of Jane Austen's response to contemporary literature it would not be surprising to find the genesis of a scene in her reading of another novel, though treated with a tact and moral awareness distinctively her own. But whether Jane Austen had or not, the scene at Pemberley serves as a useful kind of parallel to make precise the differences in fictional treatment between a sentimental novelist like Mrs Roche and a novelist of Jane Austen's calibre. Both scenes share the same setting—that of a large mansion which bears witness both to the wealth and character of its owner, the difference being that everything about Pemberley and Darcy is 'handsome' and 'ample' whereas Tudor Hall, Lord Mortimer's stately home, is 'antique, quite in the Gothic style' with a romantic prospect of ruins from its windows (corresponding no doubt to the 'tincture of romance' in Mortimer's disposition). In both cases it is the heroine who is trespassing and the surprise encounters between the lovers provoke the same feelings of confusion and embarrassment in all parties. However, for Jane Austen such a meeting is to be treated with a delicate sense of emotional responsiveness and tact all contained within the decorum of social ritual:

> They were within twenty yards of each other, and so abrupt was his appearance, that it was impossible to avoid his sight. Their eyes instantly met, and the cheeks of each were overspread with the deepest blush. He absolutely started, and for a moment seemed immovable from surprise; but shortly recovering himself, advanced towards the party, and spoke to Elizabeth, if not in terms of perfect composure, at least of perfect civility.
> She had instinctively turned away; but, stopping on his

approach, received his compliments with an embarrassment
impossible to be overcome.

(Pride and Prejudice, OEN, III, i, 221)

Mrs Roche treats a similar situation very differently, for when
Amanda, delicately sketching in Mortimer's music room, hears
a 'deep and long-drawn sigh' behind her, her surprise is not
controlled by decorum but is registered in the most exaggerated
behaviour:

> Amazed, unable to speak, to move, almost to breathe, she
> stood, motionless and aghast—the pale statue of Surprise, as
> if she neither durst nor could believe the evidence of her eyes.
>
> (IV, viii, 164)

Mortimer himself is not merely embarrassed but is presented as
a typical despairing lover ghastly and dishevelled in the Hamlet
style:

> In the pale countenance of Lord Mortimer scarce a vestige
> of his former self (except in the benignancy of his looks) re-
> mained; his faded complexion, the disorder of his hair, his
> mourning habit, all heightened the sad expression of his
> features—an expression which declared that he and happi-
> ness were never so disunited as at the present moment.
>
> (IV, viii, 164)

The tone of their meeting has nothing of Jane Austen's 'civil-
ity', nor is Mrs Roche capable of registering the 'silence' into
which Elizabeth and Darcy lapse when all attempts at conversation fail; instead of presenting the strong currents of
emotional disturbance with restraint, Mrs Roche drowns
individuality with lingering pathos. In a scene reduced to
stylised slow-motion movement her lovers cannot separate nor
keep quiet, yet their dialogue does nothing to illuminate misunderstanding, interrupted as it continually is by Amanda's
'streaming tears' and Mortimer's expressions of 'mingled horror
and wildness' as he groans 'in the excruciating agony of his
soul'.

In such an atmosphere of 'breathless emotion' Amanda swoons
twice under the strain, both occasions providing the author

with the opportunity to appeal to her readers' sympathetic imagination, for the faintings are presented in great visual detail with Mortimer catching Amanda in his arms. Incidentally, to erotic suggestiveness is added the hint of illicit love for both Amanda and the reader believe that Mortimer is now married to somebody else:

> Amanda trembled . . . her respiration grew faint; she could not support herself, and made a motion to sit down upon the grass; but Lord Mortimer eagerly caught her to his bosom. She had not strength to resist the effort, and her head reclined upon his shoulder; but who can speak her feelings, as she felt the beating heart of Mortimer, which, from its violent palpitations, seemed as if it would burst his bosom to find a passage to her feet? (IV, viii, 169)

Of course as soon as Amanda recovers she is overwhelmingly 'sensible of the impropriety of her situation' and resolves to leave Mortimer 'for ever'. But having played with the improper suggestion and delivered the heroine's response, 'Oh, my lord, you shock, shall I say more? You disappoint me', Mrs Roche withdraws such a possibility by revealing that Mortimer is not married and so is free to address Amanda honourably after all. It hardly needs adding that Amanda faints more freely into his arms a second time:

> She sunk, beneath surprise and joy, into the expanded arms of her beloved Mortimer.—It is ye alone, who, like her, have stood upon the very brink of despair, who, like her, have been restored, unexpectedly restored to hope, to happiness, that can form any judgment of her feelings at the present moment, at the moment, when, recovering from her insensibility, the soft accent of Lord Mortimer saluted her ear, and made her heart, without one censure from propriety, respond to rapture as he held her to his bosom. (IV, viii, 171)

Even when the crisis has passed there is no diminution of the 'tears of impassioned tenderness'—not for Mrs Roche the restraint of Jane Austen:

The happiness which this reply produced, was such as he

had probably never felt before; and he expressed himself on the occasion as sensibly and as warmly as a man violently in love can be supposed to do. (*Pride and Prejudice*, III, i, 325)

Mortimer's behaviour is much closer to Mr Collins's (though entirely without Jane Austen's parodic dimension):

> Alternately he fell at the feet of Amanda, alternately he folded her to his bosom, and asked his heart if its present happiness was real? (IV, viii, 172)

In such a bath of sentimentality all possibility of registering individual responses is lost so that Amanda and Mortimer, unlike Elizabeth and Darcy, recede into the stereotypes of the sentimental novel, ready to take part in the happy-ever-after ending which Mrs Roche provides.

Sentimentality pervades the ending. We feel the mollifying influence of the author's presence as the conflicting sets of values explored in the novel are brought into exquisite balance by narrative artifice. The strong arm of Providence having stripped the wicked of happiness and honour and brought 'terror and amazement' appropriately upon them, the righteous are exalted to their proper place in the world. As we might expect, the ending is preoccupied with marriages of 'honour and reason'; with Amanda's marriage to Mortimer in the village church of her childhood her happiness is 'completed', the author informs us. In her indestructible innocence Amanda would have appealed to the reader's sense of the peculiar strength of women which lies behind their fragile exteriors, for Mrs Roche, though critical of society was by no means subversive and did her best to confirm prevailing social myths: 'She looked, indeed, the child of sweet simplicity, arrayed with the unstudied elegance of a village maid; she had no ornaments but those which could never decay, namely, modesty and meekness' (IV, x, 221). As this description suggests, the narrative turns decisively away from urban society to what we can only call the symbolic landscape of the pastoral retreat. The romance and marriage of Oscar, the other Child of the Abbey, is in every way a parallel to Amanda's, the brother and sister sharing the same inheritance of tragic romantic love from their parents but fulfilling in their generation the destiny of their ancient house. Oscar, now Lord Dunreath, marries his Adela in the chapel where his parents were married and takes her to live in his ancestral home. In their prosperity these 'sweet descendants of the Dunreath family' assume once more an emblematic rôle: 'their example inspires others with emulation to pursue their courses' (IV, xi, 256).

In *The Children of the Abbey* Mrs Roche has illustrated the orthodox eighteenth-century moral and social assumptions in the most fashionable form of fiction available to her; she is, as Michael Sadleir described her (in his pamphlet on the Northanger Novels, 1927), 'an out and out sensibility writer but with a Gothic accent'. Though her novel contains potentially disturbing elements of social criticism and emotional awareness, its final poise is meant no doubt to reassure its readers who after all read for entertainment. And reading such fiction was, as another Minerva writer Mrs Meeke admitted in 1802, 'a very innocent, if not a very profitable recreation' (Preface to *Midnight Weddings*).

Manfroné; or, The One-Handed Monk

In contrast to the well-regulated sentimental Gothic of *The Children of the Abbey*, *Manfroné; or, The One-Handed Monk* is a nightmare full of hallucinatory terrors and sexual violence presented like a melodrama, lurid and simplistic. Written in 1809 when 'Gothic' had become synonymous with 'sensational', it is very much a product of its time. In fact its author, Mary-Anne Radcliffe, had been the compiler some few years before of *Radcliffe's New Novelist's Pocket Magazine*, one of those short-lived periodicals of chapbook productions specialising in melodramatic Gothic fiction. (Incidentally, Mary-Anne Radcliffe is no relation to Mrs Ann Radcliffe of *Udolpho*, though the confusion over authorship was inevitable, indeed perhaps intended by the second writer.) The violence of *Manfroné*, though symptomatic of fictional trends in general, was not typical of Minerva Press fiction and it is interesting that A. K. Newman, Lane's successor, only accepted *Manfroné* for republication under the Minerva name in 1819, after ten years of popularity under the imprint of J. F. Hughes of Oxford Street had given it a measure of familiarity if not of respectability. Montague Summers condemned *Manfroné* as 'an utterly worthless compilation of ill-digested horrors and ranting absurdities' in his *Essays in Petto* (1928). It is true that *Manfroné* is a very bad novel but it is also a very interesting one, possessing an extraordinary emotional compulsiveness in its displays of neurotic sexuality, all this presented under the ingenious disguise of a 'whodunnit'. Though there is nothing very new about its materials or its technique, what is strange is the peculiar fascination which this spendid thriller exerts; it is this which is worth our consideration for it reveals much about the Gothic state of mind and about the techniques of sensationalism in a wider reference.

The world of *Manfroné* is a nightmarish feudal world of arbitrary tyranny and dark threats, with the narrative interest focussing on the harassments of the heroine Rosalina. She is the consistent suffering figure throughout, while the forces threatening her undergo an astonishing process of metamorphosis. Sometimes they appear as the malicious Prince Manfroné her rejected lover, sometimes as a mysterious grey-hooded monk from a neighbouring monastery, once indeed as her father who tries to murder her, and frequently as the fearful black monk Grimaldi. There is a dreadful hallucinatory quality about many of the crisis scenes, filled as they are with indistinct gigantic forms gliding swiftly and silently about Rosalina, but like the figures of a nightmare, never actually harming her. As the novel works its devious way to solving the initial mystery of Rosalina's midnight attacker who loses his hand in a sword-fight with her father, there is little sense of a narrative continuum as crises in the action succeed one another with seeming arbitrariness and alarming rapidity. It would be false to one's experience of the book to pretend that two interrupted midnight weddings, several savage murders and innumerable attempts to abduct the heroine form any evident kind of logical patterning; all we discern as the action heaves along is that the sinister figure of Grimaldi emerges as the supreme manipulator of people and events: 'He seemed to take pleasure in acts of cruelty and black and horrible revenge.'

This very neurotic novel is in fact structured like a nightmare, not upon action or character, but upon two key images: a severed hand which becomes a skeleton hand with the passing of time, and Grimaldi's black mask which suggests mysterious evil lurking behind it. Everything depends on discovering the identity of the owner of the hand and on the removal of the mask; incidentally we might remark that the title of the novel is ineptly revelatory, giving us the vital clue which it takes the author four volumes to divulge through the action! Of course Grimaldi is Manfroné, who has been acting throughout from motives of revenge and frustrated lust. From the moment of Rosalina's discovery that Grimaldi has only one hand, the novel runs quickly to its conclusion with the revelation of his true identity, his imprisonment of Rosalina in his castle, and his attempted rape prevented at the very point of its accomplishment by her lover Montalto bursting into her dungeon. With a 'death-dealing blow' he lays Manfroné on the ground, where he has to lie in agony watching the lovers embrace. The author comments, perhaps laconically, perhaps innocently: 'What a sight was this for the dying Manfroné!' The lovers immediately escape from Manfroné's castle and by morning are far beyond the confines of nightmare back in the security of Rosalina's home. What follows is the conventional happy ending which has little relation in tone or feeling to the main fantasy; Rosalina and Montalto are married with full Gothic splendour and 'Heaven smiled on their union and never did a pair enjoy more real felicity than they did'.

Clearly Mary-Anne Radcliffe is relying on her readers' familiarity with a certain kind of novel, playing on predictable responses to stock situations to obtain emotional effects without holding up the pace of the narrative. By 1809 readers knew what associations were expected of them when confronted with castles and abbeys in picturesque Italianate settings, and they had no trouble in recognising the main characters and in identifying their rôles and moral values from their appearance and behaviour. *Manfroné* is no exception to this commercialised patterning: readers would immediately recognise Rosalina, that 'loveliest of created beings', as the heroine with her 'white arms' and 'expressive eyes', and they would know that the dashing young cavalier who rescues her from the band of ruffians is her fit companion in a sentimental love relationship. As soon as Prince Manfroné appears, the dark stranger of 'colossal height' shooting 'dark meaning looks' at the heroine, they would be equally certain that he is the villain, only perhaps to be surpassed in sinister intent by the mysterious monk Grimaldi, the wearer of the black mask who spends a lot of time intently viewing Rosalina 'through the narrow aperture of his cowl'. Readers would not have been disappointed and the very predictability of the pattern has the simple appeal of recognition, which is of course felt just as strongly today in various forms of popular entertainment. It is the delight of surrendering to a familiar fantasy world and Mary-Anne Radcliffe's readers would have enjoyed the fiction with which they were presented; Thackeray's Miss Caroline and the maid Becky were still going pale and goggle-eyed over it in *A Shabby Genteel Story* in 1840. The author is very conscious that she is constructing a fiction and makes no attempt to be realistic; indeed realism was specifically not a criterion of excellence for her, much of *Manfroné*'s appeal lying in its promise of escapism. Everything is distanced from real life by the very conventionality of its Gothic presentation, so that the reader's rôle is analogous to that of a spectator at a play becoming involved to a certain degree yet always conscious that he is watching an artefact, a constructed fiction. Surely part of the appeal of Gothic terror must be the reader's ultimate sense of safety, something which Burke had taught people to appreciate in his aesthetic definition of the 'delightful horror' of the sublime.

The justification for this form of fiction was the moral lesson to be drawn from the action and Mary-Anne Radcliffe continually and somewhat defensively reminds her readers that she is showing violent passions in action only so that they may be warned against vicious elements in their own experience. This is the orthodox moral defence of the Gothic novelist, although endearingly this author's protestations are accompanied by a rather shaky confidence in her own efforts: 'whether [these volumes] answer that purpose or not, there is a consoling reflection which will ever remain to alleviate the disappointment, and which is, that their intent was good' (Ch. ix, p. 166).[4] She makes both a scrupulous moral translation of every crisis and structures

her events so that the narrative is an unambiguous illustration
of the triumph of good over evil. Moral forces are polarised in
the main protagonists whose behaviour is totally in keeping
with them, the angelic heroine representing 'goodness' as an
absolute and rather passive quality, supported by the active
fighting arm of the hero who embodies 'goodness' in its com-
bative rôle, and 'evil' being exaggerated in the gigantic figure
of the villain. The balance does not shift throughout the novel;
indeed it has the schematic rigidity of a moral fable.

The aura of nightmare which surrounds all the contacts between the heroine and the villain suggests that moral insight is
less the issue here than something more intuitive. It would
appear that the hallucinatory terrors of *Manfroné* are based not
on any rational morality but on the heroine's sexual fears. *Manfroné* must be classed as one of those rare English Gothic novels,
along with Lewis's *Monk* and Charlotte Dacre's *Zofloya*, where
women's sexual neuroses and male feelings of aggression and
frustration are actually brought to the surface and enacted. For
the most part in Gothic fiction the villain's rages and the heroine's morbid fears of him indicate tensions without actually
stating them. Mary-Anne Radcliffe treats these emotions with
a naive directness, though at the same time refusing to understand the significance of what she is describing.

The figure of the One-Handed Monk epitomises these sexual
neuroses in a way that is at once typical of the Radcliffe-Lewis
pattern and unique in its explicitness. The fashion for monkish
fiction had been set by *The Monk* and *The Italian* where the
main characters hide their particular forms of hypocrisy behind
the mask of monasticism. In *Manfroné*, however, we have the
figure of the secular villain who assumes the monastic garb simply as a disguise, completing the image by wearing at all times
a black mask under his cowl. With her usual ineptness the author
underlines this mechanism for us about halfway through:

> He, it will seem, did indeed only assume the religious habit
> he wore, as a cloke to the forwarding of his unfathomable
> schemes; for the accomplishment of which, his remorseless
> and cruel disposition shrunk not at the perpetration of the
> most horrible deeds.   (xiii, 97)

In his dual rôle of monk and frustrated lover, Manfroné represents the conflation of superstitious and sexual fears which are
the basic stuff of Gothic fiction. Despite his gigantic form, Manfroné has no stature as a character; possessing neither Ambrosio's
talent for self-destruction nor Schedoni's Machiavellian ambition, he functions more as a ubiquitous threatening force than
as a personality. His sinister machinations, though varied in
their forms to include murder, betrayal and blasphemy, are all
directly related to his prime motive of revenge which in turn is
the result of his frustrated passion for the heroine. The immensely complicated intrigue can ultimately be reduced to a series of
elaborations on Manfroné's sexual frustrations. From the first
crisis to the last (both of them attempted rape) his purpose remains constant, while the aura of dread surrounding him is
heightened by all the heroine's intuitive fears. As the basic
framework of the novel, this theme exerts a powerful emotive
force which is, I think, the secret of its peculiar fascination.

Of course, in talking about the emotional appeal of *Manfroné*
we must consider too the form in which it is presented. From the
very beginning we notice its theatricality and it is interesting to
see how the author exploits the dramatic clichés of Gothic to
enhance the vividness of her narrative. In *Manfroné* we have an
almost perfect example of the contemporary stage melodrama
in prose fictional form; not that the novel has a tight dramatic
structure, but that it is built out of a series of crisis scenes, each
one presented with great visual skill and appealing directly to
the reader for an immediate emotional response. In fact, many
of these scenes have their exact parallels in contemporary melodramas. To say that *Manfroné* is 'theatrical' is to praise and to
criticise it at the same time: it has dramatic immediacy but is
guilty of frequent staginess and a lack of any sense of continuity
in the action.

Despite these reservations, 'theatrical' seems to describe best
the most distinctive quality of this novel—its extraordinary and
almost exclusively visual technique. Certainly the vividly-
realised dramatic scene had always been an important part of
Gothic fictional convention from *Otranto* onwards, where Walpole had acknowledged the influence of Shakespearean drama in
helping to shape his new kind of romance; combined with the

8

interaction between the Gothic novel and the Gothic melodrama, this led by 1800 to fiction which employed many
dramatic conventions of gesture, behaviour and scenery. What
is unusual about *Manfroné* is the degree to which its effectiveness
depends on the reader's imaginative response to the visual
quality of the scene presented. Dedicated as she is to dramatic
effects, Mary-Anne Radcliffe has evolved a notation of external
forms which almost entirely replaces the common novelistic
method of verbal commentary and analysis, an example of this
being her precise description of a character's appearance, which
contains a built-in silent moral commentary derived from conventions of dress and facial expression. As in a dream, there is a
continual shift in focus: sometimes the images are there haunt-
ing us as vague 'soul-harrowing forms' or 'dark savage presences', and at others they appear in such precise detail that we
cannot avoid staring straight into the eyes behind the monk's
black mask or seeing 'the dagger in the breast, encircled by the
ghastly fingers of a skeleton hand'. With the action leaping
apparently inconsequentially from one crisis to another, this
hallucinatory quality holds our attention almost in spite of ourselves and casts an ambiguous shadow of the supernatural over
events which are in fact prompted by the basest of human
motives.

A striking illustration of theatrical qualities in the novel is to
be found in the opening chapter, where we are presented with
a dramatic scene outside the time sequence of the narrative
which works exactly like the curtain-raiser of a melodrama:

> Rosalina, for some time lost in thought, rested her head on
> her white arm, till the increasing gloom of her chamber
> made her look to her expiring lamp; hastily she arose to trim
> it, for she feared to be left in the shades of darkness, as her
> thoughts were sorrowful, and sleep seemed not inclined to
> 'steep her senses in forgetfulness'.
>
> Her apartment was spacious and lofty; the wainscoting
> was of dark cedar, and the ceiling was formed of the same.
> The uncertain light of the lamp, which doubtfully fluttered
> round the wick, scarcely shed its faint lumen farther than the
> table on which it was placed.

An almost nameless sensation, but in which terror held a share, disturbed Rosalina; for, as she gazed around, she almost fancied the distant shades as the shrouds of spectral forms, gliding along with noiseless pace; and fancy made her listen in idea to the hollow tones of their sepulchral voices.

She had some time dismissed her servant, who had retired to her bed; and whether it was the effect of the tale she had been perusing, or some presentiment of ill which arose in her breast, and which filled her bosom with a secret dread, is uncertain; but she was going to summon her domestic to remain with her during the night, when a noise at the further extremity of her chamber fixed her, trembling, to her seat.

(I, 1–3)

The stagey quality comes across immediately in our view of the beautiful heroine sitting pensive and alone beside her flickering lamp. In the rapid transition from nameless fears to the first crisis of the action the reader is encouraged to feel the same responses as the heroine at every moment of her adventure. Her reactions are not difficult to follow for the point is quickly conveyed that Rosalina is a typical heroine in temperament as well as in physical appearance, with the peculiarly febrile nervous system which characterised these ladies. What is interesting is the way that the author relates Rosalina's imaginative terrors to actual events, exploiting the ambiguity between her natural fears of the dark and her private intuitions. The notation is purely 'sensational' in the way it insists on the direct relation between physical experience and psychological tensions, the gloom and darkness of the room becoming crude equivalents for the heroine's state of mind. The conventional stage prop of the lamp has a new importance here, operating as the mode of transition from one phase of the action to the next; from the flickering dimness of the opening it flares up suddenly to illuminate the terrifying vision of the tall figure in the sable mantle, but it is rapidly extinguished, plunging reader and heroine alike into utter darkness and impenetrable mystery. Though the author is keen to give her readers an incidental frisson of the supernatural, she is in reality much more interested in human beings and in the actions to which they may be led by their passions. It is the physicality of the ensuing fight that is stressed; there is nothing supernatural about the 'large and muscular' human hand which the villain leaves behind him as he escapes. With this shock of physical revulsion the action of the first chapter comes to an end. As we disengage from the crisis, we can appreciate the variety of effects achieved: the author has plunged us directly into the central mystery, she has suggested the physical power of the villain and the carnal nature of his threat to the heroine, and has compelled our attention by the double appeal to our curiosity and our fears. We may be reminded of the dramatic openings of Gothic novels like Mrs Parsons' *The Mysterious Warning* or Mrs Radcliffe's *The Italian*, and surely it is part of the author's intention that we should be. She is relying on an immediate response from her readers and a ready-made structure of expectations which it will be the purpose of the novel to fulfil.

Mary-Anne Radcliffe was immensely indebted to contemporary writers for some of her most striking effects and indeed for the main image in her story. A severed hand had already appeared in C. R. Maturin's first novel *Fatal Revenge* (1807), when the lover of Count Montorio's wife has his sword hand cut off in a fight with the count's men. The opening chapter may well have been inspired by a scene in a melodrama produced at Drury Lane in 1807, 'Monk' Lewis's *One O'Clock! or, The Knight and the Wood Daemon* which, though not the curtain-raiser, has some remarkable similarities in stage machinery and action with the *Manfroné* opening. Act III, Scene 1 of *The Wood Daemon*, where the villain breaks in at dead of night to kidnap a child, takes place in a high dark chamber with a secret sliding panel by which he enters, 'wrapped in a black cloak and masked'; the woman's screams for help and the ensuing struggle all happen in the dark as the villain's lantern is thrown down, and his dramatic exit (through a trapdoor) differs from Manfroné's in its effect only to the extent that he has been successful in his mission and carries the child off with him. There is more dialogue in Lewis's play than in Mary-Anne Radcliffe's novel, where the reported action is entirely devoid of any human sound but the most primitive exclamations: screams, deep groans and gasps for breath; but though Lewis's characters are

voluble, their language is as cliché-ridden as Mary-Ann Radcliffe's authorial voice, and *The Wood Daemon* would have provided a model where language as a vehicle of feeling breaks
down before the display of passion in action. The ending of
Lewis's play with its confrontation between heroine and villain
in a cavern is also quite close to the ending of *Manfroné*, though
I suspect it is to another melodrama, George Colman's *Blue
Beard* (Drury Lane, 1798), that the author has turned for the
details of her final action.

To draw attention to Mary-Anne Radcliffe's borrowings
from stage melodramas has, I hope, a positive aspect as well as
the negative one of emphasising her lack of originality, for
through her very naiveté she manages to translate these models
into prose without losing their crude directness of emotional
assault. The novel could serve as the script for a Hammer film,
where no doubt full justice would be done to the awful climax
of the narrative; this is the scene when Rosalina makes the
crucial discovery of the possessor of the 'dismembered arm'. It
is a moment unsurpassed in Gothic fiction, a moment of imaginative realisation so intense that it borders on madness. After a
massive accumulation of intuitive fears and strange eventuali-
ties, among which are the murder of her father and her abduction from his castle, Rosalina finds herself entirely in the power
of the monk Grimaldi. It is during an evening's respite at a
'wretched hovel' in the country after a long coach journey with
Grimaldi that, being a girl of some initiative, she decides on a
desperate escape attempt.

> She now, as silently as she was able, got out of the casement,
> and holding by the rope, put her foot softly on the bench,
> which trembled with the agitation of her body: the man was,
> however, still undisturbed—and the next moment she stood
> on the ground. She then stepped lightly on, intending to go
> round the cottage, and so reach the peasant; but in doing
> this, she passed by a low casement, which was open, and at
> which, horror-struck, she encountered the gaze of the padre
> Grimaldi, whose cowl being thrown back, disclosed the sable
> mask he wore.
> The monk, starting from his seat, hastened to the door, and

Rosalina flew towards the place where she had observed the peasant had seated himself; but he was no longer there, and probably had fled on perceiving the approach of the monk, through a dread of his resentment. He advanced nearer to her every moment, and at length caught her by her garments, as they waved in the wind.

Rosalina, exerting all her strength, at length succeeded in tearing her garments from his hold; but as she was struggling with him, what was her horror on perceiving he had but one hand, and that his other arm was shorn at the wrist!

Her sensations at this discovery were far beyond the weak efforts of the pen to describe. To her distended gaze, she instantly imagined, appeared the vile assailant of her honour, the intended assassin of Montalto, and, to sum up the horrid catalogue, the murderer of her parent!

She wildly shrieked at seeing the dismembered arm, and, with a dreadful groan, fell senseless on the earth.

(xxi, 124–6)

Mary-Anne Radcliffe takes the stock Gothic situation of the imprisoned heroine frustrated at the very moment of escape by the villain himself, and reanimates the cliché with daring explicitness. Her technique of accurate visual notation is peculiarly evident here and is combined with an excellent sense of pace. From Rosalina's cautious stealthy movements to her shock of horror at seeing the monk's face at the window the action speeds up as she is pursued, so that we watch appalled as he closes in on his victim. Unusually for this type of novel, he does actually catch her. As she struggles to free herself, all the facts and feelings that have been repressed throughout the novel emerge: the masked monk is indeed the man who had tried to rape her earlier and who had killed her father and wounded her lover, so all her religious superstitions and her sexual fears are telescoped into one terrible moment of realisation. For once, authorial apologies about 'the weak efforts of the pen' are needless, for she does catch the force of the split second of time when Rosalina's physical horror and moral revulsion are heightened to such a pitch that they make possible an imaginative perception of the truth; the 'distended gaze' describes not only Rosalina's physical response to panic but also her suddenly widened awareness at this crucial moment. It is no wonder that she falls down in a fainting fit, for her world is totally shattered; morbid fantasy and reality are frighteningly brought together, with reality shown to be as terrible as nightmare just as it was in *The Monk*.

From this point on, the narrative becomes the explicit enactment of sexual obsession, being the fulfilment of an interrupted nightmare of Rosalina's described earlier in the novel. As the action accelerates the focus clears, with the villain at last unmasked. 'The dark ferocious features of the Prince di Manfroné, so long supposed dead' now terrify Rosalina as the living man leaps out of the reaches of nightmare and death to molest her in her waking hours. His sudden appearances as he strides about the castle where he has her imprisoned are indeed more to be feared than nightmares or ghosts, augmented as they are by the real sexual threat of his presence: 'She had proceeded half way down the marble stairs, when she suddenly stopped, for to her terrified gaze appeared, when far remote from her thoughts, the Prince di Manfroné' (xxii, 168–9). Having tried unsuccessfully to coerce Rosalina into marrying him, he is finally reduced to physical assault and attempted rape, in a last crisis scene which is very reminiscent of *The Monk*:

'Now, proud fair, I mean to possess the lovely habitation of your scornful soul; nor longer will I wait to reap the harvest of my toils.'

Thus having said, he caught hold of the trembling Rosalina, and dragged her towards him: she screamed with affright, and long did she resist his dark intents; her agonizing sensations gave her fresh strength, and by a sudden effort she disengaged herself, and, opening the door of the dungeon, fled to the farther extremity of the cave: but the prince was resolved to perpetrate the dreadful deed which had long been the subject of his meditations, and he hastily pursued and brought her back. The strength of the hapless maid was fast decreasing, when suddenly the blast of a horn echoed through the cave. The prince started at the sound—hasty footsteps were heard—the door of the dungeon was burst open—and

Manfroné, drawing his sword, prepared to punish the un-
welcome intruders; but an arm, far superior to his in skill and
strength, with a death-dealing blow laid his gigantic form on
the ground, gasping for life.   (xxii, 194–6)

Here we find the same display of male physical power and
terrified female resistance as Lewis used in the rape of Antonia,
the same dramatic action without dialogue, and the same
authorial reticence about the use of the word 'rape'. Mary-Anne
Radcliffe refers to it as 'the dreadful deed which had long been
the subject of his meditations' (a circumlocution which emphasises the duration of the sexual threat to Rosalina and indeed
validates her own morbid intuitions). There is nothing however
that readers would not have encountered before and the real
shock comes only with the sudden blast of the horn and the
'death-dealing blow' that sends Manfroné crashing to the
ground. (Of course it is Montalto, Rosalina's lover, who has
come to her rescue once more.) It is a superbly sensational encounter, so totally theatrical in its effect that we ought not to
be surprised to find a very similar dénouement in a contemporary melodrama, George Colman's *Blue Beard*, where the villain's
attempt on the heroine's life is suddenly interrupted by horns
sounding loudly, walls falling down, and the appearance of the
hero:

> Drums—gong—crash.—Selim and Abomelique fight with
> scimitars ... After a hard contest, Selim overthrows Abo-
> melique at the foot of the skeleton. The skeleton instantly
> plunges the dart, which he had suspended, into the breast of
> Abomelique, and sinks with him beneath the earth.—A
> volume of flame arises, and the earth closes.—Selim and
> Fatima embrace.   (*Blue Beard*, ii, vii)

Mary-Anne Radcliffe follows Colman's model with only
slight variations (having used the skeleton hand earlier in a
different connection) up to the point when Rosalina 'recognising her lover, almost fainted with excess of joy, and hung with
rapture on his arm' (xxiii, 207). Manfroné is ultimately powerless
and dies in this knowledge, gazing on the lovers. When we consider the sexual basis of his aggression, this embrace reads like

the final blow in the tale of his frustrated passion. But the author immediately draws away from the significance of this climax, turning her story into a moral fable, for she translates Manfroné's defeat into an example of how justice always overtakes the wicked at the moment of their greatest triumphs. It is a crude distancing reaction away from the emotional raw material of her fiction, typical of Minerva writers' attempts to repress the implications of the neurotic fantasies which so fascinated them. *Manfroné* is not really moral at all, which is why the final moral aphorism—'To be good is to be happy!'—sorts so ill with the preceding narrative.

For Gothic sensationalism in both the psychological and the fictional sense, *Manfroné* cannot be outdone. We may object to the author's imposition of a Providential moral patterning on events which seem to have their own emotional logic but this does not at all affect the main lines of force in the novel. Even when Mary-Anne Radcliffe leaves behind her murky fantasy world, returning Rosalina and Montalto to safe marital bliss and reminding her readers of her moral intentions, she cannot easily dispel the gigantic shape of her title figure. *Manfroné* remains as the most explicit embodiment of sexual neurosis in Gothic fiction.

Jane Austen, *Northanger Abbey*

Charming as were all Mrs. Radcliffe's works, and charming even as were the works of all her imitators, it was not
in them perhaps that human nature, at least in the midland counties of England, was to be looked for.
                      (*Northanger Abbey*, ii, x, 177)[1]

Jane Austen was nothing like so irascible in her criticism of
Gothic fiction as Coleridge, who in 1797 condemned its 'shrieks,
murders, and subterraneous dungeons' manufactured with so
'little expense of thought or imagination',[2] nor was she so
coarse-grained as her contemporary Mrs Parsons whose *Castle of
Wolfenbach* actually subverts Gothic effects by revealing how the
'ghost' had been charged on oath to 'rattle a chain, groan, and
make such kind of noises as may appal' any visitors to the castle.[3]
Instead Jane Austen views Gothic with a wide imaginative
awareness, keenly perceiving its absurdities and its comic potential yet at the same time giving it credit for its often bizarre insights into human nature. She is always aware of the paradoxical
nature of the art of the novel: that while taking its substance
from real life situations it aspires to evoke a more satisfying order
than is available in life. She was never so simple-minded as to
believe that on the one hand there are novels and on the other
is life; rather that there is a complex interrelatedness between
living and imagining and that readers and novelists should both
cultivate a lively awareness of their interplay. It is in this context that we can most easily understand her response to the
Gothic craze which was at its height when she was writing
Northanger Abbey, a response which in some measure adds to our
appreciation of Gothic as well as focussing attention on its more
dangerous inanities.

Northanger Abbey is the most self-consciously literary of all Jane
Austen's novels. It depends for some of its distinctive effects on

specific allusions to Gothic fiction; it shows a craftsman's serious concern with the uses and abuses of language;[4] and throughout we see Jane Austen as the reader as well as the writer of novels investigating the central problem of the novelist: how fiction relates to real life.[5] Through the account of Catherine Morland's reading and education Jane Austen is using her own literary awareness to do a great deal more than merely parody the circulating library fiction that her heroine so much admires; though, like *Emma*, to some extent it presents a case against the imagination, *Northanger Abbey* is also a demonstration of the importance of imagination in Catherine's response to life. In Catherine's naive attempts to translate the crises of Gothic fiction into real situations, in the irresponsible and destructive gossip of Isabella and John Thorpe, and in General Tilney's ambitious mercenary delusions, Jane Austen is exploring the imaginative propensities of the ordinary human mind, showing the extent to which imagination colours daily experience and judgement. All these characters, Jane Austen makes it plain, have a great deal in common with the novelist; what they lack is 'genius, wit and taste' and the ability to wield 'the best-chosen language' for their imaginative fictions, those very points on which her spirited defence of the novel rests in *Northanger Abbey*. Her own stated awareness of her rôle as omniscient author at the end confirms her delight in fiction making but it also indicates her balanced awareness of precisely what kind of activity she is engaged in. As a responsible storyteller she shapes her artefact with humane awareness and exercises a strong imaginative control over it, a talent she clearly thought lacking in her characters and that Gothic novelists were deficient in as well.

To attack Gothic fiction as the current literary fad in the late 1790s was nothing unusual, but to criticise it with such creative insight was certainly peculiar to Jane Austen. She is not condemning the imaginative element of Gothic fantasy; rather she is criticising the irresponsibility of those writers who trivialise their important insights into human behaviour merely to frighten silly girls. Like them, her own heroine Catherine is left 'to the luxury of a raised, restless and frightened imagination over the pages of Udolpho'. That she should focus her attack on

Mrs Radcliffe, the best and most influential of these writers, is characteristic of Jane Austen's discernment, for between Mrs Radcliffe and herself there is really a great deal of common ground, not least in the subtlety of their techniques, but more obviously in their shared assumption of the importance of both feeling and reason to moral awareness. The difference lies in Mrs Radcliffe's flagrant abuse of the very imaginative faculties that Jane Austen praises, for Mrs Radcliffe finally abandons her readers to uncertainty whereas Jane Austen is always careful to argue for discrimination and discipline. Indeed she does so here in *Northanger Abbey* through comedy, with supreme literary tact trying to laugh readers out of their errors by showing what happens to her heroine when she indulges in too much Gothic fiction.

It is perhaps worthwhile clarifying *Northanger Abbey*'s area of literary reference; Jane Austen certainly thought it worth drawing attention to in her Advertisement prepared for the novel's expected publication in 1816. Though *Northanger Abbey* was not published till 1818 (with *Persuasion*), we know that she began it in the late 1790s and had it ready for publication by 1803. It did not appear then, and thirteen years later she wrote her authorial advertisement reminding her readers that some of the 'places, manners, books, and opinions' in it had 'undergone considerable changes' since the writing and that some parts of the work were already 'comparatively obsolete'. What was out of date was the particular list of fashionable Gothic novels that Isabella recommended Catherine to borrow from the circulating library in Bath, because the titles on her list were all published by 1798.[6] These girls are reading in the heyday of Mrs Radcliffe and her imitators, while John Thorpe, in an attempt to be very risqué, says that he has just finished Lewis's *Monk* (1796). He is such a liar that we cannot believe him even in this, and it is perhaps a veiled judgement on that novel that its only possible reader could have been the braggadocio John Thorpe! These are very much the enthusiasms and sensibilities of the late 1790s. By 1816 the fashionable literary figures were Sir Walter Scott and Byron, writers to whom Jane Austen refers in *Persuasion*, and given the modishness of *Northanger Abbey* it is quite noticeable that there is no reference to either of them. If the novel had been up to date, we might have expected that

Catherine would have liked history more (or at least historical novels), and we might also have expected that Catherine and Isabella would have found a Childe Harold figure in Bath—though by that time they most likely would have been following the Prince Regent to Brighton anyway! Instead, we find them enthusing over Mrs Radcliffe, and Catherine being frightened by a very traditional elderly villain with 'the air and attitude of a Montoni'. No doubt these are the reasons why Jane Austen felt it necessary to apologise to her readers. Her areas of reference would have been much more obviously outmoded than they are for us at this distance in time. What is interesting to us is the way she presents and explores the Gothic in *Northanger Abbey*. She moves far beyond literary burlesque and begins to investigate the very area of the irrational that the Gothic novelists always claimed as their own.

We know that one of Catherine's first discoveries in Bath was Mrs Radcliffe's *Mysteries of Udolpho*, and we also know with what delight she read it: 'While I have *Udolpho* to read, I feel as if nobody could make me miserable' (I, vi, 36). Indeed I think it very likely, judging from what she refers to later, that Catherine never got beyond Mrs Radcliffe and that Isabella's list of 'ten or twelve more of the same kind' were not begun, though in fact there were only seven on her list of promising Gothic titles! Jane Austen is keenly alive to the comic potential of Catherine's enthusiasms, always showing how her burning interest in Mrs Radcliffe's fantasy world mixes incongruously with the triviality of her everyday life. For instance, instead of paying attention to Isabella's gossip in the Pump Room, all Catherine is worrying about is what is behind the black veil in the castle of Udolpho. Their conversation, as Norman Page has noticed (*The Language of Jane Austen*, pp. 117–18), recalls the dialogue of eighteenth-century stage comedy:

'Have you gone on with *Udolpho*?'

'Yes, I have been reading it ever since I woke; and I am got to the black veil.'

'Are you indeed? How delightful! Oh! I would not tell you what is behind the black veil for the world! Are not you wild to know?'

'Oh! yes, quite; what can it be?—But do not tell me—I would not be told upon any account. I know it must be a skeleton, I am sure it is Laurentina's skeleton. Oh! I am delighted with the book!'   (I, vi, 34)

In this interchange, the humour is both on the surface in the dialogue and in the specific literary allusion. Isabella's provocative exclamations and Catherine's innocent curiosity culminate in her hilarious juxtaposition of her horror of the skeleton and her delight in the book. Jane Austen is laughing at the evident gap between Catherine's imaginative life and her palpable inexperience, a point she makes very clearly by her allusion to the veiled picture in *Udolpho*. Readers who knew *Udolpho* well would remember Emily's adventure and what it was that provoked this response:

> Emily went towards the picture, which appeared to be enclosed in a frame of uncommon size, that hung in a dark part of the room. She paused again, and then, with a timid hand, lifted the veil; but instantly let it fall—perceiving that what it had concealed was no picture, and before she could leave the chamber, she dropped senseless on the floor.
>
> (II, vi, 248–9)

What Emily had seen was the waxen image of a worm-eaten corpse 'dressed in the habiliments of the grave'. Isabella Thorpe is much more disingenuous than Catherine; clearly she wants to shock her by telling her about the corpse in order to gratify her own delight in morbid sensationalism.

In that Pump Room conversation between Catherine and Isabella the words 'horrid' and 'delightful' are used with gay abandon. Their meanings merge as they become synonyms; this language is a kind of debased currency minted by Burke in his treatise on the Sublime. It is a characteristic feature of Jane Austen's criticism of Gothic literary conventions to work by juxtapositions. By thus linking two concepts as seemingly opposed as 'horror' and 'delight' she shows not only the primitiveness of the emotions displayed but also their inappropriateness as ways of response to the banal events of everyday life. Such juxtaposition also provides a rich source of comedy, especially as the characters are somewhat prone to giving indiscriminate and effusive expression to what they feel.

Jane Austen is certainly laughing at Catherine's excessive enthusiasm for Gothic buildings when she is invited to visit Northanger Abbey:

> Northanger Abbey!—These were thrilling words, and wound up Catherine's feelings to the highest point of extasy.
>
> (II, ii, 123)

and

> With all the chances against her of house, hall, park, place, court, and cottage, Northanger had turned up an abbey, and she was to be its inhabitant. Its long, damp passages, its narrow cells and ruined chapel, were to be within her daily reach, and she could not entirely subdue the hope of some traditional legends, some awful memorials of an injured and ill-fated nun. (II, ii, 125)

Catherine comes to Northanger fresh from reading *Udolpho* and having her imagination enlivened on her journey by Henry Tilney's zestful Gothic tale set in the real abbey, which is really a teasing burlesque. Her inflated ideas of the place are modelled on those of Emily, Mrs Radcliffe's heroine, as she approaches the castle of Udolpho in the wilds of the Apennines. It might indeed be Emily who muses:

> As they drew near the end of their journey, her impatience for a sight of the abbey . . . returned in full force, and every bend in the road was expected with solemn awe to afford a glimpse of its massy walls of grey stone, rising amidst a grove of ancient oaks, with the last beams of the sun playing in beautiful splendour on its high Gothic windows. (II, v, 142)

Mrs Radcliffe's very phraseology is echoed here, for Emily had also gazed with 'melancholy awe' on 'mouldering walls of dark grey stone', seeing the evening sun's rays 'streaming in full splendour on towers and battlements'. The only change Jane Austen has wittily made is to make the landscape more familiar, for even Catherine would be realistic enough not to look for mountain pines in the midland counties of England but rather for 'a grove of ancient oaks'. (For the full text of the *Udolpho* passage, see p. 33 of this book.)

Jane Austen begins by showing how inappropriate Catherine's expectations are. Her technique is deliberately and crudely anti-Gothic: Northanger is decidedly not 'the sovereign of the scene'; instead, 'so low did the building stand' and with 'such ease' did Catherine and Henry approach 'along a smooth level road of fine gravel' that Catherine finds herself in the very pre-cincts of the abbey without feeling any fears at her arrival: 'There was something in this mode of approach which she cer-tainly had not expected'. Catherine is actually inside the hall being warmly welcomed by Eleanor and the General before she has time to be assailed by any 'awful foreboding of future misery . . . The breeze had not seemed to waft the sighs of the murdered to her; it had wafted nothing worse than a thick mizzling rain'.

The interior of Northanger is just as disillusioning; whereas Emily had gone into 'an extensive Gothic hall, obscured by glooms of evening' with everything vast, dilapidated and cheer-less, the common drawing-room of Northanger is furnished 'with all the profusion and elegance of modern taste' and with a fireplace 'contracted to a Rumford'. Things are so different in reality that Catherine wonders if 'anything within her obser-vation would have given her the consciousness' of being in an abbey at all. No wonder she looks at the Gothic windows 'with a peculiar dependence'; but she is again disappointed: 'To an imagination which had hoped for the smallest divisions, the heaviest stone-work, for painted glass, dirt and cobwebs, the difference was very distressing' (II, v, 143).

Catherine's silly expectations are mocked; Jane Austen shows them to be silly because they are so inappropriate to the living context. But Jane Austen is sympathetic as well; indeed it seems to me that both Catherine and her creator honestly acknow-ledge that despite her expectations, she does not feel, or even pretend to feel, Emily's emotions. After all, Catherine had 'not one moment's suspicion of any past scenes of horror' on entering Northanger. Despite her propensity for fantasising, Catherine does not live in a world of literary delusion; she is perfectly cap-able of perceiving that Northanger is not like an ancient Gothic edifice (unlike the obsessional Cherry Wilkinson in E. S. Barrett's burlesque *The Heroine* (1813)), and assisted by General Tilney's demands for her attention her fantasies subside as she gently returns to the comforts and anxieties of actuality. After all, the General insisted on the strictest punctuality for dinner at 5 p.m.!

Jane Austen is more indulgent to Catherine on her first night at Northanger; at least she grants her a stormy night and a high old-fashioned black cabinet in her room, precisely those features for which her imagination had been primed by Henry's tales that morning. It is at this point that Catherine is first described as 'well-read', a tongue-in-cheek description which recurs throughout the period of her Gothic fantasising. Prompted by Radcliffian memories, she manages to work herself up into a real fright as she examines the Japan cabinet, Jane Austen exploiting both the emotional and the comic potential of Catherine's enterprise as she records her dialogue with herself in her anxious and unprofitable search through the drawers of the cabinet. It is a marvellous example of deliberate self-deception:

> Though she had 'never from the first had the smallest idea of finding anything in any part of the cabinet, and was not in the least disappointed at her ill success thus far, it would be foolish not to examine it thoroughly while she was about it'.
> (II, vi, 150)

But Catherine gets her reward:

> And not vain, as hitherto, was her search; her quick eyes directly fell on a roll of paper pushed back into the further part of the cavity, apparently for concealment, and her feelings at that moment were indescribable. Her heart fluttered, her knees trembled, and her cheeks grew pale. She seized, with an unsteady hand, the precious manuscript, for half a glance sufficed to ascertain written characters; and while she acknowledged with awful sensations this striking exemplification of what Henry had foretold, resolved instantly to peruse every line before she attempted to rest. (II, vi, 150–1)

This adventure is reported with a superb command of syntax, beginning with Catherine's lengthy fumblings, followed by a

9

quick registration of her discovery, then the revelation of the object itself. The whole episode smacks of cliché, confirmed by a reference to the archetypal Gothic discovery. At this point, Jane Austen parodying the Gothic novelists' pretensions of linguistic inadequacy says of Catherine's feelings that they were 'indescribable'. She lets Catherine play the heroine rôle with all its behaviouristic attributes of fluttering heart, trembling knees, pale cheeks and unsteady hand. Catherine is acting exactly like Adeline in Mrs Radcliffe's *Romance of the Forest* (which Harriet Smith had tried to persuade Robert Martin to read in *Emma*). Adeline also found a small roll of paper when impelled by a dream to explore the ruined abbey in which she had been imprisoned; it turned out to be a manuscript written by her father before he was murdered by his brother, the very Marquis who was harassing Adeline with his amorous attentions.

Being so 'well-read', Catherine immediately knows what to do, for 'half a glance' is all she needs. We then move into a conventional Gothic scenario:

> The dimness of the light her candle emitted made her turn to it with alarm; but there was no danger of its sudden extinction, it had yet some hours to burn; and that she might not have any greater difficulty in distinguishing the writing than what its ancient date might occasion, she hastily snuffed it. Alas! it was snuffed and extinguished in one. A lamp could not have expired with more awful effect. Catherine, for a few moments, was motionless with horror. It was done completely; not a remnant of light in the wick could give hope to the rekindling breath. Darkness impenetrable and immoveable filled the room. A violent gust of wind, rising with sudden fury, added fresh horror to the moment. Catherine trembled from head to foot. In the pause which succeeded, a sound like receding footsteps and the closing of a distant door struck on her affrighted ear. Human nature could support no more. A cold sweat stood on her forehead, the manuscript fell from her hand, and groping her way to the bed, she jumped hastily in, and sought some suspension of agony by creeping far underneath the clothes. (II, vi, 151)

All the Gothic words and images are here in the dim candlelight which gives way to 'darkness impenetrable', leaving the heroine 'motionless with horror' then 'trembling from head to foot'. What undermines the seriousness of it all is the author's making it abundantly clear that the crisis is all Catherine's own fault. She carefully traces the stages of the rapid growth of Catherine's terrors to utter panic, only to end with the deflating information that she had jumped hastily into bed! This is a delightfully childish reaction, bringing out the full disparity between 'agony' and its remedy. Jane Austen's strategy is clear: she playfully allows Catherine to indulge her 'raised, restless, and frightened imagination', but always preserves an ironic awareness of its absurdity. It is also an astute analysis of night fears, the very kind of distortion that Gothic novelists relied on so often to generate irrational terrors. In this case the terrors prove to be totally ill-founded. Catherine finds in the cold light of morning that her Gothic roll is only an old laundry list, and feels very ashamed of 'the absurdity of her recent fancies'.

However, Catherine still has not really learnt to control or to look critically at her own powers of fantasising, a foible that Jane Austen thinks relatively unserious until there is a real danger of allowing romance to colour her judgements and lead her into moral absurdity. Having conceived the idea that General Tilney is like Mrs Radcliffe's villain Montoni and so must have either poisoned his wife or locked her up secretly, she goes to explore the former Mrs Tilney's apartments, only to have her suspicions refuted by the evident simplicity and comfort of the bedroom. It is not enough, however, for Catherine to perceive again her own 'folly'—this time she is discovered in her fantasising by Henry, who seriously takes her to task. Whereas before he had joked with her about the Gothic, now he gently but firmly points out its absurdity.

> 'If I understand you rightly, you had formed a surmise of such horror as I have hardly words to—Dear Miss Morland, consider the dreadful nature of the suspicions you have entertained. What have you been judging from?'   (II, ix, 175)

This is Catherine's *éclaircissement*, her crisis of self-realisation, where she is startled out of her Gothic fantasising and startled into a more active awareness of her feelings for Henry, hence the energy of her repudiation of Gothic.

> The visions of romance were over. Catherine was complete-ly awakened. Henry's address, short as it had been, had more thoroughly opened her eyes to the extravagance of her late fancies than all their several disappointments had done. Most grievously was she humbled. Most bitterly did she cry. It was not only with herself that she was sunk—but with Henry. Her folly, which now seemed even criminal, was all exposed to him, and he must despise her for ever. The liberty which her imagination had dared to take with the character of his father, could he ever forgive it? The absurdity of her curio-sity and her fears, could they ever be forgotten? She hated herself more than she could express. He had—she thought he had, once or twice before this fatal morning, shewn some-thing like affection for her.—But now . . .   (II, x, 176)

Here Jane Austen comes very close to Catherine's feelings, giving us an almost physical sense of their intensity and motion. The sentence-structures are carefully patterned: short staccato sentences at the beginning, then longer ones later, sometimes interrupted by dashes and sometimes resolving themselves into questions. This pattern surely reflects Catherine's emotions. She begins in tears, believing her world to be dashed; as she takes stock of her folly, her thoughts turn inwards toward her own humiliation, and then they gradually move outwards as she realises that her fantasising has perhaps killed the genuine warmth of feeling that was growing between Henry and her-self. The language conveys the oscillation of her thoughts as she swings between a recognition of her gullibility and its possible effects on Henry. The balance between the two poles of Cather-ine's thought is beautifully maintained, as Jane Austen trans-lates movements of feeling into the novelist's 'best-chosen language'.

If we look analytically at the words Jane Austen lends Catherine here, words like 'folly', 'criminal absurdity', 'she hated herself', 'this fatal morning', we may think them very strong, unnecessarily cutting for the somewhat trivial nature of the offence. Through her heroine's language Jane Austen is once again making an oblique comment on the dangerous effects of Gothic reading, showing the grip that it had on the emotions of its uncritical devotees like Catherine. It is not Gothic extravagance itself that is being criticised now but Catherine's own exaggerated feelings. Jane recognises that Catherine believes them to be genuine, though she hints that they cannot continue at this pitch for long. Indeed they don't: 'In short, she made herself as miserable as possible for about half an hour.' This rather deflating insight lowers the emotional key. Later, when Catherine meets 'the formidable Henry' again, the language definitely assumes comic overtones when we see how kindly he behaves to her: 'Catherine had never wanted comfort more, and he looked as if he was aware of it.'

There is a gentle modulation back into the everyday patterns of social intercourse as 'the evening wore away with no abatement of this soothing politeness', so that instead of fierce lonely self-castigation, Catherine is led into a more rational appraisal of her silliness, as suggested in the comfortably balanced sentence which sets her worst fears at rest: 'She did not learn either to forget or defend the past; but she learned to hope that it would never transpire farther, and that it might not cost her Henry's entire regard.' When she begins to acquire the ability to see cause and effect in her own behaviour patterns and to connections between past and present, fiction and reality, Catherine is described as actually 'learning'. Perceiving how the 'voluntary, self-created delusion' arose, she undertakes an analysis of her whole fantasising process, coming to a criticism of Gothic fiction which is surprisingly mature for her and close to Henry's:

> Charming as were all Mrs. Radcliffe's works, and charming even as were the works of all her imitators, it was not in them perhaps that human nature, at least in the midland counties of England, was to be looked for.

Catherine's attempts to make discriminations are still a little inadequate; after all, 'all' Mrs Radcliffe's works are still 'charming', as are those of 'all' her imitators, but at least the girl who had earlier loved *Sir Charles Grandison* returns to a sense of human nature which is very Augustan and very much Jane

Austen's own. As Norman Page points out, it is one which stresses 'the common element in men which it was the true province of literature to delineate' (p. 87). She is still timid in her judgements:

> Of the Alps and Pyrenees, with their pine forests and their vices, they [Gothic novels] might give a faithful delineation; and Italy, Switzerland, and the South of France, might be as fruitful in horrors as they were there represented. Catherine dared not doubt beyond her own country, and even of that, if hard pressed, would have yielded the northern and western extremities.   (II, x, 177)

Catherine excludes all Gothic territory as unknown, but within her own limited range she tries hard to assimilate Henry's advice. He suggested that she consult her own understanding, her own sense of the probable, her own observation, and by doing so, she comes up with the sensible conclusion that 'among the English ... there was a general though unequal mixture of good and bad'. From there she progresses to a more balanced assessment of the Tilney family, though hero-worship is not entirely absent; at most, she thinks, there might be 'some slight imperfection' in Henry.

The transition in Catherine's feelings from utter desolation to self-forgiveness and a determination 'to be happier than ever' is astonishingly quick: it all happens within 'the course of another day'. Certainly the Gothic leaves her with a feeling of vulnerability, for there were still some subjects which she believed would always make her spirits tremble, not through terror but through remembered folly. In a marvellously balanced sentence Jane Austen returns her heroine to the real world: 'The anxieties of common life began soon to succeed to the alarms of romance' (II, x, 178).

The result of Catherine's commonsense reflections is that she absolutely rejects Gothic fiction as irrelevant to her understanding of life. But her author is wiser, for Jane Austen makes plain Catherine's limitations and immaturity; she still has something to learn which will enable her to transcend her own literalmindedness. Maybe the tales of the Alps and Pyrenees will complement the resolution she so uncritically takes over from

Henry 'to always judge and act in future with the greatest good sense'. Henry's voice sounds so authoritative in Catherine's ears that we might assume as she does that right is all on his side, but Jane Austen deftly shows us that after all sometimes he is wrong. Whatever the security to be derived from the social context to which Henry appeals, people do not always act rationally; after all, gossip does not rely on 'understanding and observation' for its power, and that 'neighbourhood of voluntary spies' actually fosters misunderstanding. John Thorpe told lies about Catherine and General Tilney did not stop to consider that Thorpe's tales might be self-flattering or spiteful fantasisings.

In the narrative it emerges that real life and Gothic fiction are not so totally apart as Henry had asserted them to be. Though some fictional structures might break down when brought into the light of common day, the converse is not necessarily true: real people and real situations often retain some resemblance to novels. Catherine's own career is very like that of the heroine in any sentimental novel. In this, Jane Austen's most explicit and liveliest exploration of the relatedness between fiction and real life, she has constructed a narrative which works rather like a set of Chinese boxes: the setting of the novel has direct interplay with the real world, and the world of Gothic fantasy contained within the novel also draws its substance from life but is shown to be dangerous and subversive.[7] Jane Austen does not reject Gothic because it is different from life, but because it can so easily distort one's real life responses. Henry has maintained that the world of Gothic is separate, untrue to life, yet as Catherine discovers, General Tilney really is as unscrupulously ambitious as a Montoni when he finds that she is not the heiress he had assumed her to be. If his behaviour in virtually turning her out of Northanger is not so melodramatic as that of a Gothic villain, it is surely only because real life did not present the same possibilities for violence as a pseudo-medieval fantasy world.

As a result of the General's tyrannical behaviour, Catherine on her last night at Northanger is as isolated and fearful as any Gothic heroine, but here the genuineness of her feelings is spelled out in explicit contrast to her first night of imagined terrors in the same room:

Heavily past the night. Sleep, or repose that deserved the name of sleep, was out of the question. That room, in which her disturbed imagination had tormented her on her first arrival, was again the scene of agitated spirits and unquiet slumbers. Yet how different now the source of her inquietude from what it had been then—how mournfully superior in reality and substance! Her anxiety had foundation in fact, her fears in probability; and with a mind so occupied in the contemplation of actual and natural evil, the solitude of her situation, the darkness of her chamber, the antiquity of the building were felt and considered without the smallest emotion; and though the wind was high, and often produced strange and sudden noises throughout the house, she heard it all as she lay awake, hour after hour, without curiosity or terror. (II, xiii, 201)

The tone is totally serious, as the weight of the present crisis on Catherine's spirits emerges through sentences which balance the agitations of 'now' against those of 'then'. 'Then' it was a 'disturbed imagination' but 'now' Catherine is face to face with 'reality and substance', with 'fact' and 'probability'. In her confrontation with 'actual and natural evil' (and for the first time the word 'evil' is used instead of 'shocks' or 'horrors'), she can hastily catalogue all the trappings of romance and dismiss them 'without curiosity or terror'. The anxiety and fear are genuine now; they have the substance their Gothic shadows lacked; it is a change in feeling analogous with that displacement of sublime awe by real fear which Emily experienced on her first sight of Udolpho. Interestingly, Jane Austen is employing a Radcliffian technique for registering Catherine's emotions but here she defines feeling more precisely than Mrs Radcliffe had done.

So, in spite of having decided to act and judge with the 'greatest good sense', Catherine does have to modify her decision as she begins to learn that real life is often no more rational than fiction. Just as there are villains, so there are heroes who marry heroines, not out of rational judgement but prompted by irrational motives; Henry himself marries Catherine. And plenty of things happen privately if not secretly in Jane Austen's

world, under the very noses of that 'neighbourhood of voluntary
spies' by whom everybody is surrounded. Henry manages to
propose to Catherine while on a most decorous walk from her
father's parsonage to Mrs Allen's house. It reminds us both of
the reconciliation between Emily and Valancourt in the tower
at the end of *Udolpho* and also of the way Elizabeth Bennet and
Mr Darcy's meetings are organised by Mrs Bennet!

The ending of *Northanger Abbey* is a comic exploitation of conventional novel endings, both the happy-ever-after promise and
the moral message. It is a way of provoking readers into looking
again at the connections between real life and fiction. With
characteristic irony, Jane Austen glances critically at the irresponsibility of many novelists and the cliché-istic expectations
of her readers: 'I leave it to be settled by whomsoever it may
concern, whether the tendency of this work be altogether to
recommend parental tyranny, or reward filial disobedience.'
Such a criticism is in the same comic vein as her earlier wry
comment on the presentation of the gradual development of
Henry's love for Catherine, where the distance between romance
and common life is defined by the author's daringly attributing
to herself all the qualities of the fantasist:

> It is a new circumstance in romance, I acknowledge, and
> dreadfully derogatory of a heroine's dignity; but if it be as
> new in common life, the credit of a wild imagination will at
> least be all my own. (II, xv, 216)

What Jane Austen has done in *Northanger Abbey* is quite mis-
chievously wise: if she has criticised Gothic novelists for their
emotional extravagance and for the way they deliberately sever
connections between real life and fiction in the interests of
sensationalism, she has also got under the skin of the Henry
Tilneys of this world by demonstrating the truth of the Gothic
novelists' perceptions into the psychology of feeling and the
dimensions of human irrationality. In no sense does Jane
Austen deny the validity of feeling and imagination, least of all
the authorial imagination; *Northanger Abbey* is a spirited defence
of the novel as her praise of Richardson, Fanny Burney and
Maria Edgeworth suggests. But when Jane Austen talks about
'the common feelings of common life' she sounds deceptively

ordinary, for as *Northanger Abbey* shows, common life is full of very strange feelings indeed. What Jane Austen wants for her readers as much as for her heroine is a balanced awareness of the interplay between imagination and reason; as we might expect, she is arguing for sensitivity and discrimination as crucial factors in the cultivation of right judgement.

C. R. Maturin, *Melmoth the Wanderer*

The drama of terror has the irresistible power of convert-
ing its audience into its victims.
> (*Melmoth the Wanderer*, III, xii, 257)[1]

The fascination of that distinctively Gothic knot of feelings,
Love, Mystery, and Misery, survived all its ardent exponents and
vigorous detractors to find its most powerful imaginative treatment in *Melmoth the Wanderer*, published twenty-five years after
Udolpho and *The Monk*, in 1820. Written by the flamboyant
Irish clergyman Charles Robert Maturin, protégé of Scott,
admirer of Byron, and incidentally Oscar Wilde's great-uncle,
Melmoth gives the fullest expression to that obsession with intense private experience that characterises Gothic fiction and
relates it to the wider currents of Romanticism.[2] In Maturin's
dark imagination all the Gothic neuroses are exacerbated:
crises of suffering are embodied in a romance which marks the
high point of extravagant Gothic rhetoric. A contemporary reviewer called Maturin 'a passionate connoisseur in agony',[3]
while Mario Praz in *The Romantic Agony*, treating him together
with Swinburne in a chapter entitled 'The Shadow of the
Divine Marquis', makes a suggestive connection between
Maturin's imagination and that of Sade. Being a clergyman and
a Christian moralist, Maturin rationalised his concern with pain
and suffering by claiming that it was the only sure means to
spiritual growth, though the exclusiveness of his preoccupation
with the 'dark abyss' as he calls it, argues for a very peculiar
sensibility indeed. We must call his fiction Gothic, but it is
Gothic energised by the pathological intensity of its explorations
into the darkest regions of human consciousness and presented
in language that is wholly in keeping with the hyperintensity
and resonance of the writer's psychological perceptions.

None of Maturin's contemporaries doubted that he was a

writer of the unfashionable terror school, and all perceived his disturbing superiority over other writers in the genre. When Scott reviewed Maturin's first novel, *Fatal Revenge; or, The Family of Montorio* (1807), he praised the writer's talents and added a note of regret that he should waste them on the Gothic romance:

> We have at no time more earnestly desired to extend our voice to a bewildered traveller, than towards this young man, whose taste is so inferior to his powers of imagination and expression, that we never saw a more remarkable instance of genius degraded by the labour in which it is employed.[4]

And ten years later when *Melmoth the Wanderer* was published, a note of unwilling admiration creeps into the voice of the *Monthly Review* critic:

> The taste for horrors, or for tales abounding in supernatural events and characters, compacts with the devil, and mysterious prolongations of human life, has for some years past been on the decline in England. The necromancers of the Rhine, the Italian assassins of Mrs. Radcliffe, the St Leons of Mr. Godwin, etc. etc., had indeed begun to disappear, overwhelmed by their own extravagance, but these still retain their station in the first rank of the provincial circulating library.
>
> Still, however, it is confessedly possible for a man of decided genius to revive for a while, this exploded predilection for impossibility, even among better readers ...
>
> Influenced by these considerations, and still more by the passion for the violent, the ferocious, and dreadful in poetry, which our contemporaries have so eminently displayed ... Mr. Maturin has again appeared before the public as the author of a most extravagant work—Melmoth.[5]

Finally, the delightfully urbane criticism in the *Athenaeum* which appeared in 1892 at the time of a new edition of *Melmoth* shows that Maturin was still honourably remembered as an eccentric talent long after the demise of traditional Gothic:

> A new edition of *Melmoth the Wanderer* is not exactly one of those things for which there is a crying need; but it may be

welcomed, all the same, as a contribution towards the curiosities of literature.

Distinctly the most remarkable of the British Triumvirate which, in the early part of the century, won a momentary fame as the school of horror, Maturin is much less known to the readers of today than either Monk Lewis or Mrs. Radcliffe.[6]

Maturin's fascination with the supernatural and his consistent preoccupation with dread, fear and terror would make him a Gothic writer by any definition, but the imaginative range of his psychological speculations and the minutiae of his emotional analyses give him a superiority over those novelists who used the techniques of sensationalism with no other purpose than to shock and frighten their readers. As a practitioner of the craft, Maturin was perfectly aware that the spell of Gothic fiction lay in its power to arouse certain feelings in its readers and he is quite explicit about the compulsion that terror in art exerts, as the remark from *Melmoth* at the beginning of my chapter shows. He used traditional Gothic techniques in a conscious attempt to stimulate his readers into a state of total empathy with his characters but he also used such techniques as instruments for exploration into hitherto uncharted areas of psychology. As in those other romantic novels, Mary Shelley's *Frankenstein* and James Hogg's *Confessions of a Justified Sinner*, Gothic machinery becomes in Maturin's hands a metaphorical language for describing new insights into human suffering and conflict.

Certainly the images and vocabulary of Gothic are peculiarly suitable for accommodating the insights of such a morbidly fantastic imagination as Maturin's. E. M. Forster's description, in his essay on T. S. Eliot in *Abinger Harvest*, of possible ways of confronting horror provides, I think, a suggestive framework for defining the quality of Maturin's sensibility, while it also offers us a way of distinguishing variations in the range of Gothic fiction to which Maturin's romances are related:

> In respect to the horror that they find in life, men can be divided into three classes. In the first class are those who have not suffered often or acutely; in the second, those who have

escaped through horror into a further vision; in the third, those who continue to suffer.

Maturin undoubtedly belongs, along with Lewis, in the third class, whereas Mrs Radcliffe and the Minerva novelists belong in the first, and Charlotte Brontë possibly in the second. Maturin's fiction never escapes beyond the agony of existence, hence the obsessional insistence on man as a victim and the universality of suffering and fear throughout human history.

With *Melmoth the Wanderer* Maturin has constructed a fiction which gives him the freedom to pursue his speculations into psychology and morality in the literary form traditionally associated with fantasy and nightmare. *Melmoth* is really a collection of tales all dealing with the wanderings and temptations of Melmoth, an Irish Faust figure who has sold his soul to the devil and is then given a reprieve of one hundred and fifty years to find someone to change places with him in the afterlife. The damned tormented figure of Melmoth wanders through the novel, isolated from mankind and independent of space and time, to confront human beings in their worst moments of agony to offer his impossible bargain. The narrative structure is extremely loose; when it appeared, critics accused it of having no structure at all. As the *Blackwood's* reviewer noted:

> The truth is that it is mere courtesy to call Melmoth 'a Romance', for the four volumes contain as many or more stories which, with the exception of the agency of one character common to them all, have no sort of connection with each other, their personages being otherwise quite different, and their scenes laid at different periods, and in quite different parts of the world.[7]

Certainly the reader's first impression is of a number of separate tales, every one treating a different emotional crisis. The frame story is set in Ireland in 1816 when the Wanderer comes home to die, and there are various excursions back in time which cover the period of his wanderings, changing in locale from Inquisition Spain, to Restoration England, to an exotic Indian island, and returning to Ireland at the end.

In the extravaganza of its conception, *Melmoth* is a romance of epic proportions, for Maturin had an eclectic and imaginative view of history. We find episodes that enact the great myths of human history, like the Garden of Eden and the Fall, the sufferings of Satan and forebodings of the Day of Judgement, all woven into the texture of historical fact in the detailed accounts of Melmoth's experiences on earth from the early 1600s to 1816. As a historical novelist, Maturin has a great deal in common with Scott (who doubtless influenced him, both by his fiction and in their private correspondence);[8] both of them give life to their evocations of the past by minute historical detail, yet both of them believe in the need for history to be recreated in the crucible of the individual imagination. Such a creed provokes some of the most brilliant scenarios in the novel, such as the recreation of the panic caused by the Great Fire of London, or the animated decadence of the Restoration stage. However, the author's obsession with but a single area of feeling—as opposed to the many and varied historical settings—changes his romance into an allegory of a world where the chief preoccupations of man are guilt, suffering and care. Like its central figure, the novel wheels about free of the ties of time and place, thus missing the sustained grandeur of epic or tragedy, though it has hints of both. According to the hostile condemnation of the *Quarterly* reviewer, 'Mr. Maturin's tales are involved and entangled in a clumsy confusion, which disgraces the artist and puzzles the observer'.[9]

However, though there is no obvious linear structure, there is a clear Christian moral patterning, as the preface to the first edition suggests:

The hint of this Romance (or Tale) was taken from a passage in one of my Sermons, which (as it is to be presumed very few have read) I shall here take the liberty to quote. The passage is this.

'At this moment is there one of us present, however we may have departed from the Lord, disobeyed his will, and disregarded his word—is there one of us who would, at this moment, accept all that man could bestow, or earth afford, to resign the hope of his salvation?—No, there is not one—

not such a fool on earth, were the enemy of mankind to traverse it with the offer.'

This passage suggested the idea of 'Melmoth the Wanderer'. The Reader will find that idea developed in the following pages, with what power or success *he* is to decide.

The tales illustrate the text by providing a series of situations of trial or temptation. The Tale of the Indians and the Lovers' Tale are parallels, both of them being about women torn by the conflict between human and divine love, while the three tales about men (Stanton's Tale, The Tale of the Spaniard and The Tale of Guzman's Family) all deal with crises of suffering which bring their victims to the point of madness or spiritual despair.[10] As one of the characters tells another, 'We are all beads strung on the same string', the string of Melmoth's temptations. Melmoth's own statement just before his death points back to the place of each tale as a demonstration of the original sermon text:

> No one has ever exchanged destinies with Melmoth the Wanderer. *I have traversed the world in the search, and no one, to gain that world, would lose his own soul.*—Not Stanton in his cell—nor you, Monçada, in the prison of the Inquisition—nor Walberg, who saw his children perishing with want—nor —another— (538)

In the dislocated time scheme of the narrative Melmoth remains uncannily the same and ever present. Though one critic thought it lamentable that a clergyman should allow the Devil 'to be such a prodigious favourite with him',[11] what emerges is a moral statement about the permanent features of the human condition—about suffering and pain, human resilience and man's need for faith in God.

So *Melmoth* is in one sense a *roman à thèse*, indeed a Gothic sermon. As a Christian moralist, Maturin believed with a profoundly religious conviction in the inevitability of suffering. Indeed, he gives as clear a statement of the theological justification for his beliefs in *Women*, written two years before *Melmoth*, as he does in his *Sermons*, published 1819:

> The Bible reconciles us to suffering, by showing not only

that it is the path all must tread, but the path the best have
trod—a path consecrated by the steps, the tears, the blood
of those to whom humanity looks up for solace and for eleva-
tion. Patriarchs and prophets, saints and martyrs, and Him
whose name must not be named in a page so light, they were
all destitute, afflicted, and tormented, and shall we repine?

(III, 143)[12]

In the same novel, Maturin proclaimed the value of suffering
as part of God's plan for man's salvation: 'Joy leads us to communion with man, who can share it; and grief to communion
with God, who alone can relieve it.—Which is best?' (III, 180).

While the narrative of *Melmoth* is certainly contained within
this structure of belief, the imaginative impact of the book
comes not from the idea of salvation and damnation but from
the description of human responses to fear, terror and oppression. All Maturin's tales are about human beings struggling for
survival in a world where man's rôle is that of a victim, tormented by external agents both human and supernatural, and
always in danger of betrayal by his own passions and instincts.
'What is Man?', asks Maturin, fascinated by the duality of
man's nature, rather as Hamlet marvels that man so capable of
love and goodness is also capable of evil and agony, caught
between beauty and horror, suspended between Heaven and
Hell. The paradox of the human condition is the real area of
Maturin's exploration, which has as its starting-point a desperate faith in God's mercy as the only possible means of man's
salvation. Given his tormented awareness, it is no wonder that
his most powerful literary effects are those of terror and horror,
and that the main character is the agent of moral chaos, himself
a pray to monstrous spiritual despair.

Suffering for Maturin is more than a religious belief; it is an
obsession which he transforms into a literary aesthetic, so that
in his hands it becomes nothing less than the raw material for
psychological enquiry. There is even the suggestion (made by
one of the characters and italicised by the author) that a man
may actually derive his sense of consequence from the sufferings
inflicted on him: '*While people think it worth their while to torment
us, we are never without some dignity, though painful and imaginary*'

(III, xii, 251). This surely is a psychological insight into the masochistic temperament rather than any religious truth. Robert Kiely in a persuasive analysis has shown how Maturin's imagination, stimulated by painful subjects, makes each narrative in Melmoth 'the history of a mind newly made by misery', so illustrating 'a whole phase of romantic psychology and the creative process'.[13] Maturin pursues human beings to the extremes of their emotional, mental or physical endurance, in order to gaze intently on what remains as distinctively human when 'the tenth wave of suffering' is reached. The evidence recorded in *Melmoth* suggests that the 'varieties in moral botany far exceed the wildest anomalies in the natural [world]' (III, xvii, 311), a metaphor which aptly characterises Maturin's own genuinely scientific curiosity and the merciless precision of his dissections of human feelings. He isolates all his characters by pushing them beyond the normal range of sympathetic human comprehension into a dark inner world of which Melmoth's alienation is merely the most extreme example. From the depths of such experience emerge the products of the agonised imagination, the obsessions and the dangerously distorted dream worlds which form the substance of the novel.

I think we can best appreciate Maturin's achievement if we see *Melmoth* as a document of its author's own pathological consciousness where everything—character, narrative design, feeling and style—is made to express that paradox which he saw as the central truth of the human condition. The description of his fictional method as 'a sort of excited psychology, an exclamatory insistence on sensation and emotion'[14] is too impressionistic, but it does describe the sense of shock and emotional violence which the novel generates. It is Maturin's style as much as the events of his narrative that is responsible for this impression, as his contemporaries were well aware: almost every reviewer of *Melmoth* commented on his 'wonderful richness of diction' and his 'eloquence of imagination', for the language is remarkable in its physical concreteness and its poetic intensity. It is the language of romance—not romance in its vague dreamlike states but in its moments of preternatural clarity, unhinged from everyday modes of perception. It allows for a close scrutiny of the feelings of someone in a state of

heightened awareness, at the extreme edge either of life or of
sanity, when the mind as well as the soul is 'trembling on the
verge'. The style generates a sense of vertigo, as images of elemental conflict and apocalypse are hurled on top of one another,
while minutely-observed psychological detail is carried in the
breathlessly insistent rhythms of the prose. The following
passage is a characteristic example:

> From the tranquil and hopeless aspect of the divinity,
> smiling on the misery it neither consoles nor relieves, and
> intimating in that smile the profound and pulseless apathy of
> inaccessible elevation, coldly hinting that humanity must
> cease to be, before it can cease to suffer—from this the
> sufferer rushed for consolation to nature, whose ceaseless
> agitation seems to correspond with the vicissitudes of human
> destiny and the emotions of the human heart—whose alterna-
> tion of storms and calms,—of clouds and sun-light,—of terrors
> and delights—seems to keep a kind of mysterious measure of
> ineffable harmony with that instrument whose chords are
> doomed alternately to the thrill of agony and rapture, till the
> hand of death sweeps over all the strings, and silences them
> for ever.—With such a feeling, Isidora leaned against her
> casement, gasped for a breath of air.   (III, xx, 341)

In this passage there are hints too of the notion of correspon-
dences, that yearning for a harmony between man and the
universe which is so characteristic of the Romantic mystique of
transcendence. But for Maturin anguish and suffering are the
permanent features of the human condition, for which antithesis is the most appropriate expression; his characters'
realisations are most frequently conveyed in paradoxes which
disturb and energise in their exploration of extreme ranges of
feeling, as in:

> I was a maniac, oscillating between hope and despair. I
> seemed to myself all that day to be pulling the rope of a bell,
> whose alternate knell was *heaven—hell*, and this rung in my
> ears with all the dreary and ceaseless monotony of the bell of
> the convent.   (II, viii, 188)

Leven Dawson has written about paradox as Maturin's means

of exploring hitherto unformulated connections between feelings usually regarded as antithetical.[15] This perception gives us I think the vital clue to understanding Maturin's insistence on 'painting life in extremes', in those moments of intensity where contradictory elements are fused together at the dynamic point of agony or ecstasy. Such intensity belongs to the lyric poem, or in a novel to the short episode—as one of Maturin's most perceptive contemporary critics pointed out:

> This is the most daring, wild, and powerful, of all the romances of its author ... Its merit is not in the *idea* (compounded of Godwin and the infernal machinery of Lewis), nor in the *plot*, which is ill-constructed, nor in the *characters*, which are for the most part impossible, but in the *marvellous execution of particular scenes*, and in thickly clustered felicities of expression, which are spread luminously over the darkness of its tenor, like fire-flies on a tropical ocean.[16]

I have chosen the most striking examples of paradox and conflict in *Melmoth* in order to show how the pattern of paradox can be seen to operate in every aspect of Maturin's creativity. Ranging widely, these include the duality of man's nature as imagined in one individual, tragic love, the aesthetic appeal of horror, and a transcendent moment when tensions are resolved in an ecstasy of pure agony at the point of death.

By the very conditions of his existence Melmoth himself is a creature of paradox; in him the dual nature of personality is exaggerated into mythic dimensions of emotional and moral torment. Both man and devil, he exemplifies the conflict between human aspiration and the prohibitive forces of destiny. His existence is a living death both literally and metaphorically, where despair, misery and misanthropy are the direct results of a half-earthly, half-hellish being. Balzac's comment in his tale, 'Melmoth Reconciled', is an excellent analysis of the 'awful melancholy of omnipotence' from which he suffers:

> That vision of the infinite left him forever unable to see humanity and its affairs as other men saw them. The insensate fools who long for the power of the Devil gauge its desirability from a human standpoint; they do not see that

with the Devil's power they will likewise assume his thoughts; and that they will be doomed to remain as men among creatures who will not understand them.[17]

Melmoth retains the desire for human sympathy but his destiny compels him to self-imprisonment and to denial of those very impulses he wants to express:

> One generous, one human feeling, throbbed in his veins, and thrilled in his heart. He saw her in her beauty,—her devotedness,—her pure and perfect innocence,—her sole feeling for one who could not, by the fearful power of his unnatural existence, feel for mortal being. He turned aside, and did not weep; or if he did, wiped away his tears, as a fiend might do, with his burning talons, when he sees a new victim arrive for torture; and, *repenting of his repentence*, rends away *the blot* of compunction, and arms himself for his task of renewed infliction.   (III, xxi, 366)

His resulting torments give him the tragic appeal of the Satan figure so admired by the Romantics. Melmoth is specifically identified with Satan, both by the nature of his sin, 'pride and intellectual glorying', and by the intensity of his suffering; Maturin actually defines the power of Melmoth's attraction as the sublime agony of the Satan figure:

> He clasped his hands with a fierce and convulsive agony, that might have pictured the last struggles of the impenitent malefactor,—that agony without remorse, that suffering without requital or consolation, that, if I may say so, arrays crime in the dazzling robe of magnanimity, and makes us admire the fallen spirit, with whom we dare not sympathise.
>   (II, viii, 190)

The author's attitude is just as awe-stricken and only slightly less sympathetic than Shelley's in his essay 'On the Devil and Devils' (written *c.* 1820):

> He [the Devil] is forever tortured with compassion and affection for those whom he betrays and ruins; he is racked by a vain abhorrence for the desolation of which he is the instrument; he is like a man compelled by a tyrant to set fire

to his own possessions, and to appear as the witness against, and the accuser of his dearest friends; and then to be their executioner, and to inflict the most subtle and protracted torments upon them . . . God is represented as omnipotent and the Devil as eternal. Milton has expressed this view of the subject with the sublimest pathos.

For Maturin's readers, the Satanic aspect of Melmoth undoubtedly merged with the appeal of glamourised violence that distinguished the behaviour of the Byronic hero, for Melmoth has the dark lowering expression, the piercing eyes, the withering sneer and the contemptuously curled lip which characterise what Coleridge referred to in his criticism of Maturin's play *Bertram* as 'the modern misanthropic hero'. His moods oscillate wildly between meditative gloom and outbursts of fierce passion and his behaviour is excessively violent and tempestuous; everything about him suggests the agony of a soul in torment. Like Childe Harold and the Wandering Jew, he is cursed with a life of eternal restlessness as he wanders in haughty solitude and weariness of soul through Spain and on to the East. To the Childe Harold image are added the characteristics of Byron's later heroes, as one critic's description of them suggests:

> Manfred is the Byronic Hero in the process of maturing, of taking on a philosophical and psychological depth which he certainly did not have in *Childe Harold* I or II or in the romances. This is shown in the accession of the Faust theme of knowledge and sorrow, in the hero's Titanism, and his defiant questioning not only of political and moral authority (as in the romances), but of ultimate philosophical and religious authority as well, and finally it is shown in the Satan-Prometheus themes of the 'mind as its own place'—free to create its own scheme of order and value.[18]

Melmoth's qualities of mind represent a similar fusion of Romantic characteristics, with the difference that Melmoth knows that he is damned. Like Goethe's Faust, he has a specific reason for his fatalism and ultimately dies a Faustian death. Melmoth is in fact the conflation of many Romantic types, so that the associations of fatality, fallen angels and diabolism which were used metaphorically by Byron and Mary Shelley are here taken up literally to provide a religious explanation for the fascination of the Byronic hero.

The unnaturalness of Melmoth's emotional and moral reactions are the direct result of his spiritual condition. Indeed, he takes an intellectual delight in contemplating the irony of his own position, one that paradoxically brings his agonies as a damned soul very close to the ecstasies of the saints, as his daring speculation on feeling suggests:

> Infidel and scoffer as I may appear to you, there is no martyr of the Christian church, who in other times blazed for his God, that has borne or exhibited a more resplendent illustration of his faith, than I shall bear one day—and for ever. There is a slight difference only between our testimonies in point of duration. They burned for the truths they loved for a few moments—not so many perchance. Some were suffocated before the flames could reach them,—but I am doomed to bear my attestation on the truth of the gospel, amid fires that shall burn for ever and ever.
>
> (IV, xxiv, 389–90)

His encounters with human beings are terrifying, not only for the dreadful bargain which he offers them and the sweet music which precedes his approach to his victims. There is another sort of unnaturalness which is not specifically connected with his devil rôle and which has more in common with the perversity of the parricide in the Spaniard's Tale than with anything non-human. Maturin describes the motivation as 'the fiery thirst of the soul for communication' (195) and discusses the need to relieve the condition of alienation by the illusion of human contact, which is only to be got by the sufferer's making other people as miserable as himself. In the words of the parricide:

> By watching their motions, and flattering their passions, and promoting their interest, or setting up my own in opposition to them all, while I made them believe it was only theirs I was intent on, I might make shift to contrive as much misery to others, and to carve out as much occupation to myself, as if I were actually living in the world.   (II, ix, 208)

Melmoth's desire to possess Immalee has a similar explanation, which gives it a ring of emotional truth which would have been absent in a supernatural demonic urge to destroy: 'As he felt this, and gazed on her, he cursed himself; and then, with the selfishness of hopeless misery, he felt that the curse might, by dividing it, be diminished' (III, xx, 353).

The love affair between Melmoth and Immalee explores the emotional aspects of Melmoth's cosmic despair, while at the same time translating tragic romantic love into an emblem of the spiritual condition of mankind. As a love 'begotten by despair upon impossibility', it is the longest and most strenuous demonstration in the novel of moral and emotional paradox. It has the strong imaginative appeal of myth, for Melmoth is literally a demon lover and Immalee, the innocent maiden on her Indian island, represents the lost ideal of the Edenic world, the only happy being in Maturin's fiction. It is significant that happiness is presented as a very fragile state and our first view of Immalee is of a being other than, and indeed less than, human in her 'existence of felicity, half physical, half imaginative, but neither intellectual nor impassioned'. She is like a flower but she is also like Eve in *Paradise Lost*, doomed to fall into a knowledge of her human condition: the fall, precipitated by her love for Melmoth, is recorded in language which strangely mingles Milton's moral seriousness with Maturin's morbid sentimentality:

> She had, indeed, tasted of the tree of knowledge, and her eyes were opened, but its fruit was bitter to her taste, and her looks conveyed a kind of mild and melancholy gratitude, that would have wrung the heart for giving its first lesson of pain to the heart of a being so beautiful, so gentle, and so innocent. The stranger marked this blended expression, and exulted.
>
> (III, xvii, 308)

The structure of the conflict between good and evil in their love is continually drawn to our attention by authorial comments, by imagery, and by Melmoth's own repeatedly stated awareness of his role as destroyer. But the real interest lies not in the traditional moral fable but in the working out of a particular emotional relationship through a detailed analysis of the fantasies and frustrations contained within sexual love.

Like all Maturin's lovers, they are ill-fated, for he saw sexual passion as the supreme paradox of optimism and despair, the most exquisite form of suffering known to mankind. Lying at the conjunction of Man's finite nature with his infinite longings, love embodies the essential conflict between human desires and the prohibitive forces of destiny, so the condition of being in love inevitably precipitates a crisis of awareness where the lovers try to escape from human limitations by the only means available to them—fantasy or death. In common with other Gothic novelists, Maturin associated sexuality with fears of destruction, so great appeared to him the power released by instinctual urges; unlike the others he pushes this fear to its extreme, adding to the usual Gothic mixture of eroticism and guilt a dimension of metaphysical speculation. In his earlier novels, Maturin treated tragic love as an entirely human problem, investigating its confusion of anguish and delight and the romantic reasons for the death urge. As the heroine in *The Milesian Chief* says:

> A soul like mine, devoured with love, regards death without consternation; death alone can give it that promise of perfect and perennial security which life denies, and of which the want makes life more terrible than death to the souls of those that love.   (III, 131)[19]

In the same novel there is a suggestion of that necrophiliac dimension to passionate love of which Lewis at least was aware:

> Can this be death! Oh, how the fools who dread it are deceived: never was life so lovely! Is he indeed dead? Why should not the dead love? . . . Why should not the dead love, when death is so lovely!   (IV, 201–2)

In *Melmoth*, tragic love goes beyond the strictly human situation into one which is fatal by definition. Melmoth is a phantom (not, I would suggest, a 'fleshless phantom' as Kiely describes him but a very 'fleshful' one); he has already died one hundred and fifty years before he meets Immalee, and he constantly reminds her of the death-doomed quality of their love, 'Who can be mine and *live*?'. No real unity is possible for these lovers, locked as far apart as the worlds of life and death in a relationship which is based on the consequent emotional torment. It is to this context that the crises of fury and rapture belong and in which raging storms, a midnight wedding performed by a dead priest, and exotic tropical gardens are the imaginatively appropriate correlatives.

However their love is more than a darkly Romantic fantasy and it is worth noticing as symptomatic of Maturin's realistic if somewhat overdramatised psychology that there are real emotional reasons for the initial attraction between Melmoth and Immalee, just as there are reasons for the inevitable failure of their relationship. Melmoth is attracted to Immalee because her Innocence brings him his only moments of relief from his private hell and she finds in his Experience a new stimulus for her emotions and imagination. Though he may return to her island moved by 'what feelings it would be beyond human conjecture to discover', it is equally certain that 'when seated beside her listening to her questions or answering them, he seemed to enjoy the few lucid intervals of his insane and morbid existence' (298). And as she tells him later in Spain:

> You were the first human being I ever saw who could teach me language, and who taught me feeling. Your image is for ever before me, present or absent, sleeping or waking. I have seen fairer forms, I have listened to softer voices,—I might have met gentler hearts,—but the first, the indelible image, is written on mine, and its characters will never be effaced till that heart is a clod of the valley . . . I loved you because you were my *first*,—the sole connecting link between the human world and my heart,—the being who brought me acquainted with that wondrous instrument that lay unknown and untouched within me, whose chords, as long as they vibrate, will disdain to obey any touch but that of their first mover.   (III, xxii, 375)

Melmoth is Immalee's mentor, giving her that education of sensibility through suffering which to Maturin was the criterion of being human. The supreme irony is that Melmoth's success has an effect precisely the opposite of his original intention; instead of awakening Immalee from her dream world of innocence to destroy her soul, he becomes the agent of her salvation.

True, he destroys her physically by plunging her into a terrible dream world as life-denying as even he could have wished, but in the end Immalee wins, dying a Christian death in the prison of the Inquisition.

Every encounter between Melmoth and Immalee is a situation of conflict, made the more intense by the powerful sexual attraction between them and the inevitable failure of any impulse towards harmony and union. Melmoth's last visit to Immalee on her tropical island is typical of the crises which form the pattern of their relationship, where the inherent violence of frustrated passion gives Maturin the opportunity for the kind of sensational display of feeling in which he revelled. Melmoth's grand emotional assault lasts through a fierce tropical storm and is abandoned only when the girl, 'exhausted by emotion and terror', falls senseless at his feet. Maturin deploys all the standard Gothic visual techniques to create an immediate impact on his readers and to glamourise emotional violence. The tumult of the raging storm coincides with the rise and fall of their passions, and becomes not only the means by which feeling is amplified but a way of realising the emotional experience itself. As the *Monthly Review* critic remarked in his review of *Melmoth*:

> That this scene manifests an extravagance passing all the sober bounds of sense, we are as ready to acknowledge as the reader will be to discover: but does it not also exhibit eloquence and imagination, with a strong perception of the powers and energies of nature and of their corresponding impulses in the heart of man? It is not everyone who can so feel and so describe these secret harmonies.

This fragment of Melmoth and Immalee's conversation when she is kneeling at his feet in a ruined pagan temple illuminated by the 'red and jagged lightnings' of the raging storm dramatically illustrates the kind of feeling generated between such incompatible lovers:

> The Indian remained prostrate and aghast. 'Immalee', said the stranger in a struggling voice, 'Do you wish me to tell you the feelings with which my presence should inspire

you?'—'No—no—no!—' said the Indian, applying her white and delicate hands to her ears, and then clasping them on her bosom; 'I feel them too much.'—'Hate me—curse me!' said the stranger, not heeding her, and stamping till the reverberation of his steps on the hollow and loosened stones almost contended with the thunder; 'hate me, for I hate you —I hate all things that live—all things that are dead—I am myself hated and hateful!'—'Not by me', said the poor Indian, feeling, through the blindness of her tears, for his averted hand. 'Yes, by you, if you knew whose I am, and whom I serve.' Immalee aroused her newly-excited energies of heart and intellect to answer this appeal. 'Who you are, I know not—but I am yours.—Whom you serve, I know not, —but him will I serve—I will be yours for ever. Forsake me if you will, but when I am dead, come back to this isle, and say to yourself, The roses have bloomed and faded—the streams have flowed and been dried up—the rocks have been removed from their places—and the lights of heaven have altered in their courses,—but there was one who never changed, and she is not here.'

As she spoke the enthusiasm of passion struggling with grief, she added, 'You have told me you possess the happy art of writing thought.—Do not write one thought on my grave, for one word traced by your hand would revive me. Do not weep, for one tear would make me live again, perhaps to draw a tear from you.'—'Immalee!' said the stranger. The Indian looked up, and, with a mingled feeling of grief, amazement, and compunction, beheld him shed tears. The next moment he dashed them away with the hand of despair; and, grinding his teeth, burst into that wild shriek of bitter and convulsive laughter that announces the object of its derision is ourselves. (III, xviii, 318–19)

Such a meeting belongs to grand opera rather than to the novel, with its tumultuous movements of feeling orchestrated by elemental conflict. This is a very strenuous demonstration of the paradox which lies at the heart of tragic love, threatening death and destruction on a vast scale yet specifically located within the emotional experience of two individuals. Like opera, it has a very tight formal structure, one that works entirely by anti-theses—in speech, gesture and feeling. There is an obvious visual contrast between Immalee's stillness and Melmoth's violent movements, between her gentle tear-filled eyes and his wild shrieks of laughter. He continually warns her against himself in full knowledge of her danger and she, blinded by love and tears, consistently fails to understand his threats. Both of them talk in the same absolutes of love and hate and death but Melmoth's expression of feeling is negative and static in contrast to the range and variety of Immalee's. To his declaration of universal hatred, Immalee replies with her declaration of undying love, an intensely lyrical affirmation of present feeling which also contains a promise for the future. Her sensuous imagery drawn from nature conveys at once the delicacy and vigour of her love, which is akin to nature in its organic life but also superior to the natural cycle in its unchangingness. Immalee's love has a resonance beyond death but as optimistic romantic fantasy it is worlds away from the negation of feeling that Melmoth encompasses. All he can do is to invoke her name but whether in pity or in appeal it is not clear. His exclamation is, incidentally, a most eloquent demonstration of that failure of language under extreme pressures of feeling with which all the Gothic novelists had been obsessed. The convention is used more convincingly here, for the superhuman dimensions of Melmoth's despair can find expression only in his violent and unaccountable behaviour. What he does is indeed astonishing for one who claims to be devoid of all human feelings: 'disinherited child of nature' that he is, he manages to find the common vocabulary of the senti-mental lover and to shed tears. But Melmoth's humanness is only a vestigial reminder of a former state, a refinement on a torment which Immalee cannot begin to comprehend and as he dashes his tears away he gives that terrible laugh which so haunted Baudelaire in its paroxysm of despair, that 'explosion perpetuelle de sa colère et de sa souffrance' ('De l'Essence du Rire' in *Critique d'Art*). Strenuous denial is the only way that Melmoth can testify to the strength of his passion: he is the negation of every natural feeling—but a negation fired by the dynamic energy of chaos.

He is the death-bringer and storm and fire are the elements

with which he is always associated. Such imagery has strong sexual as well as religious overtones, as Maturin simultaneously exploits its double associations to emphasise the dangers inherent in sexual love. Melmoth insistently uses the metaphor of the storm to try to make Immalee understand his threat to her:

'Love,' he cried, extending his arm towards the dim and troubled sky, 'love the storm in its might of destruction—seek alliance with those swift and perilous travellers of the groaning air,—the meteor that rends, and the thunder that shakes it! Court, for sheltering tenderness, those masses of dense and rolling cloud,—the baseless mountains of heaven! Woo the kisses of the fiery lightnings, to quench themselves on your smouldering bosom! Seek all that is terrible in nature for your companions and your lover!—woo them to burn and blast you—perish in their fierce embrace, and you will be happier, far happier, than if you lived in mine! *Lived!*—Oh who can be mine and live!'   (III, xviii, 322)

Such rhetoric fails, however, to make any impression on Immalee, and the storm continues to roll until the scene rises to its crescendo in Melmoth's marriage proposal:

Amid thunder I wed thee—bride of perdition! mine shalt thou be for ever! Come, and let us attest our nuptials before the reeling altar of nature, with the lightnings of heaven for our bed-lights, and the curse of nature for our marriage benediction!   (III, xviii, 323)

Melmoth can offer Immalee a transcendent love but it will be the ideal perverted into its demonic opposite—an eternity of loving celebrated not in heaven but in hell. His later rhapsody of the consummation of love in death far surpasses the usual Gothic necrophiliac flirtings or even rapes among the tombs: it has the intensity of paradox energetically pursued to the point where contradictions are fused in a nightmare vision:

Perish to all the world, perhaps beyond the period of its existence, but live to me in darkness and in corruption! Preserve all the exquisite undulation of your forms! all the indestructible brilliancy of your colouring!—But preserve it for me alone!—me, the single, pulseless, eyeless, heartless

embracer of an infertile bride,—the brooder over the dark
and unproductive nest of eternal sterility,—the mountain
whose lava of internal fire has stifled, and indurated, and
inclosed for ever, all that was the joy of earth, the felicity of
life, and the hope of futurity!   (III, xx, 354)

Melmoth's cosmic despair and the operatic mode of presentation heighten our awareness of the unreality of this love affair
but through all the emotional violence there are glimpses of
real feeling. The author manages to present the emotional
effects of a breakdown of communication between two individuals where each is imprisoned in a private world of innocence
or guilt. The failure of the relationship is shown to be psycho-
logically as well as morally inevitable. The measure of their
incompatibility may be seen when Immalee's perfect devoted-
ness is contrasted with Jane Eyre's love for Rochester: whereas
Jane could say 'I am akin to him', Melmoth remains for
Immalee 'that mysterious being whose presence inspired her
equally with terror and with love' (IV, xxxiv, 513).

The only possible proof of his love that Melmoth could give
would be to abandon Immalee, which he does when he flings
her down senseless on the sand. The final tableau is the appropriate finale, very theatrical in its presentation of a love where
no future or growth is possible:

> 'Is she dead?' he murmured, 'Well, be it so—let her perish
> —let her be any thing *but mine*!' He flung his senseless burden
> on the sands, and departed—nor did he ever revisit the
> island.   (III, xviii, 324)

Like the storm clouds, Melmoth rushes away 'carrying their
diminished burden of wrath and terror where sufferings were
to be inflicted', the author's final comment providing our only
insight into the apparent contradictoriness of Melmoth's behaviour. The emphasis in this tale is on the power of romantic
love to disarm even diabolical temptation, although there is
nothing life-affirming about this love: it is perverted into a
triumph which can be celebrated only in death.

The love between Melmoth and Immalee shows that attraction of opposites which for Maturin expressed the truth about

man's dual nature. He pursues his speculation on tragic love
and desire when the lovers meet against three years later in
Spain, where Immalee has been transported back to her family
(and her name changed to Isidora) to live a life of 'imbecility
and mediocrity'. When Melmoth renews his temptations, he
offers her the most dangerous release of all, a retreat into the
dream world of her lost innocence:

> She had renewed, in these nightly conferences, her former
> visionary existence. Her whole day was but a long thought of
> the hour at which she expected to see him. In the day-time
> she was silent, pensive, abstracted, feeding on thought—with
> the evening her spirits perceptibly though softly rose, like
> those of one who has a secret and incommunicable store of
> delight; and her mind became like that flower that unfolds
> its leaves, and diffuses its odours, only on the approach of
> night . . . At night alone she existed.   (III, xxi, 356)

As she slips away from life, her romantic dream world darkens
into Gothic nightmare with her midnight marriage to Melmoth,
leading her through a wasteland of suffering to the prisons of
the Inquisition and the death of her child until she dies 'of a
broken heart'. Her death is the final statement of paradox, for
she dies kissing the crucifix and declaring her love for Melmoth,
while the heavenly paradise which she envisages closely resem-
bles that lost world of innocence of her Indian island where she
had first met Melmoth; even the movement heavenwards is for
Isidora a regression:

> 'My daughter', said the priest, while the tears rolled fast
> down his cheeks—'my daughter, you are passing to bliss—
> the conflict was fierce and short, but the victory is sure—
> harps are tuned to a new song, even a song of welcome, and
> wreaths of palm are weaving for you in paradise!'
> 'Paradise!' uttered Isidora, with her last breath—'*Will he
> be there!*'   (IV, xxxvii, 533)

Maturin's analysis of the paradoxical nature of our response
to terror and suffering extends from a contemplation of its
victims to an interest in the feelings of its spectators. It is a disturbing truth that the spectacle of mental or physical agony can

operate as a powerful imaginative stimulus, and the range of
Maturin's speculations on this area of feeling is so wide as to
establish it as a morally neutral fact about human psychology.
It is an awareness shared by the most depraved and the most
decent characters in the novel, and also exploited by the author
as an essential part of his technique for stirring the feelings of
his readers. In the words of a particularly vicious monk who
specialises in voyeurism:

> It is actually possible to become *amateurs in suffering*. I have
> heard of men who have travelled into countries where hor-
> rible executions were to be daily witnessed, for the sake of that
> excitement which the sight of suffering never fails to give,
> from the spectacle of a tragedy, or an *auto da fe*, down to the
> writhings of the meanest reptile on whom you can inflict
> torture, and feel that torture is the result of your own power.
> It is a species of feeling of which we never can divest ourselves.
>
> (II, ix, 207)

The following incident, which describes the torments of a
novice in a Spanish monastery, is a particularly striking example of the imaginative and moral complexity involved in
Maturin's aesthetic of suffering:

> A naked human being, covered with blood, and uttering
> screams of rage and torture, flashed by me; four monks pur-
> sued him—they had lights. I had shut the door at the end of
> the gallery—I felt they must return and pass me—I was still
> on my knees, and trembling from head to foot. The victim
> reached the door, found it shut, and rallied. I turned, and
> saw a group worthy of Murillo. A more perfect human form
> never existed than that of this unfortunate youth. He stood
> in an attitude of despair—he was streaming with blood. The
> monks, with their lights, their scourges, and their dark habits,
> seemed like a group of demons who had made prey of a
> wandering angel,—the group resembled the infernal furies
> pursuing a mad Orestes. And, indeed, no ancient sculptor
> ever designed a figure more exquisite and perfect than that
> they had so barbarously mangled. Debilitated as my mind
> was by the long slumber of all its powers, this spectacle of

horror and cruelty woke them in a moment. I rushed forward
in his defence. (I, v, 108)

Moral indignation and horror mingle strangely here with
aesthetic delight, as the spectator numbed in mind and body by
devotional exercises gazes passively on this scene of torment.
His human sympathies momentarily suspended, he keeps at an
emotional distance as the scene crystallises into an instant of
stasis when the novice turns at bay on his persecutors. Emotional violence is filtered through images of art in this contemplation of physical agony as the scene is compared with the
paintings of Murillo, with sculpture, with figures of religious
and pagan myth. The dramatic lighting effects emphasize the
picturesque formal grouping of the victim and his tormentors,
who only secondarily take on the symbolic resonance of an
opposition between good and evil. Then, quite suddenly, the
stasis dissolves into violent movement as the current of human
feeling returns to the spectator and he rushes to the victim's
defence.

There are two quite separate kinds of movement in this passage, one physical and the other emotional. There is the chase
itself which stops at the locked door and then resumes in the
struggle at the end; there is also the emotional change in the
spectator from passivity to active participation. The point of
stasis is coincident for both kinds of movement and allows for
the aesthetic contemplation of physical beauty mutilated in the
full agony of consciousness. It is the length and precision of the
spectator's detached view which is so suspect, for though he does
finally resolve emotional tension into moral commitment there
remains that pause of pure delight in horror. As Kiely says of
this passage:

What complicates the scene is that the narrator [whom I
have called the spectator] relishes, with an artist's eye, precisely what the monks seem to enjoy doing to the beautiful
novice . . . As artist, the speaker is with the victimisers even
if, as moralist, he disapproves of them. (op. cit., 195)

It is an interesting comment on Maturin's psychological
realism that he can make the most bizarre and horrible situa-

tions emotionally credible. *Melmoth* creates a world of subjective experience but it is far from the escapism of earlier Gothic novels; it is a world of nightmare not unlike the 'Nighttown' of Joyce's *Ulysses*, where anxieties and fears take on the exaggerated dimensions of obsessional fantasy. The following dream vision of being burned alive in a Spanish *auto da fe* is fantasy of this kind, pushing Gothic delight in morbid sensationalism to a new point of extravagant horror. It is an avid speculation on feeling on the knife-edge between life and death, at that dynamic point in time 'that condenses and crowds all imaginable sufferings in one brief and intense pang, and appears exhausted itself by the blow is has struck' (216):

> The next moment I was chained to my chair again,—the fires were lit, the bells rang out, and litanies were sung;—my feet were scorched to a cinder,—my muscles cracked, my blood and marrow hissed, my flesh consumed like shrinking leather,—the bones of my legs hung two black withering and moveless sticks in the ascending blaze;—it ascended, caught my hair,—I was crowned with fire,—my head was a ball of molten metal, my eyes flashed and melted in their sockets,— I opened my mouth, it drank fire,—I closed it, the fire was within,—and still the bells rang on, and the crowd shouted, and the king and queen, and all the nobility and priesthood looked on, and we burned, and burned!—I was a cinder body and soul in my dream. (II, xi, 236)

This is a dream flash of 'one wild moment of yelling agony', all contained within a single breathless sentence as every detail of the physical sensation of burning crowds in, to the terrible climax in the long final clause, 'and still the bells rang on . . .' The burning man assimilates everybody into his private world of annihilation, 'we burned, and burned'. The curse of isolation and separateness is thus lifted in the victim's agonised consciousness at that moment of synthesis when life is transcended by death. The whole experience is remarkably contained within the dreamer's double vision, from inside the intense agony of the burning but with the final comment made as it were from a great imaginative distance. The dreamer is still there at the end to record quite objectively, 'I was a cinder body and soul in my dream'. The dynamic moment has exhausted itself.

Another important psychological perception that this passage illustrates is the extraordinary elasticity of time as a feature of human consciousness: a moment like this can contain an infinity of suffering, while on the other hand monotony can reduce large tracts of time to nothingness in the mind, as the same character perceives: 'Day followed day for many a month, of which I have no recollection, nor wish to have any. My life was a sea without a tide' (I, v, 99). The discrepancy between chronological time and time experienced through the rhythms of feeling is a symptom of that paradoxical relation between the objective world and subjective reality which is a feature of the human condition. Melmoth, in so many ways the monstrous paradigm of man's duality, is himself a being outside time yet bound to it as part of his Faustian bargain; it is an important aspect of his torment that he must contemplate human suffering within time while enduring an eternity of despair that the other characters experience only imaginatively.

At the end, time closes in on Melmoth: he returns to Ireland to die in the room where he was born, his supernatural existence having come to an end. Quite suddenly he becomes very old: 'His hairs were as white as snow, his mouth had fallen in, and the muscles of his face were relaxed and withered—he was the very image of hoary decrepid debility' (IV, xxxix, 540). But the climax of horror is not the natural horror of physical death; it is the spiritual horror of Melmoth's vision of timelessness in hell. The collision of time and eternity at the moment of death is a paradox that can only be stated in a metaphysical image, the striking of the giant clock which Melmoth envisages:

> He saw the mysterious single hand revolve—he saw it reach the appointed period of one hundred and fifty years—(for in this mystic plate centuries were marked, not hours)—he shrieked in his dream, and, with that strong impulse often felt in sleep, burst from the arm that held him, to arrest the motion of the hand.   (IV, xxxviii, 539)

In the Wanderer's Dream, time explodes into an eternity of

agony in the most terrible visionary landscape in the novel, where souls shriek forever on fiery billows at the bottom of a vast gulf. Melmoth's death is imaged as a vertiginous plunge down into chaos, where he is pushed by a gigantic black arm belonging to some being 'too vast and horrible even for the imagery of a dream to shape'. The language of the dream is surely inspired by Milton's vision of Satan's fall down into hell with its fiery lake and 'darkness visible' but the intensity of Maturin's dramatic description recreates spiritual dread in a new and frighteningly concrete form.

Melmoth's death is very Faustian in its mixture of mysterious happening and graphic outline of events. Recorded in fragments of evidence—shrieks and yells at midnight, footprints leading to an Irish clifftop overlooking the sea, and Melmoth's white handkerchief fluttering halfway down the cliff—it provokes the reader into an imaginative reconstruction of the actual death scene which gathers resonance from the Wanderer's Dream as well as from its Faustian prototype. We are compelled to gaze into the abyss, like the two witnesses of Melmoth's last appearance on earth who, having followed his tracks, find themselves confronting 'the wide, waste engulphing ocean' beneath them. Then '[Young] Melmoth and Monçada exchanged looks of silent and unutterable horror, and returned slowly home' (IV, xxxix, 542).

That look of horror is a strange ending even for a Gothic novel and certainly a very strange one for a novel based on any kind of optimistic Christian premise. It is a very open ending in the sense that it explains nothing, either about Melmoth or about the paradoxical nature of man as it is uncovered in the narrative. Nor does it hint at any possibility of reconciliation: it ends on a note of terrified speculation about the mystery of death, which we as readers share with the two witnesses. We are perhaps the more horrified, in that we know the details of Melmoth's dream which transform the Irish scene for us into a visionary landscape, the abyss of Melmoth's own mind. Suffering stretches to infinity.

There is surely a contradiction in the author's own mind, caught as he is in a dilemma between his duty as a Christian moralist and the urges of his own dark Romantic sensibility.

Whatever the rationale of his imposed religious framework, every situation develops its own momentum as an exploration of suffering, conflict and frustration. Maturin makes some disturbing discoveries about man's emotional potential which give his own desperate faith in the possibility of man's salvation something of the aura of paradox in which he delighted. Because there are no rational or moral explanations for the psychological insights he records, the novel is a series of isolated *aperçus* into dream states, schizoid states and paranoic fantasy. *Melmoth* is full of the shocks of collision between emotional and moral opposites, between life and death, between the objective reality of fact and the subjective reality of feeling. It is as though the author can only create the sensation of being alive when poised on the very edge of experience where 'the soul [or the mind] trembles on the verge'. 'Perhaps it is amid the moments of despair, that imagination has most power, and they who have suffered, can best describe and feel' (ii, xi, 242).

Maturin's is an agonised sensibility that insistently probes the mystery of man, ranging widely through a panoramic vision of history for its examples but always turning inwards on itself to discover new areas of a psychological terrain as vast as Melmoth's own vision of hell. That trilogy of feelings Love, Mystery, and Misery assumes new dimensions here: it is no longer merely the stuff of emotional crisis but rather spells out the terrible conditions of human existence. At the end we can only look with horror over the precipice down into the abyss of death, so that we are left, more like victims than spectators, 'tembling on the verge' at the extreme limits of morbid Gothic fantasy.

Charlotte Brontë, *Jane Eyre*

Then, too, imagination is a strong, restless faculty, which
claims to be heard and exercised: are we to be quite deaf
to her cry, and insensate to her struggles?
(Charlotte Brontë to G. H. Lewes, November 1847)

Coming to *Jane Eyre* after reading *Melmoth the Wanderer* is like
walking out into the open air, away from the imprisonment of
morbid fantasy towards a comprehensive view of feeling,
imagination and reason all integrated in a fictional presentation
of complex individual lives. Though the novel stands at a distance both chronologically and imaginatively from Gothic
fiction, it still retains so many traditional features that I think
we can wisely treat it as a 'good Gothic novel' which at once
realises the potential of this type of fiction and far surpasses the
earlier simplified concepts of Love, Mystery, and Misery in its
subtlety and emotional range. *Jane Eyre* treats irrational experience with full confidence in its value and by doing so marks a
significant progress beyond private fantasy and alienation back
to the fully integrated personality. With this novel, Gothic
fiction may be seen to have broken through into the world of
everyday life and humane social awareness which are the
recognised major concerns of fiction.

Charlotte Brontë was conscious of writing within the sensa-
tionalist tradition, as is evident from a letter of hers to G. H.
Lewes (November 1847) shortly after *Jane Eyre* was published.
In reply to a criticism of his she wrote:

You warn me to beware of melodrama, and you exhort me
to adhere to the real. When I first began to write, so impressed
was I with the truth of the principles you advocate, that I
determined to take Nature and Truth as my sole guides, and
to follow to their very footprints; I restrained imagination,
eschewed romance, repressed excitement.[1]

The result of her efforts was that six publishers refused her novel, *The Professor*. So, though it would be wrong to think that in *Jane Eyre* she was merely writing to a sensationalist formula popular with the circulating libraries, this earlier criticism no doubt helped her to recognise her own capacity to write imaginative fiction. In the same letter to Lewes she asserts the value of imagination, in full awareness of the tension that exists in the mind between the rival claims of imagination and reason (see the quotation at the beginning of this chapter).

Across the distance of nearly thirty years with an imagination influenced as much by Scott and Byron and the wild romantic engravings of John Martin in Haworth parsonage as by old Gothic novels, Charlotte Brontë retains in her fiction discernible links with Gothic attitudes as well as with Gothic techniques. Her novels preserve the conflict between imagination, feeling and reason which was the rationalist inheritance of the Gothic novelists and the Romantic poets, but for Charlotte Brontë the duality of human nature did not necessarily tend to destruction (as it did for Lewis and Maturin); it can also be a condition of adventurous struggle toward wider human awareness. She certainly has in mind the traditional character types of Byronic hero and sentimental heroine, though her response to these stereotypes in Rochester and Jane Eyre is original enough. The most important similarity with Gothic modes is in her emphasis on feeling for as David Lodge says in his *Language of Fiction*, 'the dominant energies and sympathies of this novel are on the side of passion'. But here too comes an interesting development beyond traditional Gothic: whereas the earlier novels were made of emotional crises and of moments 'where the soul trembles on the verge', these crises occur in *Jane Eyre* only as part of a whole range of feelings, a range that widens to include such everyday states as mild depression and even boredom, and times of meditation on feelings. The Gothic features in *Jane Eyre* make the novel an interesting commentary on the preceding genre but it would be doing it an injustice to restrict one's comments to that alone. Gothic conventions assume their proper importance when we see them as only part of a subtle and economical technique for realising the components of individual feeling set within the context of everyday life.[2]

Jane Eyre is cast as an autobiography, a study in the growth of awareness of Jane herself as a credible individual. Not being a romance, it escapes the digressions so characteristic of that genre and has a formal coherence which was lacking in the earlier Gothic novels. It shows the emergence of a personality from childhood to adulthood with all the crises and reassessments that that entails. Melmoth was a wanderer but Jane is a traveller to a specific goal. Her journey is on the one hand a moral and spiritual one towards true independence and integrity and on the other an emotional one from alienation and longing for love to emotional fulfilment as Rochester's wife.[3] The focus on a single consciousness immediately brings to mind Lewis's *Monk* which was also concerned almost exclusively with one personality, Ambrosio the Monk himself. *The Monk*, as we have seen, is a characteristically Gothic study in obsession, showing the appalling growth of neurosis into criminal madness, the monastic cell being only the outward sign of Ambrosio's psychological imprisonment. Ambrosio never seems to remember his past experiences, let alone come to terms with them, so that he continually reacts with shock and horror to the revelations of his own criminal potential. His final confrontation with the devil may be seen as a demonstration of his utter lack of self-awareness and moral irresponsibility throughout. Jane on the other hand insistently remembers, assesses and anticipates, so that we have a clear sense of a continually developing personality, excited by the potential within her own nature and growing outwards in her appreciation of other people and in her ability to form ever more varieties of human relationship.

There is another kind of awareness which develops in Jane and which is of fundamental importance in distinguishing this novel not only from other Gothic novels but from all other romantic novels as well. This awareness is something other than moral or emotional but an intimately related analytical awareness best described by D. H. Lawrence (in his Foreword to the American edition of *Women in Love*): 'Any man of real individuality tries to know and to understand what is happening, even in himself, as he goes along. This struggle for verbal consciousness should not be left out in art.' And Charlotte

Brontë does not leave it out; indeed the novel is very much concerned with exploring feelings and finding the words to describe them precisely, however odd the feelings may be. The novel as fictional autobiography is after all the result of Jane's remembering, recreative process, in which her earlier feelings can be described and understood more adequately than she was able to do at the time of the experience. This is very clear when she talks about her inadequacy as a child to explain to the friendly apothecary exactly why she is unhappy; there is no question of her not feeling intensely, but there is a lack of verbal skills to shape her experience meaningfully:

> How much I wished to reply fully to this question! How difficult it was to frame any answer! Children can feel, but they cannot analyse their feelings; and if the analysis is partially effected in thought, they know not how to express the result of the process in words.   (I, iii, 23–4)[4]

It is precisely this verbal skill that the older Jane possesses: in her private meditations, in the witty language of her conversations with Mr Rochester, in her wrestling with St John Rivers, and we also see it in the remarkable concreteness of language with which she describes the workings of feeling and its force. Jane is character and author, so she can on occasions both relive an experience and distance herself from it in order to evaluate it. We have the sense that the writer has achieved that balance between feeling and judgement for which we have seen her striving throughout the various crises in the novel.

There is a very clear instance of the distancing and judging process when Jane is remembering her response to Mr Rochester's first proposal. She recreates her passionate involvement and also from ten years' distance measures her romantic dream against the intimations of reality, something which was impossible for her at the time:

> And if I had loved him less I should have thought his accent and look of exultation savage: but sitting by him, roused from the nightmare of parting—called to the paradise of union—I thought only of the bliss given me to drink in so abundant a flow.   (II, viii, 258)

It is only much later that Jane can admit the metaphysical flaw in this first stage of their relationship: 'I could not, in those days, see God for his creature: of whom I had made an idol' (II, ix, 277). So Jane adds in her telling a perspective and an interpretation of events which are formed long after the experience itself. I think this reshaping in terms of a specifically Christian ethic gives to the novel a moral structure which the events and feelings do not obviously possess in themselves. Indeed, the way Jane sees things at the time they happen and the way she understands them later as part of the pattern of her whole experience are not exactly the same; we should not expect them to be, as the novel is a record of the remembered process of growth and realisation.

The energy of the novel springs from the immediacy of Jane's registration of feelings and events for she writes 'to the moment' as minutely as Richardson's Clarissa had done. Jane has none of the overwhelming guilt of an Ambrosio or a Melmoth, nor has she the timid prudishness of a Radcliffian heroine; instead, she is robustly human with all her energies on the side of life. Her most intense feelings are directed towards human beings and the novel ends (as it has proceeded) with the triumph of feeling in this world. The point is that Jane is a survivor: physically (as Rochester said, she 'must have been tenacious of life' at Lowood school) and emotionally and spiritually, after her victories over Rochester and St John Rivers. Jane and her author too have full confidence in the value of feeling and in the power of human beings to communicate and find fulfilment through love. Indeed, love may raise human beings to superhuman heights, as Jane and Rochester's telepathic communication near the end suggests, and their happy marriage is not called a 'supreme blessing' lightly. It is witness to a dimension of awareness in them both, painfully developed through harsh experience, that the individual has both a separate emotional identity and a spiritual affinity with powers beyond himself: man is God's creature in a truly life-affirming sense.

Jane has none of the morbid fears of death which so obsessed the Gothic heroines. Although in times of stress she sometimes wishes she were dead, she always reacts vigorously against these negative moments and never really considers the possibility of her own death. Such an attitude is clear in her determination to survive when she is wandering desolately on the moors after leaving Mr Rochester and Thornfield:

> Hopeless of the future, I wished but this—that my Maker had that night thought good to require my soul of me while I slept; and that this weary frame, absolved by death from further conflict with fate, had now but to decay quietly, and mingle in peace with the soil of this wilderness. Life, however, was yet in my possession; with all its requirements, and pains, and responsibilities. The burden must be carried; the want provided for; the suffering endured; the responsibility fulfilled. I set out. (III, ii, 329)

There are various deaths in the novel and Jane's reactions to them are a measure of her own maturity at the times of their occurrence. The first is that of Helen Burns when Jane is at Lowood. It is a child's view of death, lacking the realisation of the possibility before it occurs and separated from the physical phenomenon itself. Jane goes to sleep in Helen's arms and when she wakes up she is being carried away by the nurse. The account includes no more than a childish awareness allows and the emphasis is placed on what is important at the time: the way Jane is guided by Helen to see death as a spiritual release. The final comment, made fifteen years after the event, is a description of Helen's grave and her epitaph: 'A grey tablet marks the spot, inscribed with her name, and the word "Resurgam" ' (I, vii, 83). It is a delicate fusion of the young Jane's inability to accept the finality of death and the mature Jane's realisation that there is no spiritual finality in it.

There are two reported deaths—a suicide and the death of Jane's uncle in Madeira who leaves her his fortune, but Jane's next experience of death is that of her Aunt Reed when she is already governess at Thornfield. Her return to Gateshead where she had spent her early childhood revives many unhappy memories but she is no longer at their mercy:

> The fact was, I had other things to think about: within the last few months feelings had been stirred in me so much more potent than any they could raise—pains and pleasures so

much more acute and exquisite had been excited, than any it was in their power to inflict or bestow.   (II, vi 231)

She can view her dying aunt with a disinterestedness which is yet not without compassion. Her account of the death, devoid as it is of any false emotion, is an entirely realistic appraisal of the distance between the living and the dead:

> A strange and solemn object was that corpse to me. I gazed on it with gloom and pain: nothing soft, nothing sweet, nothing pitying, or hopeful, or subduing, did it inspire; only a grating anguish for *her* woes—not *my* loss—and a sombre tearless dismay at the fearfulness of death in such a form.
> (II, vi, 242–3)

There is no danger however, that Jane could be accused of that lack of feeling which she condemns in her cousin Eliza:

> Feeling without judgment is a washy draught indeed; but judgment untempered by feeling is too bitter and husky a morsel for human deglutition.   (II, vi, 239)

We are aware already of her developing emotional attachment to Mr Rochester, so can give full credence to the assertion she makes to her aunt:

> I am passionate, but not vindictive. Many a time, as a little child, I should have been glad to love you if you would have let me; and I long earnestly to be reconciled to you now: kiss me, aunt.   (II, vi, 242)

With her energies directed toward life and love she will not recognise death as a stimulus for conventional emotions of grief which she does not feel. Later she hears about the dreadful suicide of mad Mrs Rochester by report only. Her reaction is confined to the brief exclamation 'Good God!' at the physical horror of the inn-keeper's description but her attention turns immediately to Rochester, as her next question 'And afterwards?' indicates. The novel ends with the expectation of St John Rivers's death as a missionary in India and Jane's attitude is a clear expression of her intuitive sympathy with Rivers's nature, at once so like and so dissimilar to her own:

> And why weep for this? No fear of death will darken St. John's last hour: his mind will be unclouded; his heart will be undaunted; his hope will be sure; his faith steadfast. His own words are a pledge of this . . .　　　　　(III, xii, 458)

Jane's honesty is the final measure of her achievement of tolerance and spiritual comprehension.

Jane's lack of fear at the idea of death frees the novel from the morbid terrors of the supernatural so characteristic of Gothic fiction. This does not mean, however, that irrational experience in *Jane Eyre* is confined within what we would regard as the normal bounds of probability, for all through the novel the presence of the supernatural world is felt, both in the characters' awareness of inexplicable forces and in the structuring of narrative events. As Kathleen Tillotson says, the idea of the supernatural world lies across the whole novel, if only half-perceived, and she quotes Helen Burns as its spokesman:

> Besides this earth, and besides the race of men, there is an invisible world and a kingdom of spirits: that world is round us, for it is everywhere; and those spirits watch us, for they are commissioned to guard us . . . and God waits only the separation of spirit from flesh to crown us with a full reward.[5]

While Jane's interpretation of this other world is as different from Helen's as their particular personalities must dictate, she has a similar awareness of spiritual forces.

Jane is very explicit about the importance of the affinity between man and mysterious cosmic forces when she talks about 'presentiments, sympathies, and signs'. Her statement about the ways in which these affinities operate is absolutely central to the design of the novel:

> Presentiments are strange things! and so are sympathies; and so are signs: and the three combined make one mystery to which humanity has not yet found the key. I never laughed at presentiments in my life; because I have had strange ones of my own. Sympathies I believe exist: (for instance, between far-distant long-absent, wholly estranged relatives, asserting, notwithstanding their alienation, the unity of the source to which each traces his origin) whose workings baffle

mortal comprehension. And signs, for aught we know, may
be but the sympathies of Nature with man.   (II, vi, 222)

This differs markedly from the treatment of the supernatural in
earlier Gothic fiction. Here, the awareness of supernatural
forces fuses with spiritual awareness and together they become
an integral part of Jane's personality. It is indicative of the
author's attitude as well as of Jane's that human beings occupy
a central place in the web of connections: by presentiments,
man is linked to a knowledge of his future; by sympathies, man
is linked to man; and signs, it is suggested, may be a link between
man and the natural forces of the universe. It is a human-
centred notion of man as a spiritual being and we find that the
highest states of awareness in the novel are also the moments of
greatest spiritual insight.

It is because Jane comes to realise her spiritual nature that
she can respond as she does in the extraordinary telepathic
communication with Mr Rochester. She does not minimise the
remarkable quality of her experience; indeed she emphasises
that it has all the strangeness of the supernatural but none of
the fear usually associated with it. By describing the mystery in
terms of her own sensations, she gives the experience a wonderfully tangible human concreteness. When she talks about her
excited state just before she hears Rochester's call from many
miles away, she likens her feelings to an electric shock as the
closest equivalent in known sensation, and then she proceeds to
define the difference:

> The feeling was not like an electric shock; but it was quite
> as sharp, as strange, as startling: it acted on my senses as if
> their utmost activity hitherto had been but torpor; from
> which they were now summoned, and forced to wake. They
> rose expectant: eye and ear waited, while the flesh quivered
> on my bones.   (III, ix, 424)

Her senses thrill but her awareness is heightened and not para-
lysed. As she says: 'My powers were in play and in force.' She
reacts by running outside to answer the call and, recognising
the truth of what has occurred, she quite specifically repudiates
the false shadow of superstitious fear:

'Down, superstition!' I commented, as that spectre rose up
black by the black yew at the gate. 'This is not thy deception,
nor thy witchcraft: it is the work of nature. She was roused,
and did—no miracle—but her best.'   (III, ix, 425)

For Jane, such experience comes within the bounds of the
natural and by 'nature' she means the whole structure of forces
which control the life processes of the universe, the world of
intertwining roots and magnetic attraction to which she had
previously compared her love for Rochester. Nature and mystery, human and divine caring, are fused in her realisation of
the myserious combination of forces within the human personality.

The telepathic communication is set within a curious psycho-
spiritual context of passionate feeling and Christian prayer. It
would be wrong to say that the lovers have transcended the
desires of the flesh; rather that these desires are so intensified by
desperation that passion itself effects a momentary release from
the limitations of self into that invisible world 'which is around
us, for it is everywhere'. Jane's prayer afterwards shows her
realisation of the relatedness of the individual psyche and divine
powers, for she prays with the elation of a mystic in spiritual
communion with God:

> I seemed to penetrate very near a Mighty Spirit; and my
> soul rushed out in gratitude at His feet. I rose from the thanks-
> giving—took a resolve—and lay down, unscared, enlightened
> —eager but for the daylight.   (III, ix, 425)

It is a proof of her conviction that, following this 'wondrous
shock of feeling', Jane commits the one truly irrational act of
her life: she goes back to Thornfield to answer Rochester's call,
knowing it to be against all reason and yet never doubting that
she is following her intuition of truth.

It is in the context of Jane's peculiar psychological make-up
that her frequent reference to Gothic preoccupations has to be
considered and evaluated. Her marked imaginative streak
which Rochester recognised very early in their acquaintance
gives her a remarkable openness to ranges of perception against
which her rational mind tugs, both at the time and in retrospect.

For instance, despite her crisis of hysterical fear in the Red Room as a child, Jane does not actually believe that she has seen a ghost, as her answer to her nurse's question indicates: 'Oh! I saw a light, and I thought a ghost would come' (I, ii, 17).

Jane's attitude to the mysterious happenings at Thornfield when she comes to Mr Rochester's house as a governess shows the same mixture of imagination and common sense, though by this time she is much more aware of the conflicting inclinations within herself, as befits a person nine years older. However, she is still young enough and imaginative enough to want to believe in ghosts, although she will not allow herself to do so. It is almost as if she dares herself to believe in them when she is being conducted over the old house at Thornfield by the house-keeper, Mrs Fairfax. Her conversation with that lady and her comments on Mrs Fairfax's responses show very clearly Jane's entertainment of supernatural possibilities, not unlike Catherine Morland's in some ways:

> 'One would almost say that, if there were a ghost at Thorn-field Hall, this would be its haunt.'
> 'So I think: you have no ghost then?'
> 'None that I ever heard of,' returned Mrs. Fairfax, smiling.
> 'Nor any traditions of one? no legends or ghost stories?'
> 'I believe not.' (I, xi, 107)

Certainly her desire to flirt with the notion of fear in a haunted house is encouraged by the mysterious laugh she hears on the deserted third floor. She seems consciously and deliberately to maintain a tension between her imagination and the facts with which she is faced:

> I really did not expect any Grace to answer; for the laugh was as tragic, as preternatural a laugh as any I ever heard; and, but that it was high noon, and that no circumstance of ghostliness accompanied the curious cachination; but that neither scene nor season favoured fear, I should have been superstitiously afraid. However, the event showed me I was a fool for entertaining a sense even of surprise. (I, xi, 108)

The very energy with which Jane continually tells herself she is being ridiculous in allowing the laugh to scare her suggests the undercurrent of irrational fear that remains. Jane likens it to 'goblin laughter' when one night she is awakened by the sound of it close to the key-hole: 'Was that Grace Poole? and is she possessed with a devil?' (I, xv, 149). On that occasion Jane's questions give vivid expression to the confusion and terror she feels at being awakened in such a manner. Her immediate assignment of the laugh to Grace as a rational explanation is undercut by the demonic images of her imagination. The experience occurs on the threshold of consciousness, between dreaming and waking, where it is impossible to separate fantasy from fact. The laugh may be 'unearthly', but whatever the 'ghost' is, its outbreaks of violence are real enough. On every occasion they demand from Jane a very practical response, the more readily entered into, we suspect, as a means of escaping from the notion of mysterious terror. In the first crisis, Jane discovers that an unknown person has set fire to Rochester's bed, but far from attributing the deed to the work of a ghost she blames Grace Poole for it. When Jane sees her the next day, she is 'absolutely dumbfoundered'—not at Mrs Poole's demonic qualities but rather at her 'miraculous self-possession and most inscrutable hypocrisy' (II, i, 157).

Jane's reactions to the mysterious occurrences at Thornfield are in no way conventionalised however, either as fear of the supernatural or as rational repudiations of it. They are entirely credible responses to the particular demands of every situation. On the occasion of Mr Mason's attack, Jane registers her initial terror at the cry from the upper storey in language which is at once evocative of her sensations and suggestive of her emotions:

> My pulse stopped: my heart stood still; my stretched arm was paralysed. The cry died, and was not renewed. Indeed, whatever being uttered that fearful shriek could not soon repeat it: not the widest-winged condor on the Andes could, twice in succession, send out such a yell from the cloud shrouding his eyry.   (II, v, 208)

However, when she is summoned by Rochester to go up to the third floor and sit with the wounded man, her terror changes in its nature though not in its intensity. Confronted with a dangerous situation, her fear of the supernatural is replaced by a no less genuine fear for her own physical safety:

> Here then I was in the third story, fastened into one of its mystic cells; night around me; a pale and bloody spectacle under my eyes and hands; a murderess hardly separated from me by a single door: yes—that was appalling—the rest I could bear; but I shuddered at the thought of Grace Poole bursting out upon me. (II, V, 212)

All the Gothic machinery is here: the mysterious being behind the locked door, the heroine alone tending a wounded man whose eyes are 'glazed with the dullness of horror', and in a situation she cannot understand:

> What crime was this, that lived incarnate in this sequestered mansion, and could neither be expelled nor subdued by the owner?—What mystery, that broke out, now in fire and now in blood, at the deadest hours of night? (II, V, 212)

Even the pictures on the great apostle cabinet begin to assume demonic proportions, 'theatening a revelation of the arch-traitor—of Satan himself—in his subordinate's form'. The main function of such a Gothic image is to suggest how entirely Jane's imagination has been affected by mystery and horror. She is very worried, and for valid reasons: she fears for her own safety and she fears that Mason may die while Rochester is away fetching a doctor. However, as soon as he returns, Jane is capable of putting aside her imaginative fears and of answering the practical demands of the situation. Later on, in her conversation with Rochester she can dismiss all but the very real fear that someone would come out of the inner room.

The third midnight visitation brings Jane and the Thornfield ghost literally face to face. It occurs in a context where it is again impossible to separate fantasy from reality, thus exaggerating all the attributes of terror and nightmare with which Jane's mind is full on being awakened. When she is telling Rochester about the event afterwards, she does not for a moment believe that it was a ghost and she is very definite in distinguishing it from her two previous nightmares. As she tells him, they

were only the preface of which 'the tale is yet to come'. However, in her account the nightmarish apparition does not belong
quite so clearly and convincingly to the real world as she would
wish to make Rochester believe. She answers his questions in a
manner as matter-of-fact as she can manage, though her
description of the figure continually veers towards the sensational and the melodramatic:

> It seemed, sir, a woman, tall and large, with thick and
> dark hair hanging long down her back. I know not what
> dress she had on: it was white and straight, but whether gown,
> sheet, or shroud, I cannot tell.   (II, x, 286)

The 'shroud' suggests the workings of Jane's overwrought
imagination, as does her description of the figure's face:

> Fearful and ghastly to me—oh sir, I never saw a face like
> it! It was a discoloured face—it was a savage face. I wish I
> could forget the roll of the red eyes and the fearful blackened
> inflation of the lineaments!   (II, x, 286)

Her language not unnaturally provokes Rochester's mildly
ironic reply, 'Ghosts are usually pale, Jane'. The final part of
her description is as melodramatic as anything in the best
Gothic tradition of horror:

> 'This, sir, was purple: the lips were swelled and dark; the
> brow furrowed; the black eyebrows wildly raised over the
> blood-shot eyes. Shall I tell you of what it reminded me?'
> 'You may.'
> 'Of the foul German spectre—the Vampyre.'
> 'Ah!—what did it do?'
> 'Sir, it removed my veil from its gaunt head, rent it in two
> parts, and flinging both on the floor, trampled on them.'
> 'Afterwards?'
> 'It drew aside the window-curtain and looked out: per-
> haps it saw the dawn approaching, for, taking the candle, it
> retreated to the door. Just at my bedside, the figure stopped:
> the fiery eye glared upon me—she thrust up her candle close
> to my face, and extinguished it under my eyes. I was aware
> her lurid visage flamed over mine, and I lost consciousness:

for the second time in my life—only the second time—I became insensible from terror.' (II, x, 286–7)

The conventional elements are obvious: the midnight apparition which flees at dawn, the mirror reflection of the hideous face, and Jane's image of the vampire which unites her physical horror and her nightmarish fear. Her terror when the figure approaches her with the candle is so intense that she faints like any Gothic heroine.

The use of a Gothic vocabulary here is an extremely complex one. Whether Jane's experience is imaginative or real, the language is an appropriate register of her emotionalised perceptions and their nightmare quality. It is so close to melodrama that, even when it emerges with the factual proof of the torn wedding veil that her nightmare has the substance of reality, Rochester can almost persuade Jane to doubt the evidence of her senses by suggesting that she has exaggerated the demonic qualities of Grace Poole. The final shock comes on Jane's wedding day, when after the interruption of the ceremony she discovers that her wild 'imaginings' are not the trick of a disturbed mind but an accurate description of the object, and that all her horrors have their basis in reality. The fact is that Thornfield really is cursed and that the 'ghost' is Rochester's criminally insane wife.

The interrupted marriage had been a favourite crisis scene as far back as Mrs Radcliffe's *The Italian* (1797), and it is interesting to see how Charlotte Brontë takes the stereotype and reshapes it to define the uniqueness of Jane's experience. Indeed, I think there is convincing evidence for *The Italian* as the specific source here: we know that Charlotte Brontë had read Mrs Radcliffe's novel and we also know her responses to it from the account in *Shirley*, for in 'An Evening Out' (Chapter 23) Caroline Helstone discusses the novel with the child Rose York who is reading it. Caroline herself had read it long ago:

'Long since, when I read it as a child, I was wonderfully taken with it.'
'Why?'
'It seemed to open with such promise—such foreboding of a most strange tale to be unfolded.'

And after a short discussion of a wandering as opposed to a settled life, they return to their literary talk:

> 'But, Rose,' pursued Caroline, 'I fear a wanderer's life, for me at least, would end like that tale you are reading—in disappointment, vanity, and vexation of spirit.'
> 'Does *The Italian* so end?'
> 'I thought so when I read it.'

In *The Italian*, the secret wedding between the hero and heroine is interrupted by a summons for the lovers to appear before the court of the Inquisition on a trumped-up charge that the heroine is really a nun who has escaped from her convent. Their wedding is clouded by omens of death and disaster: it is a stormy day, the chapel has a 'funeral' look, and as the groom leads his trembling bride to the altar, the figures are shrouded in 'sepulchral gloomy light' and the heroine continually looks around in fearful expectation of seeing intruders. Suddenly, as the service is beginning, a mysterious gigantic hooded figure emerging out of the shadows, announces in a voice 'like bursting thunder' that the bridal pair are arraigned by the Inquisition. Giving a half-stifled shriek, the heroine falls fainting into her lover's arms. The situation is treated very melodramatically for there is much declamation by the hero and priest and the mysterious officials and a terrible sword fight in front of the altar when the hero is wounded. In the end, the bride and bridegroom are dragged separately out of the chapel, the bride calling 'in the piercing accents of despair', 'Farewell, Vivaldi! —O! for ever—ever, farewell!'. And her bridegroom watches in agony as her fluttering veil disappears. It is interesting that in both *The Italian* and in *Jane Eyre* there is an emphasis on the bridal veil as the key symbol of disaster. In *Jane Eyre* it is torn in half by the mad wife and in *The Italian* the heroine is condemned because of her veil, which belonged to a nun and which she had forgotten to take off before her marriage.

The Gothic stereotype is full of violent action and emotional display against which Charlotte Brontë reacts by treating her scene in a deliberately anti-Gothic way. Jane is explicitly negative about all the violent aspects, as we see in her account of the whole incident when she is sitting alone in her room after it is all over:

> The morning [of the wedding] had been a *quiet* morning enough—all except the brief scene with the lunatic: the transaction in the church had *not* been noisy; there was *no* explosion of passion, *no* loud altercation, *no* dispute, *no* defiance or challenge, *no* tears, *no* sobs: a few words had been spoken, a *calmly* pronounced objection to the marriage made; some stern, short questions put by Mr. Rochester; answers, explanations given, evidence adduced; an open admission of the truth had been uttered by my master; then the living proof had been seen; the intruders were gone, and all was over. (II, xi, 298, my italics)

Jane's account is low-toned, almost legalistic, and the intense emotional shock she has received is implied by the bare prose, which is utterly devoid of any emotional elaboration. The wedding scene had been developed in a similarly non-dramatic way. Jane had no forebodings on her way to the wedding; as she remarks, she did not even notice whether the day was fair or foul, because all her attention was concentrated on Mr Rochester and in trying to discover the reason for his peculiarly violent mood. She took no notice of the two strangers whom she saw wandering about in the churchyard, and who followed them into the church. When the interruption of the wedding service came, it was in a solicitor's voice—calm, distinct, and nasal, but 'not loud', and it was a real impediment which was announced, 'It simply consists in the existence of a previous marriage: Mr Rochester has a wife now living' (II, xi, 292). Jane did not scream or faint at the news, though she felt her nerves vibrate 'as they had never vibrated to thunder'. Rochester did not react dramatically either; he merely 'moved slightly, as if an earthquake had rolled under his feet'. All the 'subtle violence' of intense emotion is there in the imagery but there is no outward expression of it. Instead of being dragged from the church, Rochester, still grasping Jane, leads the party out saying, 'I invite you all to come up to the house and visit Mrs. Poole's patient, and *my wife*!' (II, xi, 295).

He leads them straight up to the room where the 'ghost' is

imprisoned, and there the terrible wrestling match takes place between Rochester and his mad wife. Jane immediately recognises her as the woman who had torn her wedding veil in two: 'The maniac bellowed: she parted her shaggy locks from her visage, and gazed wildly at her visitors. I recognised well that purple face,—those bloated features' (II, xi, 296). After a desperate struggle, Rochester finally ties her down into a chair, then he turns to Jane and his accusers with a Byronic smile 'both acrid and desolate': ' "That is my *wife*," said he. "Such is the sole conjugal embrace I am ever to know" ' (II, xi, 296). Here is the explanation of the interrupted marriage and of the mystery of Thornfield. The actuality has a horror far beyond Gothic fantasy. Rochester was right when months earlier he had called Thornfield 'accursed':

> Thornfield Hall—this accursed place—this tent of Achan —this insolent vault, offering the ghastliness of living death to the light of the open sky—this narrow stone hell, with its one real fiend, worse than a legion of such as we imagine.
>
> (II, i, 304)

Well might Charlotte Brontë feel disappointed at Mrs Radcliffe's failure of imagination when we see how she manages to fuse nightmare with the tangibility of fact to create an emotional reality of agony against which Radcliffian ideal terrors have no more substance than shadows.

The deliberate reshaping of Gothic convention in the events which bring the first stage of Jane and Rochester's relationship to its disastrous end leads us inevitably to a fuller consideration of their feeling for each other, and of the effect Charlotte Brontë achieved by presenting them as human beings in 'the language of Truth in preference to the jargon of Conventionality'.[6] As Harriet Martineau indicated, Charlotte Brontë's creation of her new kind of heroine was a deliberate response to a challenge which was both moral and aesthetic:

> She once told her sisters that they were wrong—even morally wrong—in making their heroines beautiful, as a matter of course. They replied that it was impossible to make a heroine interesting on other terms. Her answer was, 'I will show you a

heroine as small and as plain as myself who will be as interesting as any of yours.'[7]

Jane insists on her plain face and her plain speaking, and instead of having the conventional feminine qualities of docility
and submissiveness, she is restless, indomitable and independent. Possessing none of the 'impregnable innocence' of traditional heroines, she has a refreshing frankness and a degree of
self-knowledge which they lack. She is also much more sexually
aware than any of her predecessors and without their neurotic
fears, all of which shows in her lively response to Mr Rochester
and in the combination of playfulness and passion she displays
towards him. Jane is in fact Mr Rochester's ideal of an 'intellectual, faithful, loving woman' (That Rochester ranks intelli-
gence in a woman first is surely without precedent in the demands made on a heroine, with the possible exception of Mr
Darcy and Elizabeth Bennet in *Pride and Prejudice*). The sufferings Jane has to endure force her to scrutinise her feelings in a
way that no heroine in Gothic fiction had been obliged or able
to do before and as a result her romantic love is toughened as
her personality develops. In the full acceptance of each other
by Jane and Rochester that finally emerges, the focus is on
mutual happiness tried and tested by ten years of marriage, a
marriage in which Jane's demands for recognition of herself in
her wholeness are fulfilled.

Inevitably, Rochester is presented less completely than Jane,
for after all we see him through her eyes. Much has been made
of his Byronic characteristics,[8] but it seems useful to distinguish
between conventionalised Byronic behaviour and realistically
passionate behaviour for which Byronic images help to provide
an adequate vocabulary. For instance, Jane's description of
Rochester addressing his destiny outside Thornfield early in
their relationship is a very good example of the creative re-use
of stereotyped language, both to describe passion observed and
the observer's emotionalised perception of it. Jane's intuitive
analysis is certainly coloured by her perplexity as to why her
employer should feel so intensely about his own house:

Lifting his eye to its battlements, he cast over them a glare
such as I never saw before or since. Pain, shame, ire—

impatience, disgust, detestation—seemed momentarily to hold a quivering conflict in the large pupil dilating under his ebon eyebrow. Wild was the wrestle which should be paramount; but another feeling rose and triumphed: something hard and cynical; self-willed and resolute: it settled his passion and petrified his countenance.   (I, xv, 143)

When it does come, Rochester's comment is deliberately mystifying, transmuted as it is into a literary analogy:

During the moment I was silent, Miss Eyre, I was arranging a point with my destiny. She stood there, by that beech-trunk—a hag like one of those who appeared to Macbeth on the heath of Forres. 'You like Thornfield?' she said, lifting her finger; and then she wrote in the air a memento, which ran in lurid hieroglyphics all along the house-front, between the upper and lower row of windows. 'Like it if you can!' 'Like it if you dare!'
    'I will like it,' said I. 'I dare like it.'   (I, xv, 143)

As it emerges later, Rochester has very good reasons for explaining nothing to Jane at this stage and his melodramatic language suggests his own tensions, regrets and guilts as he tries to make up his mind about Jane. At the time Rochester's behaviour appears quite mysterious but this is only because of Jane's ignorance and her recorded opinion of him soon after suggests that she did not regard him as a fearful and mysterious being for all his Byronic traits. Though he was 'proud, sardonic, harsh to inferiority of every description' and 'moody', Jane is sure that the reasons for this would be perfectly credible if known and her final judgement salutes him as a human being:

But I believed that his moodiness, his harshness, and his former faults of morality . . . had their source in some cruel cross of fate. I believed he was naturally a man of better tendencies, higher principles, and purer tastes than such as circumstances had developed, education instilled, or destiny encouraged. I thought there were excellent materials in him.
                                                        (I, xv, 148)

It is quickly established that both Jane and Rochester are

tough and alive, with nothing ideal or conventionalised about them. G. H. Lewes at least paid their author the compliment of believing in their authenticity at a time when many other critics refused to recognise what are their most distinctive qualities—their freedom from sentimentality in attitude or presentation:

> Her genius finds its fittest illustration in her 'Rochesters' and 'Jane Eyres'; they are men and women of deep feeling, clear intellects, vehement tempers, bad manners, ungraceful, yet loveable persons.[9]

Jane and Rochester fall passionately in love with each other. There is never any doubt in our minds about the real emotional compatibility between them since their whole relationship is analysed before our eyes by Jane as she attempts stage by stage to come to terms with her feelings and with external circumstances. She always combines intense emotion with an attempt at rational assessment in her continual awareness of the tension between 'imagination's boundless waste' and 'the safe fold of common sense'. It is with scrupulous fairness that she examines emotional situations not, like a Radcliffian heroine, to distance herself from her feelings and so transform them into something more manageable, but rather to understand them more fully.

As a very practical person, Jane does not have a romantic disregard for convention at all; on the contrary, she realises very clearly both the social realities of her position vis-à-vis Rochester and also their inadequacy in terms of human relationship. Initially she refuses to name her feelings for Rochester —after all, it would be easier not to admit them, for her own peace of mind and for social reasons. What she does instead is to convey all the excitement of feeling through images, the very concreteness of which displays her intense emotional energy and anticipation while also embodying her rational caution. This is well seen in a short passage that occurs after Jane, early in her career at Thornfield, has saved Mr Rochester from being burned alive in his bed. A brief dialogue occurs preserving all the proprieties of manner, and then Jane escapes to her room where in privacy the currents of feeling sweep through her:

'My cherished preserver, good night.'

Strange energy was in his voice; strange fire in his look.

'I am glad I happened to be awake,' I said; and then I was going.

'What, you *will* go?'

'I am cold, sir.'

'Cold? Yes,—and standing in a pool! Go, then, Jane; go!' But he still retained my hand, and I could not free it. I bethought myself of an expedient.

'I think I hear Mrs. Fairfax move, sir,' said I.

'Well, leave me:' he relaxed his fingers, and I was gone.

I regained my couch, but never thought of sleep. Till morning dawned I was tossed on a buoyant but unquiet sea, where billows of trouble rolled under surges of joy. I thought sometimes I saw beyond its wild waters a shore, sweet as the hills of Beulah; and now and then a freshening gale, wakened by hope, bore my spirit triumphantly towards the bourne: but I could not reach it, even in fancy,—a counteracting breeze blew off land, and continually drove me back. Sense would resist delirium: judgment would warn passion. Too feverish to rest, I rose as soon as day dawned.   (I, xv, 153)

Here Jane gives us a minute analysis of her feelings without once naming the sexual energy which prompts them. And she ends, characteristically, with an explanatory gloss on such romantic feeling done in a very balanced eighteenth-century way, though still presented in concrete energetic images: 'Sense would resist delirium: judgment would warn passion'. Perhaps the gloss has been added in the re-telling to explain the tensions which are absolutely central to this love affair.

The whole process of admitting her love to herself through examination and assessment of strong crises of feeling is really one of growth. As she says, 'I had learnt to love Mr. Rochester: I could not unlove him now merely because I found that he had ceased to notice me' (I, iii, 187). If anything, her rigorous attempts at self-discipline only contribute to develop her awareness of being in love and though such efforts serve to control her behaviour they do not really help at all when she is confronted by Rochester himself. This emerges very clearly when he returns with his house party to Thornfield and demands that Jane sit in his drawing room every evening after dinner, where, ignored by his guests, she is condemned to watch his flirtation with Miss Blanche Ingram, the woman he is expected to marry. Here Jane's situation brings to mind Fanny Price being forced to watch Mary Crawford and Edmund Bertram, though Jane does have a certain hardy conviction of emotional equality which makes her hold Blanche Ingram at a 'mark beneath jealousy', something Fanny would never have dared to do. Again the force and complexity of Jane's feelings come through her discreet exterior boldly and directly in the imagery she uses:

> I looked, and had an acute pleasure in looking,—a precious, yet poignant pleasure; pure gold, with a steely point of agony: a pleasure like what the thirst-perishing man might feel who knows the well to which he has crept is poisoned, yet stoops and drinks divine draughts nevertheless.　　(II, ii, 176)

The progress of Jane's love is above all conveyed by her growing difficulties in maintaining any kind of rational judgement about Rochester, as she admits to herself:

> But in other points, as well as this, I was growing very lenient to my master: I was forgetting all his faults, for which I had once kept a sharp look-out. It had formerly been my endeavour to study all sides of his character: to take the bad with the good; and from the just weighing of both, to form an equitable judgment. Now I saw no bad. The sarcasm that had repelled, the harshness that had startled me once, were only like keen condiments in a choice dish: their presence was pungent, but their absence would be felt as comparatively insipid. And as for the vague something—was it a sinister or a sorrowful, a designing or a desponding expression?—that opened upon a careful observer, now and then, in his eye, and closed again before one could fathom the strange depth partially disclosed; that something which used to make me fear and shrink, as if I had been wandering amongst volcanic-looking hills, and had suddenly felt the ground quiver and seen it gape: that something, I, at intervals, beheld still; and with throbbing heart, but not with palsied nerves. Instead of

wishing to shun, I longed only to dare—to divine it; and I
thought Miss Ingram happy, because one day she might
look into the abyss at her leisure, explore its secrets and
analyse their nature.   (II, iii, 189–90)

Beginning very judiciously, Jane's meditation in this passage
gradually becomes an intensely lyrical insight into the mystery
of Rochester's personality. Again there are the concrete images
conveying emotional intensity which not only make us understand the feeling but add the extra dimension of the perilous-
ness of such sexual attraction and Jane's exhilaration in it.
Then, in the extraordinary last sentence Jane brings herself and
Miss Ingram together, combining the vocabulary of her own
passion with the more civilised conventions of language socially
appropriate to Miss Ingram, 'I thought Miss Ingram happy,
because one day she might look into the abyss at her leisure'.
This is not necessarily a leisurely activity, and is indeed belied
by Jane's own energetic language which ends the paragraph,
'explore its secrets and analyse their nature'. Obviously Jane is
trying to see Miss Ingram as Rochester's bride but the activities
attributed to her are, significantly, all Jane's own.

I have chosen to look at this passage rather than any of the
obvious crises in Jane and Rochester's love because it is important to show how Jane's intensity of feeling causes us to remember their whole relationship as one of heightened emotional
crisis, even though much of the time the external context is quite
sober and commonplace. After all, Jane is sitting quietly in the
Thornfield drawing-room at this point meditating on her feelings but doing so with such energy that the everyday frame of
living is totally obliterated. It is one of the peculiar strengths of
the novel that it engages in such intense scrutiny of feeling
behind discreet exteriors. Jane's individuality both as character
and as fictive author is all the stronger for it.

It is certain that the first love between Jane and Rochester
was real and that their interrupted marriage ceremony is a crisis
of the keenest agony for them both. Although Jane is able to see
through hindsight that this is no gratuitous crisis but a necessary
process of purgation, an enlargement of spiritual understanding,
the direct experience of the event is of heightened emotion when

the passions rage furiously 'like true heathens, as they are' (II, iv, 203). There is nothing to mitigate the shock of the interrupted ceremony when Rochester at the altar 'only moved slightly, as if an earthquake had rolled under his feet', nor Jane's own agony of loss and disillusion, which she describes as the freakish-ness of snow in midsummer:

> A Christmas frost had come at midsummer: a white December storm had whirled over June ... and the woods, which twelve hours since waved leafy and fragrant as groves between the tropics, now spread, waste, wild, and white as pine-forests in wintry Norway. (II, xi, 298)

Again we seen Jane's peculiar power of conveying her feeling through images which both intensify and enlarge the emotion itself.

When Jane, alone in her locked room, raises her head many hours after the would-be wedding, she knows immediately that she must leave Thornfield and abandon Rochester. The decision is her own, based on her instinct for survival, whatever super-natural powers or visions she may refer to. In the last terrible battle of wills between Jane and Rochester his pleading traverses the whole emotional range from violent passion which makes her feel 'powerless as stubble exposed to the draught and glow of a furnace' to gentleness 'that broke me down with grief'. There is but one way out of this 'madness' as she calls it and that is to leave before her determination and her physical strength ebb, even if to do so she must 'crack her heart strings'. Only when Jane has made her independent decision is she aware of any spiritual guidance. It comes first in the form of a moon vision of a woman who speaks with the peremptory accents which are akin to Jane's own when she has endeavoured to subdue her feelings for Rochester:

> 'My daughter, flee temptation!'
> 'Mother, I will.' (III, i, 324)

The voice comes from that region within herself which later enables her to enter into telepathic communication with Rochester. It comes from that mysterious world of 'pre-sentiments, sympathies, and signs' which erupts into human consciousness at its most highly charged points of crisis.[10] But when Jane stumbles away from Thornfield at dawn, her only feeling is agony:

> Gentle reader, may you never feel what I then felt! May your eyes never shed such stormy, scalding, heart-wrung tears as poured from mine. May you never appeal to Heaven in prayers so hopeless and agonised as in that hour left my lips: for never may you, like me, dread to be the instrument of evil to what you wholly love.   (III, i, 326

Jane's struggle for survival is attended by glimmerings of spiritual awareness, as when lying on the desolate moors she realises for the first time that her love for Rochester is part of the universal pattern of God's love, and later, when she is rescued at the point of exhaustion by the Rivers family, she acknowledges this as God's caring for her. But the dominant interest of the final part of the novel is human rather than religious; through all her experiences, spiritual realisation is nothing like so intense for Jane as her own unhappiness at being separated from Rochester. Established as school-mistress at Morton, she is quietly miserable, with the misery that comes from the exertion of rigorous self-restraint, as her musings outside her cottage one summer evening suggest:

> Meantime, let me ask myself one question—Which is better?—To have surrendered to temptation; listened to passion; made no painful effort—no struggle;—but to have sunk down in the silken snare; fallen asleep on the flowers covering it; wakened in a southern clime, amongst the luxuries of a pleasure-villa: to have been now living in France, Mr. Rochester's mistress; delirious with his love half my time—for he would—oh, yes, he would have loved me well for a while. He *did* love me—no one will ever love me so again. I shall never more know the sweet homage given to beauty, youth, and grace—for never to any one else shall I seem to possess these charms. He was fond and proud of me—it is what no man besides will ever be.—But where am I wandering, and what am I saying: and, above all, feeling? Whether is it better, I ask, to be a slave in a fool's paradise at

Marseilles—fevered with delusive bliss one hour—suffocating with the bitterest tears of remorse and shame the next—or to be a village-schoolmistress, free and honest, in a breezy mountain nook in the healthy heart of England? (III, v, 364)

This is Jane's desperate attempt to survive, by controlling her grief and adhering to the moral standards necessary for her own self-respect. Even when she uses language biassed against an illicit union, it still has an energy lacking in the description of her present situation in 'the healthy heart of England'. Though Jane as the sober-voiced commentator speaking ten years later is able to 'thank Providence' for its guidance, when she tells what she felt then (not, significantly, what she 'feels now' while writing), we see only the emotional difficulties attending right conduct, difficulties which always burst upon her no matter how hard she tries to persuade herself out of them: 'While I looked, I thought myself happy, and was surprised to find myself ere long weeping—and why? For the doom which had reft me from adhesion to my master' (III, v, 364).

Jane cannot 'turn the bent' of her nature: she believes it would be a 'monstrous martyrdom' for her to abandon her feeling for Rochester and go with St John Rivers as his wife to do missionary work in India. For her, love comes first, though in desperation she seems to be willing to fling the final responsibility for her choice on to God. When she prays, 'Show me, show me the path!', the answer comes not as a call from God but from Rochester. Certainly Jane sees it as part of the same cosmic harmony between natural and psychic forces as the earlier 'signs' of the lightning-struck chestnut tree or her moon vision, but crisis moments of genuine religious feeling like this one do not turn the novel away from psychology to religion. In her rejection of Rivers and her return to Rochester, Jane's sense of following God's will is strongly supported by her own passionate inclinations.

And Jane returns 'home'—not to Thornfield which has been destroyed by fire but to Rochester who is her 'only home'. Their reunion has all the naturalness of loving mutual acceptance:

'Jane suits me: do I suit her?'
'To the finest fibre of my nature, sir.'

13

'The case being so, we have nothing in the world to wait for: we must be married instantly.' (III, xi, 451)

Though there is wish fulfilment in the ending, there is nothing of romantic fantasy in Rochester's maimed physical condition or Jane's hardy assertion of her own independence. Instead there is the real delight of honest recognition and harmony:

> There was no harassing restraint, no repressing of glee and vivacity with him; for with him I was at perfect ease, because I knew I suited him: all I said or did seemed either to console or revive him. Delightful consciousness! It brought to life and light my whole nature: in his presence I thoroughly lived; and he lived in mine. (III, xi, 442)

The novel does not end on their wedding day, described with Jane's characteristic lack of feminine delicacy, 'Reader, I married him'. Instead, it is written from the distance of ten years' happy marriage celebrated in language which frankly embodies passion and sexuality; the elemental joy that Jane describes belongs to a new kind of Eden, attained through the fulfilment of human love:

> I know what it is to live, entirely for and with what I love best on earth. I hold myself supremely blest—blest beyond what language can express; because I am my husband's life as fully as he is mine. No woman was ever nearer to her mate than I am: ever more absolutely bone of his bone, and flesh of his flesh. (III, xii, 456)

Jane and Rochester's marriage affirms life and love and social relationships, giving them the central place in a wide range of emotional imperatives. For instance, Jane's final notation of St John Rivers's choice of 'the wild field of mission warfare' suggests that this answered the needs of his nature, just as marriage answers hers. The quality that distinguishes *Jane Eyre* from the Gothic novel is its acceptance of the need to take all kinds of feeling into account in a realistic presentation of human experience. Jane, the central consciousness, has resolved the duality within herself in a tolerant and humane maturity which recognises man as both a rational and emotional, a physical and spiritual being, God's creature in the fullest sense.

In its happy ending *Jane Eyre* offers no facile solution of the Radcliffian sentimental variety where 'rational happiness' is achieved by the neglect of emotional imperatives; nor in its recognition of human passion is it a tale of exhaustion, frustration and death, like the novels of Lewis and Maturin. Charlotte Brontë has succeeded in re-tying Donne's 'subtle knot which makes us man' in such a way that ambiguities, doubts and conflicts which form the penumbra of experience are resolved in the end for her principal characters. The synthesis that is finally achieved is not one that transcends human limitations but one that increasingly accepts them in a remarkable process of emotional and spiritual growth. *Jane Eyre* places the early Gothic novels in perspective, admitting Gothic states of mind and feeling but insisting also on a tough recognition of the world and its complex demands, so that it gives a new definition of such experiences within a realistic context of character and environment. Imagination *is* 'a strong, restless faculty' which extends the bounds of what is 'natural' to man into wider ranges of feeling than any of the earlier Gothic novelists had dared to do. Imagination also gives expression to feeling by the concreteness and range of the novel's language. In its minute registration of immediate perception and its keen scrutiny of remembered feeling, *Jane Eyre* presents a more convincing map of the irrational life than do any of the extravagantly indulgent Gothic scenarios.

With *Jane Eyre* Gothic fiction is normalised into the mainstream of literature, and fantasy and realism fused in a statement about awareness of the irrational in man. But the spell of Gothic still persists for modern readers as it did for Jane; there is something about its murky fascination that makes it a very appealing fantasy form.[11] It still speaks with its old underground voice through the host of modern Gothics in what is perhaps its truest tone, arousing suspense and fear as it addresses the irrational element in all of us which is our connecting link with 'that mystery to which humanity has not yet found the key'.

Selective List of Gothic Novels

A list of Gothic novels from which quotations in the text are taken, with details of the edition used. The original publisher and date are given in brackets. Most of the editions used belong to one of the following: Oxford English Novels, Northanger Set of Jane Austen Horrid Novels, ed. D. P. Varma (Folio Press, 1968), and the Gothic Novels collection of rare Gothic reprints, ed. D. P. Varma (Arno Press, New York).

The best catalogues of Gothic titles are in: Dorothy Blakey, *The Minerva Press, 1790–1820* (1939), which contains a complete catalogue of Minerva Press novels 1790–1820; and Maurice Lévy, *Le Roman 'Gothique' Anglais 1764–1824* (Toulouse, 1969), which contains a comprehensive catalogue of English Gothic novels 1764–1824.

Brontë, Charlotte, *Jane Eyre*. An autobiography. Edited by Currer Bell. OEN, ed. Margaret Smith, 1973 (Smith, Elder & Co., 1847)

Holstein, A. F., *Love, Mystery, and Misery!* A novel (Minerva, 1810)

Lewis, M. G., *The Monk*. A romance. OEN, ed. Howard Anderson, 1973 (John Bell, 1796)

Maturin, C. R., *Fatal Revenge; or, The Family of Montorio*. A romance (Longman, 1807)

   The Milesian Chief. A romance (Colburn, 1812)

   Women; or, Pour et Contre. A tale (Longman, 1818)

   Melmoth the Wanderer. A tale. OEN, ed. Douglas Grant, 1968 (Edinburgh: Constable, 1820; Hurst, Robinson & Co., 1820)

Parsons, Eliza, *The Castle of Wolfenbach*. Folio Press, 1968 (Minerva, 1793)

   The Mysterious Warning. A German tale. Folio Press, 1968 (Minerva, 1796)

Radcliffe, Ann, *The Mysteries of Udolpho*. A romance, interspersed with some pieces of poetry. OEN, ed. Bonamy Dobrée, 1966 (George Robinson, 1794)

   The Italian; or, The Confessional of the Black Penitents. A romance. OEN, ed. Frederick Garber, 1971 (Cadell & Davies, 1797)

Radcliffe, Mary-Anne, *Manfroné; or, The One-Handed Monk*. Arno Press, 1972 (J. F. Hughes, 1809; Minerva reprint, 1819)

Roche, Regina Maria, *The Children of the Abbey*. A tale. 6th edition, Minerva, 1810 (Minerva, 1796)

Sleath, Eleanor, *The Orphan of the Rhine*. A romance. Folio Press, 1968 (Minerva, 1798)

Stanhope, Louisa Sidney, *The Confessional of Valombre*. A romance. (Minerva, 1812)

Notes

CHAPTER I

1 The confusion of terminology is evident in eighteenth-century writers' own usage, e.g. Horace Walpole in *Otranto* talks about 'Ancient and Modern Romance', while Jane Austen in *Northanger Abbey* calls all long prose fictions 'Novels' including Mrs Radcliffe's *Udolpho* and M. G. Lewis's *Monk*. For modern critical discussions on Romance as a literary genre, see *Pastoral and Romance*, ed. E. T. Lincoln (New Jersey, 1969). R. Kiely includes Gothic fiction in his discussion of the Romantic Novel as a genre, in *The Romantic Novel in England* (Harvard University Press, 1972).

2 See Coleridge's reviews of Gothic novels in *Coleridge's Miscellaneous Criticism*, ed. T. M. Raysor (1936); also *Biographia Literaria*, ed. J. Shawcross (1907), i, 34.

3 For an interesting discussion of Foucault's theories in relation to another novel of the period, see Tony Tanner's Introduction to Jane Austen's *Sense and Sensibility* (Penguin, 1972).

4 This information appears in Talfourd's Memoir, prefixed to *Gaston de Blondeville* (1826), p. 99.

5 This letter about *Clarissa* appears in *Letters of Samuel Richardson*, ed. J. Carroll (Oxford, 1964), p. 104.

6 Bertrand Evans, *The Gothic Drama from Walpole to Shelley* (Berkeley and Los Angeles, 1947) shows how Gothic themes and characters were developed in drama before they appeared in fiction, and C. F. McIntyre suggested the influence of Shakespearean drama on Mrs Radcliffe in 'Were the Gothic Novels Gothic?', *PMLA*, xxxvi (1921), 644–67.

7 See B. Joseph, *The Tragic Actor* (1959); J. Boaden's Memoirs of Mrs. Siddons and J. P. Kemble; W. Hazlitt's dramatic criticism.

8 *The Private Correspondence of David Garrick*, ed. J. Boaden (1831), i, 158.

9 For the full script of the soliloquy, see A. Coleman, 'Mossop as Wolsey', *Theatre Notebook* (Autumn, 1970), 11–14.

10 I quote from Amy Cruse, *The Englishman and His Books in the Early 19th Century* (1930), pp. 101–2.

11 For discussion of the psychological and symbolic significance of architecture in Gothic novels, see M. Lévy, *Le Roman 'Gothique' Anglais 1764–1824* (Toulouse, 1969), Chap. X, 'Structures Profondes', 601–45.

CHAPTER II

1 Scott's Prefatory Memoir to *The Novels of Mrs. Ann Radcliffe*, Ballantyne's Novelists' Library (1824), xvii–xviii.
2 A. Alison, *Essay on the Nature and Principles of Taste* (1790).
3 All references to *The Mysteries of Udolpho* are to the Oxford English Novels edition, 1966.
4 C. R. Maturin, unsigned article 'Harrington and Ormond, Tales by Maria Edgeworth', *British Review and London Critical Journal*, xi (1818), 37–61. Attributed to Maturin by N. Idman on the basis of a letter (27 Sept. 1817) and internal evidence, in *Charles Maturin, His Life and Work* (1923).
5 'On the Supernatural in Poetry', *New Monthly Magazine*, xvi (1816), 145–52. As the editor explains, this is not a formal essay but a collection of MS pages written by Mrs Radcliffe.
6 E. Burke, *A Philosophical Enquiry into the origin of our ideas of the Sublime and Beautiful* (1757). All my references are to *The Works of the Rt. Hon. Edmund Burke* (World's Classics), i.
7 M. Ware, *Sublimity in the Novels of Ann Radcliffe* (Uppsala, 1963), and M. Lévy, op. cit., p. 285; both discuss the relationship between Mrs Radcliffe's fiction and Burke's treatise.
8 Burke, op. cit., p. 154.
9 Alison, op. cit. (3rd edn. 1812), i, 322. See also J. Reynolds, XIIIth Discourse (1786), W. Gilpin, *Three Essays* (1792).
10 I am indebted to S. H. Monk, *The Sublime: A Study of Critical Theories in XVIIIth Century England* (Ann Arbor, 1960), p. 201, for this information.
11 *Monthly Review*, viii (1792), 82–7.
12 *New Monthly Magazine*, xvi (1826), 532–6.
13 H. W. Husbands, 'The Lesser Novel, 1770–1800' (unpublished University of London MA thesis) mentions several earlier novels which criticise the conventions of sensibility, like *The Errors of Sensibility* (1774) and *Excessive Sensibility* (1787). Marilyn Butler discusses the problem in *Jane Austen and the War of Ideas* (Oxford, 1975).
14 L. Trilling, *Sincerity and Authenticity* (1972), p. 95.
15 Coleridge's unsigned review of *Udolpho*, op. cit., p. 357.
16 *The Italian* (Oxford English Novels, 1971), p. 612.
17 While Joanna Baillie's *Plays of the Passions* remained anonymous, they were thought by some of the Bluestockings to have been written by Mrs Radcliffe. Anna Seward quotes from the letter of a Mrs Jackson: 'Before their author was known, I observed so much of the power and defects of Mrs. Radcliffe's compositions in these dramas, as to believe them hers'. (Quoted by Talfourd in his *Memoir* of Mrs Radcliffe, p. 91.)

CHAPTER III

1 All references to *The Monk* are to the Oxford English Novels edition, 1973.

2 Coleridge's unsigned review of *The Monk*, *Critical Review*, xix (Feb. 1797), 194–200; quoted in *Coleridge's Miscellaneous Criticism*, pp. 370–8.

3 For a history of the controversy surrounding the novel, see A. Parreaux, *The Publication of 'The Monk', a Literary Event, 1796–1798* (Paris, 1960); M. Lévy, op. cit., 'M. G. Lewis et ses Démons', Ch. V, pp. 357–64.

4 M. Lévy, op. cit., 305–24; O. Ritter, 'Studien zu M. G. Lewis' Roman "Ambrosio, or The Monk"', *Archiv für das Studium der neueren Sprachen und Literaturen*, cxi (1903), 106–21.

5 D. A. F. de Sade, *Idée sur les Romans*, ed. O. Uzanne (Paris, 1878).

6 Kemble starred in the stage adaptation of *The Monk* in 1798, *Aurelio and Miranda*, of which Boaden reported: 'All that I ever conceived of either the dignity or sanctity of the monacal order, was as nothing compared with the awful grace with which the whole figure of Kemble became invested'. *Memoirs of the Life of J. P. Kemble* (1825), ii, 227–8.

7 L. F. Peck, *Life of Matthew Gregory Lewis* (Cambridge, Mass., 1961), reproduces the title page of the chapbook edition on which this summary appears (facing p. 65).

8 Though the figure of a villainous monk was not original to Lewis, his version supplied a new Gothic figure, and monkish tales remained popular till well on into the 1820s as the following titles suggest: *The Italian; or, The Confessional of the Black Penitents* (1797); *The Monk of Udolpho* (1807); *Manfroné; or, The One-Handed Monk* (1809); *The Monastery of St. Columb; or, The Atonement* (1813); *The Monk of Hennares* (1817); *The Wizard Priest and the Witch* (1811); *The Abbot of Montserrat; or, The Pool of Blood* (1826).

9 —Lord Angelo is precise;
Stands at a guard with envy; Scarce confesses
That his blood flows, or that his appetite
Is more to bread than stone.   (*Measure for Measure*)

10 According to O. Ritter, op. cit., and G. Herzfeld, 'Die eigentliche Quelle von Lewis' Monk', *Archiv für das Studium der neueren Sprachen und Literaturen*, cxi (1903), 316–23, Lewis has created a clever pastiche of German Gothic models here, borrowing from sources as diverse as Musaeus, Schiller, Bürger, Wieland, and an anonymous romance *Die blutende Gestalt mit Dolch und Lampe*.

11 Lewis's description here appears to owe much to Richardson's *Clarissa*, recalling Clarissa's early nightmare about Lovelace, which incidentally marks out the whole progression of the action to the final stabbing: 'Afterwards seizing upon me, carried me into a church yard; and there, notwithstanding all my prayers and tears, and protestations of innocence, stabbed me to the heart, and then tumbled me into a deep grave ready dug, among two or three half-dissolved carcases; throwing in the dirt and earth upon me with his hands, and trampling it down with his feet.' (Everyman, i, 433).

12 Susan Sontag, *Styles of Radical Will* (1969), p. 60.

13 Veit Weber, *The Sorcerer*. A tale. From the German (1795), p. 210.

CHAPTER IV

1 Dorothy Blakey in her excellent study, *The Minerva Press, 1770–1820* (1939), traces the rapid growth of Lane's library chain.
2 Blakey, op. cit., p. 41.
3 *The Children of the Abbey. A Tale*, 4 vols., 6th edition (Minerva, 1810). All subsequent page references to the novel are to this edition.
4 *Manfroné; or, The One-Handed Monk. A Romance*, 2 vols. (Arno Press, New York, 1972). This edition is a reprint of the 3rd edition of *Manfroné* published by Lane's successor A. K. Newman in 1828 in 4 volumes. All page references to the novel are to the Arno edition, where I give references to original chapter and page numbers, not to volume numbers (which are not preserved in the Arno edition). A copy of the original edition (J. F. Hughes, 1809) is in the Alderman Library, University of Virginia.

CHAPTER V

1 All references to *Northanger Abbey* are to the Oxford English Novels edition, 1971.
2 Unsigned review of *The Monk, Coleridge's Miscellaneous Criticism*, p. 370.
3 *The Castle of Wolfenbach*, Folio Press, 1968, p. 90.
4 Of the great deal of recent work done on Jane Austen's language, the following are of particular interest for *Northanger Abbey*: N. Page, *The Language of Jane Austen* (Oxford, 1972); R. Kiely, *The Romantic Novel in England*.
5 Katrin Burlin's excellent article, ' "The Pen of the Contriver": the four fictions of *Northanger Abbey*', *Jane Austen: Bicentenary Essays*, ed. J. Halperin (Cambridge, 1975), raises many of the points about Jane Austen's awareness of the processes of fiction making which I treat in a different way by relating them directly to Gothic.
6 See M. Sadleir, *The Northanger Novels: a footnote to Jane Austen*, English Association pamphlet 68, November 1927; also D. P. Varma's introduction to *The Castle of Wolfenbach*.
7 For very persuasive and slightly different viewpoints on the problems of the relation between realism and Gothic romance in *Northanger Abbey*, see R. Kiely, op. cit., Ch. vi, and Frank J. Kearful, 'Satire and the Form of the Novel: the Problem of Aesthetic Unity in *Northanger Abbey*', *Journal of English Literary History*, xxxii (December 1965), 511–27.

CHAPTER VI

1 All references to *Melmoth the Wanderer* are to the Oxford English Novels edition, 1968.
2 For a discussion of Maturin's Dark Romanticism, see R. D. Hume, 'Exuberant Gloom, Existential Agony, and Heroic Despair: Three

Varieties of Negative Romanticism', in *The Gothic Imagination: Essays in Dark Romanticism*, ed. G. R. Thompson (Washington State University Press, 1974).

3 *New Monthly Magazine*, xiv (1820), 662–8.
4 *Quarterly Review*, iii (1810), 339.
5 *Monthly Review*, xciv (1821), 81–90.
6 *Athenaeum*, No. 3366 (30 April 1892), 560–1.
7 *Blackwood's Edinburgh Magazine*, viii (Nov. 1820), 161–8.
8 See *The Correspondence of Sir Walter Scott and Charles Robert Maturin*, ed. F. Ratchford and W. H. McCarthy (Austin, Texas, 1937).
9 *Quarterly Review*, xxiv (1821), 303–11.
10 W. F. Axton in his Introduction to *Melmoth* (University of Nebraska Press, 1966) develops the idea of a thematic unity based on analogous themes of social and religious sadism. It is the only argument I have seen which attempts to justify Maturin's use of a series of tales as a conscious structural device.
11 *London Magazine*, iii (1821), 514–24.
12 *Women; or, Pour et Contre. A tale* (Longman, 1818).
13 R. Kiely, op. cit., 193.
14 *Athenaeum* (1892).
15 L. M. Dawson, 'Melmoth the Wanderer: Paradox and the Gothic Novel', *Studies in English Literature, 1500–1900*, viii (1968), 621–32.
16 *New Monthly Magazine* (1820).
17 'The Unknown Masterpiece and other Stories', *Comédie Humaine*, ed. G. Saintsbury (1896).
18 P. Thorslev, *The Byronic Hero* (Minneapolis, 1962), 168.
19 *The Milesian Chief. A romance* (Colburn, 1812).

CHAPTER VII

1 *The Brontës: Their Lives, Friendships and Correspondence*, ed. T. J. Wise and J. A. Symington (Shakespeare Head Brontë, Oxford, 1932), ii, 152.
2 See R. B. Heilman, Charlotte Brontë's "New" Gothic', *From Jane Austen to Joseph Conrad*, ed. J. C. Rathburn and M. Steinmann Jr. (Minneapolis, 1958), 118–32.
3 J. Millgate, 'Jane Eyre's Progress', *English Studies* (Anglo-American Supplement, 1969), 21–9, points out that Jane's journey is as directed though not as limited in its objectives as Bunyan's *Pilgrim's Progress*.
4 All references to *Jane Eyre* are to the Oxford English Novels edition, 1973.
5 K. Tillotson, *Novels of the 1840s* (Oxford, 1954), p. 307.
6 *Correspondence*, ii, 255.
7 'Death of Currer Bell', *Daily News* (April 1855). Quoted in the *Correspondence*, iv, 182.
8 See Winifred Gérin, *Charlotte Brontë: the Evolution of Genius* (1967), for a discussion of the versions of the Byronic hero in Charlotte Brontë's fiction.

9 Review of *Villette*, *Westminster Review*, iii (1853), 485–91.

10 For the importance of moon symbolism in the novel, see R. B. Heilman, 'Charlotte Brontë, Reason, and the Moon', *Nineteenth Century Fiction*, xiv (1960), 283–302.

11 For studies on modern Gothic, see Russel Nye, *The Unembarrassed Muse: The Popular Arts in America* (N.Y., 1970); J. M. Keech, 'The Survival of the Gothic Response', *Studies in the Novel* (North Texas State University), vi (1974), 130–44; K. J. Mussell, 'Beautiful and Damned: The Sexual Woman in Gothic Fiction', *Journal of Popular Culture* (Bowling Green State University, Ohio), ix (1975), 84–9.

Index